להגיד בבוקר חסדך

HEROES OF FAITH
100 RABBINIC TALES OF THE HOLOCAUST

Stories of our Torah leaders who survived and
inspired during the terrible years of World War II
and under Russian rule

Rabbi Dovid Hoffman

ואמונתך בלילות

Heroes

ואמונתך בלילות

ISRAEL BOOKSHOP
PUBLICATIONS

להגיד בבוקר חסדך

OF FAITH

100 RABBINIC TALES OF THE HOLOCAUST

Stories of our Torah leaders who survived and inspired during the terrible years of World War II and under Russian rule

Rabbi Dovid Hoffman

Copyright © 2013 by Israel Bookshop Publications

ISBN 978-1-60091-261-0

All Rights Reserved

No part of this book may be reproduced in any form
without written permission from the copyright holder.
The Rights of the Copyright Holder Will Be Strictly Enforced

Book & Cover design by:

SRULY PERL • 845.694.7186
mechelp@gmail.com

Proofreading by E.M. Sonenblick
esonenblick@gmail.com

Published ans distributed by:

 Israel Bookshop Publications
501 Prospect Street
Lakewood, NJ 08701
Tel: (732) 901-3009
Fax: (732) 901-4012
www.israelbookshoppublications.com
info@israelbookshoppublications.com

Printed in the USA

Distributed in Israel by:
Shanky's
Petach Tikva 16
Jerusalem
972-2-538-6235

Distributed in Australia by:
Gold's Book and Gift Company
3-13 William Street
Balaclava 3183
613-9527-8775

Distributed in Europe by:
Lehmanns
Unit E Viking Industrial Park
Rolling Mill Road,
Jarrow, Tyne & Wear NE32 3DP
44-191-406-0842

Distributed in South Africa by:
Kollel Bookshop
Ivy Common
107 William Road, Norwood
Johannesburg 2192
27-11-728-1822

לזכרון עולם בהיכל ה'

לעילוי נשמת
ר' **נפתלי טוביה** בן ר' **ישראל** ז"ל
ורעיתו האשה **פעסל** בת ר' **יהודה ליב** ע"ה

ר' **אברהם יוסף שמואל אלטר** בן ר' **טוביה** ז"ל
ורעיתו האשה **רישא רחל** בת ר' **אברהם שלמה** ע"ה

You came from a generation of the past,
Yet the lessons you taught us endure and last.
You showed us where we came from,
You gave us a clear path to follow.

As heroes among those who perished,
As heroes among those who survived,
We are your endurance,
We are your perseverance.

We are your children and grandchildren,
YOU ARE OUR HEROES.

Reb Yosef Friedenson *z"l*
He Chronicled History and Made History

It was right before Yizkor a few short years ago. My father-in-law, Reb Yosef Friedenson *z"l*, was *davening* with us in our little *shtiebel* in Monsey and he watched in amazement as most of the attendees, who were still *zocheh* to have living parents, filed out of the shul.

When we came home for the *seudah*, he told us how, today, he once again witnessed Klal Yisrael's victory over the Nazis: "After we were liberated from Buchenwald, there wasn't one person who left the Shavuos Yizkor service; and today, be"H, there was barely a *minyan* that remained. Is this not a symbol of the eternity of Klal Yisrael?"

It has been but a couple of years since my *shver* wrote the Foreword for Rabbi Dovid Hoffman's first volume of *Heroes of Spirit*; he was so appreciative of Reb Dovid's efforts in helping disseminate the spiritual heroic stories of those who suffered through the atrocities of the Second World War. And he loved being given the chance by Reb Dovid to regale the young shul audience, every year, about Simchas Torah in the Starachowice slave labor camp (see "A Simple Declaration of Faith" on page 291 of this book).

Alas, since this past *Shabbos Zachor*, the man of *Zachor* can no longer, physically, pass on to us these messages of *emunah* and the *nitzchiyus* of Klal Yisrael.

But in his own words, videoed a few years ago for the *Zechor Yemos Olam* program:

"My children and grandchildren often ask, 'Zeidy, what does it [the Holocaust] all mean? What do we all learn from this? What **should** we learn from all this?' I have many answers. But my main answer is for you to know that we are a unique people... an eternal people... indestructible. And not only that we are, but that we should know that this is our destiny; to keep up our *emunah*, that there is a *Ribono shel Olam in this world*. And that we have to stay as close to Him as possible."

Chaval al d'avdin v'lo mishtakchin... yehi zichro baruch.

Rabbi Yosef C. Golding

In Everlasting Tribute
to
ר' שמואל יוסף בן ר' אליעזר גרשון ז"ל
Reb Yosef Friedenson *z"l*

**A survivor from the embers of the Holocaust,
he dedicated his life to rebuilding Klal Yisrael.**

Through his gifted pen and brilliant words,
through his force of intellect and warmth of heart,
he gathered the few glowing sparks
from Churban Europe and fanned
them into raging fires of *emunah*
that have warmed and enlightened
our generation…
…and generations to come.

Table of Contents

Approbations..14
Acknowledgments...21
Introduction by Rabbi Shmuel Y. Klein 29
Foreword by Rabbi Yitzchak (Isaac) Avigdor..............33

Prewar: Rise of the Aggressor

1. REB BORUCH FRANKEL: An American Tale of Salvation.................43
2. The Treasured Keepsake..46
3. RABBI DR. SOLOMON SCHONFELD: Pure Humanity to the Rescue..50
4. R' DOVID LEIBOWITZ: No *Talmid* Left Behind..........................55
5. R' MICHEL MUNK: An Indestructible People..............................61
6. LEIZER COHEN: Lighting Up..63
7. MAX SCHMELING: Righteous Gentile...66
8. SATMAR REBBE: "We Are All Alive"...70

War Begins: Oppression

9. REMA - R' MOSHE ISSERLES: The Merit of a *Tzaddik*................77
10. BELZER REBBE: "Organizing" the Blessing of a *Tzaddik*..........81
11. The Boy Who Saw the Glass Eye of the Nazi............................83
12. R' BORUCH HALEVI LEIZEROVSKI: It's All in G-d's Hands..........88
13. RAV ELCHANAN WASSERMAN: "We Are the *Korbanos* of Klal Yisrael"..90
14. KEDUSHAS ZION: The Best Way to Fulfill a Mitzvah..................93
15. BOYANER REBBE: Keeping His Word..95

16. RADOSHITZER REBBE: The Shofar of Eternity 101
17. R' CHAIM KREISWIRTH: "One Mitzvah Follows Another Mitzvah" 103
18. R' YISROEL ZEV GUSTMAN: Overcoming All Obstacles 106
19. The "Chief Physician" of the Warsaw Ghetto 109
20. BELZER REBBE: The Great Escape (1) 112
21. BELZER REBBE: The Great Escape (2) 115
22. BLUZHEVER REBBE: A Time for Blessing 119
23. KOVNO RAV: "A G-d-fearing Jew Can Never Be a Slave!" 121
24. PONEVEZHER RAV: Dedication 123
25. Saved by a Pendant 126
26. R' AHARON KOTLER: Knowing Who Is a Friend and Who Is Not 129
27. VYELIPOLIER REBBE: Survival of the Five Minzer Brothers (1) ..132
28. The "Mad Priest" of Dachau 138
29. R' YEHOSHUA NEUWIRTH: The Protective Effect of Shabbos 142
30. R' EPHRAIM OSHRY: To Die as a Jew, Not as a Gentile 146
31. BOBOVER REBBE: Last *Melaveh Malkah* in Bochnia 150
32. R' CHAIM STEIN: The Mysterious Horn Peddler 153
33. R' SHLOMO ZALMAN HOROWITZ: A Sign of Heaven 156
34. THE MASTER SHOEMAKER 158
35. BULGARIA: German Ally, Jewish Savior 163
36. R' MENASHE KLEIN: Miraculous Savior 168
37. REB ALTER KURZ: Two for the Price of One 172
38. R' MORDECHAI FRIEDLAND: Our Goal Is Eretz Yisrael 176

HOLOCAUST: DEVASTATION AND DESTRUCTION

39. KLAUSENBERGER REBBE: Anything but to Be a Nazi 185

40. SATMAR REBBE: A Giant Among Men ... 187
41. R' ELIEZER GERSHON FRIEDENSON: "*Onus al Pi Hadibbur*" ... 194
42. HUSYATINER REBBE: How the Battle Was Really Won ... 196
43. VEITZENER RAV: A Permissible Sukkah ... 199
44. UDVARI RAV: Being a "*Rabbiner*" Saved His Life ... 201
45. HARDAGA FAMILY: "Righteous Among the Nations" ... 204
46. R' AHARON DAVIDS: Eating Bread *L'shem Shamayim* ... 207
47. R' YITZCHAK AVIGDOR: Two Rocks Out of One ... 210
48. R' YISROEL MEIR LAU AND CHAZZAN YOSSEL MANDELBAUM ... 213
49. A TASTE OF FREEDOM: Sinking One's Teeth into It ... 217
50. R' YEHOSHUA MOSHE ARONSON: To Eat or Not to Eat ... 220
51. BADISCHLE RAV: A Father's Prophecy ... 224
52. VEITZENER RAV: *Tzitzis* Are "G-d's Clothing" ... 226
53. MOTELE'S REVENGE: A Tale of the Youngest Partisan ... 229
54. MINCHAS YITZCHAK: Rescue and Salvation ... 236
55. BOBOVER REBBE: Survival of the Five Minzer Brothers (2) ... 239
56. R' SHIMON SCHWAB: A *Sefer Torah* for Sale ... 244
57. KALIVER REBBE: The Power of Faith – The Power of "*Shema Yisrael*" ... 246
58. R' AVRAHAM JUNGREIS: Administering to His Flock ... 250
59. NOAM ELIMELECH: Holy Earth ... 253
60. A SOLDIER'S COMMITMENT ... 255
61. R' CHAIM STEIN: The *Goral HaGra* ... 259
62. R' AHARON KOTLER: The Heart of a Jew ... 263
63. YISMACH MOSHE: Save from the Grave ... 267
64. The Shabbos Trial ... 269
65. ARUGAS HABOSEM: A Grandfather's Promise ... 271
66. REB CHAIM YOSEF RUSSAK: Chain of Miracles ... 274

Postwar: Liberation and Beyond

67. R' YITZCHAK ISAAC HERZOG: Returning the Lost Children of Israel 289
68. R' YOSEF FRIEDENSON: A Simple Declaration of Faith 291
69. R' MOSHE SOLOVEITCHIK: The Grip of the Holy Letters 295
70. THE REICHMANN FAMILY: A Loan Repaid..................298
71. R' CHAIM SHMULEVITZ/R' SHMUEL BERENBAUM: Uninterrupted Torah Study..................301
72. KLAUSENBERGER REBBE: What Is There to Do Teshuvah For?....303
73. R' YAAKOV AVIGDOR: An Unexpected Find..................307
74. Cleansing a *Neshamah* Once and for All..................311
75. BINYAMIN WERTZBERGER: *Shamash* of the Kosel..................315
76. WHERE ARE THE CHILDREN OF THE BRISKER RAV?..................317
77. BLUZHEVER REBBE: So Much to Be Thankful For..................320
78. R' MENASHE KLEIN: A Duty to Fulfill..................323
79. RECHA STERNBUCH: A Life of Giving..................326
80. LIEUTENANT BIRNBAUM: The Feldafing Feast..................328
81. R' YOSEF FRIEDENSON: There Are None So Wise as the Jewish People..................332
82. VIZHNITZER REBBE: The Food of Paradise 335
83. BOBOVER REBBE: "So That Future Generations Should Know..."..................338
84. "For the Wish of Mortal Man Is Worms"..................342
85. REB SHRAGA FEIVEL WINKLER: Kosher Generations 344
86. CHACHAM BARUCH TOLEDANO: A *Mikvah* Built by the Germans 347

Russian Wasteland

87. RABBI YITZCHAK GARELIK: A "Moscow" Sukkah 355
88. BLUZHEVER REBBE: A "Cold" to Warm Up the Night 358
89. PONEVEZHER RAV: Undivided Attention 360
90. R' BORUCH BER LEIBOWITZ: "They're Tearing Up Holy *Sefarim*" 363
91. R' YERUCHAM LEVOVITZ: Caring for Another's Feelings 365
92. R' MOSHE FEINSTEIN: A Moscow Miracle 368
93. MAKOVA RAV: A Song for the Ages 371
94. R' YECHEZKEL ABRAMSKY: "Great Is Your Faith" 375
95. SKULENER REBBE: Recognizing the Greatness of a Jew 379
96. R' CHAIM BERLIN: Of Sheep and Shepherds 384
97. NETZIV AND R' YITZCHAK ELCHANAN SPEKTOR: To Glorify G-d's Name 385
98. STEIPLER GAON: A Small Act - A Great Reward 388
99. RIBNITZER REBBE: By Your Blood Shall You Live! 391
100. LAYCHI GLUECK AND RICHARD NIXON: The Ride of a Lifetime .. 393

Biographies 397
Glossary 425

Torah Umesorah
Committing Generations to Torah

Helen Hoffman
Holocaust Lecturer

Zechor Yemos Olam

"עטרת זקנים בני בנים ותפארת בנים אבותם" (משלי יז:ו)

In Pirkei Avos (6:8), Rabbi Shimon ben Yehudah states in the name of Rabbi Shimon ben Yochai: "Children are something which is pleasing for the righteous and pleasing for the world." As it says "Children's children are the crown of the aged and the glory of children are their fathers." (Mishley 17:6)

It is with pride and pleasure that I congratulate my son Rabbi Dovid Hoffman n"y, on the completion of his second outstanding book on the Holocaust. Although he has authored many Torah works, his Holocaust collection, "Heroes of Spirit" and now "Heroes of Faith" are of special relevance to me. Being a Second Generation Holocaust survivor - both of my parents lived through those horrific years in Europe from 1939-1945 - it is of great significance to me to see that the stories of our people and the tremendous tribulations they underwent in that dark and dismal era, be brought to the masses. Too soon will the heroic efforts of the survivors be forgotten. Too soon will the horrors of the six million who died be obliterated.

Many thanks to Holocaust educators, speakers, and authors such as Dovid Hoffman, who keep their legacy alive. He has portrayed the Holocaust not in its darkness, but in the light of the heroism and faith of those who lived and died Al Kiddush Hashem.

May my son continue to see much success in all his endeavors and continue to be a role model for his family, friends and all of Klal Yisroel.

With Much Yiddish Nachas

Mrs. Helen Hoffman

אל תשכחו בכל הדורות, עדי תזכו לראות בנחמה

The number six million is so vast that it is often too difficult to fathom its immensity, nor to appreciate every victim.

The Malbim's explanation between the two different promises Hashem made to Avraham Avinu, that his children will be like, both, the sand and the stars, may help shed some understanding to this.

The sand on a beach is so numerous that it would be impossible to quantify. However, one does recognize when a significant portion of sand is missing. When counting stars, on the other hand, each individual star is unique and recognizable; hence, it is possible to count a quantifiable number.

This, explains the Malbim, is the difference between the two promises Hashem made to Avraham Avinu. Both the sand and stars are too numerous to ascertain an exact number. Sand can only be ascertained by determining how much is missing. Stars, however, are individually discernible, and therefore can be counted separately.

The *limud* for us is very profound. The Ribono Shel Olam promised Avraham Avinu that although his descendants will be so vast, like the sand, it will still be possible to count them individually, like stars. Therefore, as vast as we may be as a nation, everyone will have his place, and has the potential to shine like a star. But their losses will be noticed.

One of the *limudim* of the Holocaust is exactly this lesson. Yes, the number six million is so vast that it is impossible to appreciate who every victim was; but each was an individual, a Jew who was shining or had the potential to shine.

And that is why we feel each and every loss.

Rabbi Hoffman's book guides us to recognize the greatness of the individual, these shining stars. By reading about the great things that these people accomplished in the depths of darkness, we are inspired to strive to shine like stars when we are faced with our own challenges.

This book is a fantastic source of inspiration for all; adult, children and students alike. May we all be *zocheh* to strive to shine like stars, and by doing so, we should be *zocheh* to never know from such atrocity again, and merit to see the coming of the *Geulah beimheirah beyamenu*.

Sholom A. Friedmann
Rabbi Sholom Friedmann
Director

5923 Strickland Avenue, Brooklyn NY 11234 | T 718.759.6200 | F 347.492.6223 | www.kfhec.org

53 OLYMPIA LANE
MONSEY, NY 10952
PHONE: 845.369.1600
FAX: 845.369.NEWS

Rabbi Pinchos Lipschutz
Editor, Publisher

Erev Shabbos, Parshas Emor, 5773

As Rav Shem Klingberg of Zalashitz was being led to his death in the Plaszow camp, the beasts knocked off his *yarmulka* in an attempt to strip him of his dignity. The *tzaddik* faced his murderer calmly. He wrapped his *tallis kotton* over his head and recited the following *posuk* from *Tehillim* (73:17), which is an expression of Dovid Hamelech's longing for the *Bais Hamikdosh*:

"*Ad avo el mikdishei Kel* - Until we come home, we will never understand. Perhaps then, when everything is clear, *avinah le'achrisom*, we will merit to understand why this is occurring. Until then, it will remain a mystery."

And the *korban* was thus readied.

We cannot know and do not know why it all transpired, but what we do know is that in their deaths, the *kedoshim* revealed the glory and splendor of the Jewish soul. They demonstrated that neither hunger nor loss, neither privation nor suffering, can dim the *neshomah's* luster.

Their lessons teach us not only who they were, but also who *we* are. They taught us the strength of the *Yiddishe neshomah* and what it means to be a *Yid*.

That's what makes these books so important.

Beyond the heroism of those who perished, we appreciate the heroism that survivors displayed in picking up the shattered bits of their heart and rebuilding.

Six million of our brothers and sisters were taken during that horrific era, but many lived and went on to recreate the glorious world that had been destroyed.

How did they do it? From where did they garner the strength and wherewithal to persist and preserve, not only going on with life, but creating and building, marrying and raising children, laughing and crying again, and remaining loyal to Torah and Hashem despite all they experienced?

Their strength was derived from the same indomitable spirit that beat in their hearts and souls that kept them alive and sane in the Nazi inferno.

The same way the *kedoshim* faced death, with dignity and strength, the survivors faced life.

It is beyond the capacity of the human mind to fathom the enormity of what they lived through and grasp how they kept themselves going as they faced the worst savagery known to man on a daily basis. The stories in these volumes open a window and permit us a glimpse of the strength of the Jew throughout the ages. The subjects of the stories in this book were heroes for their time; and they are heroes for our time and for all time.

Rabbi Dovid Hoffman, who has dedicated his life to the dissemination of Torah and its values, is to be commended for producing the *"Heroes of Spirit"* series. These books are a valuable addition to the growing Holocaust library. They remind us of our inherent greatness and inspire us to persevere as we face life's challenges.

The books catalogue the indomitable spirit of Hashem's people -our unshakable faith in Him and His in us. That we are here today reading these books, learning Torah, observing *mitzvos*, and supporting and loving each other is the greatest testament to that fact.

May we merit the speedy coming of *Moshiach* and being reunited with the *kedoshim* who gave up their lives *al kiddush Hashem*.

Rabbi Pinchos Lipschutz
Publisher, Yated Ne'eman

בס"ד

To Rabbi Dovid Hoffman, שליט״א

I read your book **Heroes of Spirit** with great interest. The 100 tales that you bring are extremely moving and span a most significant era of our history. Compiling such a comprehensive collection is an important innovation. The stories have great educational value and they reflect the times well. They are suited to be read by readers of different ages, each one learning from them at his personal level. The tales include many different values which the Jewish People has always been faithful to, and throughout the book we become acquainted with exemplary leaders, models for future generations.

From a historical point of view, it might be worthwhile adding more information which could form the background of the story, and would give it even greater significance. It might also be a good idea to categorize the tales according to subject matter or chronologically.

יישר כוחכם
Yours,
Esther Farbstein
Jerusalem, 5773

בס"ד

Survival Through Education, Inc.
2164 Victory Blvd. Staten Island, NY 10314
718-983-9272
www.survivaltrougheducation.org
Helping the Chosen People Choose ©

May 5, 2013/25 Iyar 5773

It is a privilege to extend my heartfelt admiration for my chaver, **R' Dovid Hoffman** שליט"א, who has done so much to ensure that the years that surrounded the Holocaust will be remembered as years when הקב"ה tested His children and so many passed!

How will history remember the Holocaust? As the children of survivors age, it is their sacred responsibility to insure that the generations that follow know of the 'Kiddush H-Shem resistance' offered up by their ancestors. Chazal teach us that "one who saves one life, it is as if they saved an entire world." The term utilized by Chazal is "matzil nefesh achas..." as opposed to "matzil ish achas" or "matzil guf achas" because, at our core we are neshomos dedicated to elevating our physical existence.

R' Dovid's **Heroes of Faith** will serve as a lamp to illuminate the dark period in our history when such heroes were sorely needed. Much the way our Avos and Imahos sowed the path for future generations in the form of zchus Avos, so too, these **Heroes of Faith** did much to sow the path and fan the flames of faith in the pintele yiddilach of our generation who don't even know of their heritage.

It is my brocha that **Heroes of Faith** by R' **Dovid Hoffman** be well received and inspire Yidden of all affiliations to connect or reconnect with Avinu She'bashamayim, and that all those who **died so proudly** sanctifying His Name be the catalyst for us to **live so proudly** sanctifying His Name.

Dovid Winiarz
R' Dovid Winiarz
President

Acknowledgments

I have read numerous books about the Holocaust, Kristallnacht, the death camps, the cattle cars, the years leading up to the Second World War, and the years following the war. So many books that I lost count. Anything that has any sort of remote connection to this topic. Jewish and non-Jewish. I devour these books whole and reread the ones that truly inspire me again and again. It has become almost an obsession of mine. Undoubtedly, my thirst to read more and more about this inglorious chapter in the history of the Jewish people – our history, my history – is what led me to write the first *Heroes of Spirit* book and now this, the second installment in this series.

Through my readings, I have seen and heard so many stories. Every story is precious – not just those of the survivors. Every story has a message – not just those that have a happy ending. And every story is inspiring – although some will inspire in different ways than others. I am still amazed when I read how a person went through the torture and purgatory of the concentration camps; how they watched their family members sent to the left or shot before their eyes; how their children were wrestled out of their arms and taken away, never to be heard from again. I try to put myself in that situation; to try to feel the tension, the pain, the anguish. Of course, I can't.

But I try, and when I read about how after the war, these very same people thought of little else than saying Kaddish for the lost souls, *davening* and learning Torah from a real Gemara, keeping Shabbos and keeping kosher, fasting on Yom Kippur and dancing on Simchas Torah – I wonder: How did they do it? From where did they draw their strength? They knew this was the *chevlei Mashiach* and they fully expected Mashiach to arrive that very day of liberation. Yet, when he didn't, how did they go on? How would I have gone on?

It is then that my admiration for the *she'eiris hapleitah* reaches new heights and I know that these people were not mere mortals; they are heroes, they are "Heroes of Spirit, Heroes of Faith." It is my duty and obligation to tell their stories.

In preparation for this book, I have conducted numerous interviews – live and over the phone – with survivors and children of survivors, and even grandchildren of survivors. Every single one has a story to tell, but what is truly amazing is that many, if not most, have a story or anecdote that is connected in some way to a great rabbi, a *rosh yeshivah*, or a Chassidic rebbe. In some way, fashion or form, that rabbi and/or communal leader inspired them to go on, or blessed them in a way that they knew they would live to tell about. And they did! That is the crux of this book and why I have made it a "life-mission" to document these stories. There's nothing like a great and inspiring story, made even better when it includes and involves world-famous *tzaddikim* and righteous individuals who accomplished so much for the world.

Many *rabbanim* who survived the war documented their tales of survival in the *hakdamos* (introductions) to their *sefarim*. Many stories in this book were derived and translated from these *hakdamos*, including:

> *Klei Gola* (Makova Rav), *Minchas Yitzchak, Kuntres Pirsumei Nisa* (R' Yaakov Yitzchak Weiss), *Ohr*

V'Chaim L'Yisroel (Badischle Rav), *Dvar Avraham*, *Nehi V'dimah* (Kovno Rav), *Makdishei Hashem* (Veitzener Rav), *Mishneh Halachos, Kuntres Pirsumei Nisa* (R' Menashe Klein), *Shemiras Shabbos K'hilchasa*, *Kuntres Tov L'hodos* (R' Yehoshua Neuwirth), *Alei Meroros* (R' Yehoshua Moshe Aronson), etc.

As I discussed in the introduction to my first book, *Heroes of Spirit*, in this electronic age, there is so much factual and historical information to be found if you know where to look and I attempted to utilize every possible resource at my disposal. Even for those stories that I found printed in books, I did further research to enhance and add historical perspective. I listened to numerous speeches and *shiurim* in which stories were recollected and I adapted articles and material from books, old and new, until I found a great blend of stories. The following source material is included in this book:

Faith After the Flames, R' Yitzchak (Isaac) Avigdor; *A Fire in His Soul*, Amos Bunim; *They Fought Back*, Yuri Suhl; *Nor the Moon by Night*, Devorah Gliksman; *Branded for Life*, Raize Guttman; *Witness to History*, Ruth Lichtenstein (Editor-in-Chief); *Parsha Parables*, R' Mordechai Kamenetzky; *Pearls of Light*, Joseph Pearlman; *A Path Through the Ashes*, collected from the pages of *The Jewish Observer*; *Ashes to Renewal; Hassidic Tales of the Holocaust*, Professor Yaffa Eliach; *Lieutenant Birnbaum*, Meyer Birnbaum; *Kisrah shel Torah; Rescuing the Rebbe of Belz*, Yosef Israel; *The Brisker Rav*, R' Yosef Shimon Meller; *The Klausenberger Rebbe: The War Years*, translated and adapted by Judith Lifschitz from *Lapid Aish* by R' Aaron Sorasky; *Shema Yisrael: Testimonies of Devotion, Courage and Self-Sacrifice*, Yaakov Lavon; *To Save a World*, D. Kranzler, E. Gevirtz; *From Prison to Pulpit*, R' Yitzchak (Isaac) Avigdor; *Visions of Greatness* (vol I, III, VI, VII), R' Yosef Weiss; *The Jewish Observer*; R' Yerachmiel Tilles: http://ascentofsafed.com; *The Torah Profile*; *For Love of Torah*, R' Shimon Finkelman; *Reb Elchonon: The Life and Ideals of Rabbi Elchonon Bunim Wasserman of Baranovich*, R' Aaron Sorasky; *Toras Hatmarim*; *A Consoling Thought*, R' Zeev Greenwald; *A Look Back*, Dr. Gershon Kranzler; *Rosh Hashanah: Season of Majesty*, R' Zecharia Fendel; *Rav Chaim Ozer: The Life and Ideals of Rav Chaim Ozer Grodzenski*, R' Shimon Finkelman; *Tiv Hakehillah*, Harav Gamliel Rabinowitz; *Kovetz Klaliyos*; *In the Valley of Death*, Y. Yechezkieli; *Haggadah shel Pesach Al Matzos U'merorim*, R' Chaim Benisch; *Out of the Depths*, R' Yisroel Meir Lau; *A Committed Life*, Rebbetzin Esther Jungreis; *Gut Voch*, Avraham Barash; Article from OU Shabbat Shalom, by Judith Bron; *Chain of Miracles*, Faigie Russak; *Noble Deeds and Noble Lives* (vol I, II), R' Dovid Silber; *Kovetz A'ira Shachar*, R' Yehudah Russak; *Reb Boruch Ber*, R' Chaim Shlomo Rosenthal; *Kuntres Ish L'rei'eihu*, R' Naftali Weinberger; *Haggadas HaKehillos Yaakov*, R' Sholom Wallach; *The Reichmanns: Family, Faith, Fortune and the Empire of Olympia and York*, Anthony Bianco

There are so many people that assisted in the production of this book whom I wish to acknowledge and thank personally. My parents, Rabbi Pinchos and Helen Hoffman, first and foremost. My mother is a speaker extraordinaire who has made it her life's mission to speak about the Holocaust, and specifically her mother – my grandmother's tale of survival – to high schools, women's groups and organizations all around the world. When I listen to her message of *emunah* and courage, I cannot help but be inspired to write my own stories based on the lives of our great heroes. Of course, with regard to this book, my mother has done so much more than just give lectures. She has guided me in this endeavor; she has introduced me to important people in the field of Holocaust research; she has accompanied me on appointments to meet with some of these people; and she has enabled me to receive letters of encouragement and approbation from many of them, including the beautiful introduction by Rabbi Klein of Torah Umesorah. Both my father and mother are truly wonderful guides who instruct me daily on the proper course of life, and I thank them with all my heart and wish them continued blessings in every area of their lives.

If I had to choose one person whom I would consider a "partner" in this worthwhile endeavor, I would undoubtedly be referring to my sister, Rebbetzin Raize Guttman, of Ramat Shlomo, Jerusalem. She is probably the most gifted and "*hartzig*" person I know. If you knew her, you would surely agree! I still cannot believe how many times she took buses all over Jerusalem to procure a letter, or pick up a book, or find out some tidbit or detail that I needed to complete a story. She telephoned important people in many prominent organizations if I asked her to. She stayed up until all hours of the night advising and assisting me in one way or another. But her "coup d'etat" - her most incredible accomplishment of all (as far as this book is concerned) - is surely the wondrous poems she composed to introduce each chapter of this book. I defy anyone to read them and not feel the emotion pouring forth; one feels as if he or she is actually on the cattle car or in the lime pit, or talking directly to Hashem. These poems add an invaluable effect to the tone of the book, and without them, I do not believe one can truly "get in the mood" to properly read and digest these stories of inspiration. I cannot thank her enough (although I will definitely try) and I offer my deepest and most heartfelt blessings to her and her beautiful family that they continue to follow in the footsteps of their great ancestors on both sides and learn from them how to grow in Torah and *yiras Hashem*, so that they may lead us from the forefront on our way to meet Mashiach Tzidkeinu.

The list of people that must be acknowledged, as well as those I personally wish to acknowledge is long, *baruch Hashem*. But gratitude comes first and therefore my wife and our wonderful children top the list. If Estee is my pillar of support, my rock, the one to whom I turn – I wouldn't be where I am today, nor write this book, without her – then the kids are my purpose, the reason why I do this in the first place. Yitzy, Pepi, Tzvi, Alti, Naftoli, Daniel, Yehudah, Shlomo D. and little Rosie are children of the twenty-first century, but they could just as easily have been living in the 1930s and 40s, enduring what those children endured, feeling what those children felt. Holocaust stories and education is primarily for them, and it is for them that I write these books. Hashem should continue to watch over us and bless our family with happiness and health, and an abundance of Torah, *avodah* and *gemilus chassadim*. We, and all of Klal Yisrael, should never know from such horrors.

My close and dear friend, Rabbi Yosef Chaim Golding, devoted hours upon hours of his valuable time (he claims to be Executive Director of a prominent organization!) to read through each and every story in this book and make corrections, annotations and constructive criticism throughout the entire manuscript. He would not mince words when "mincing" was uncalled for and he was clear and concise in his evaluation of the material. For an author, this is truly a "godsend" and in all earnestness, if not for his constant refrain, "*Nu*, keep sending me more," I wonder if I would have been able to complete this project in time for its release. His beautiful dedication in memory of his esteemed father-in-law, Reb Yosef Friedenson *z"l*, is special in its own right, and I wish upon him and his wife (the "other" Rosie) and children, many years of *nachas*, *simchah* and success in all areas of *parnassah* and *askanus*.

My thanks and appreciation go out to my in-laws; Reb Yisroel and Leah Blonder, my sister and brother, sisters-in-law and brothers-in-law, and all those from the family who have supported me and helped out in the compilation and production of this book. Special mention to my Uncle Teddy for committing pen to paper to write the story of his father, Reb Alter Kurz.

I offer thanks to all those who graciously gave of their time and material for inclusion in this book: Rabbi Mordechai Kamenetzky; Rabbi Shmuel Klein; Rabbi Moshe Kamin; Rabbi Yosef Weiss; Reb Ephraim Minzer and his son Tuli; Rabbi Yehudah Russak; Rabbi Pinny Lipschutz; Rabbi Sholom Friedman; Reb Chaim Kofman; Reb Mordechai Friedland, his wife, daughter and son-in-law; Rabbi Dovid Winiarz; Rabbi Shimshon Sherer; Rabbi Ben Tzion Shafier; Reb Mordechai Avigdor; Reb Yankee Hirsch; Reb Nissan and Judith Bron; Breindy Taub.

Special recognition to Rabbi Moshe Kaufman and Israel Bookshop for doing another wonderful job in producing and publishing this book. Thank you to Mrs. E.M. Sonenblick for a superb proofreading job, and to Reb Sruli Perl of Vivid Design for the graphic artistry, layout and cover design. *Baruch Hashem*, our track record speaks for itself and *b'ezras Hashem* we should continue to supply the Torah world with quality and worthwhile products.

My hope and prayer to the Al-mighty is that when we attune ourselves to the Holocaust, this dark chapter in our long and glorious history, let us read about how our great leaders, our Heroes of Faith, fought back and remained a beacon of light in an otherwise gloomy and treacherous darkness. Let us teach our children that those people who lived through that calamitous period were our own flesh and blood and that we have those very same abilities and capabilities to withstand the negativity and evil that surrounds us. And let us shine forth our light to the nations of the world and show them once and for all that "*Netzach Yisrael lo yeshaker*" - the eternity of the Jewish people will withstand any and all attempts to subjugate it. It is up to us in this day and age to live our lives like "Heroes of Faith" and then we will merit our ultimate Redemption.

Dovid Hoffman
Rosh Chodesh Sivan 5773

Introduction

By Rabbi Shmuel Y. Klein
Director of Publications and Communication
Director of *Zechor Yemos Olam*, Torah Umesorah

For decades following the conclusion of the Second World War, a shroud of silence descended upon the Torah world. It kept the would-be voices of testimony still. Save for personal accounts shared by survivors with their children and with one another – and even then, with limitation and reservation – the broad topic of the destruction of *Yahadus Europa* at the hands of the German Third Reich remained unaddressed.

Perhaps the explanation is that the Jewish world needed to devote all of its energies and attention to the rebuilding of Torah life – in America, in Eretz Yisrael, and in Western Europe. That driving sense of mission precluded a focus on the past. Alternatively, the reason might also have been the inability of survivors and non-survivors alike to deal with the painful horrors of the Holocaust. Whatever the rationale, however, the darkest chapter in the odyssey of our people waited for nearly forty years to be meaningfully unearthed within the *Chareidi* camp.

Then the time came, and we experienced a surge of interest in so-called "Holocaust studies." Diaries and personal memoirs by survivors met the light of print at the hands of religiously reliable publishing houses; noted speakers began to address the topic in public venues. And schools – particularly of the Bais Yaakov genre – started to introduce programs of study intended to familiarize young Jews with the events of the war and with their ramifications.

Gedolei Yisrael then determined that what was now needed was a program of study that would be not only informative but also a responsible portrayal of a Torah perspective regarding the subject material.

The fundamental truth is that the chronicle of *churban Europa* is not merely a chapter of Jewish history; it is a profound *masechta* in the unfolding reality of the Creator's Am Hanivchar. Consequently, the educational tools – and more importantly, the *hashkafos*, the philosophical teachings – needed to be grounded in an approach that would accurately represent a Torah viewpoint. What was needed was the guidance of Torah luminaries in establishing an entity to promote a proper study of this vital *masechta*.

With that in mind, the *Va'ad Roshei Yeshivah* of Torah Umesorah called for the founding of a special division that would handle Holocaust studies, with an emphasis not on teaching the topic directly to students, but rather on training educators, enabling *them* to do so. Thus, with the leadership of Harav Elya Svei *zt"l*, Harav Avraham Pam *zt"l*, and, *ybl"c*, the Novominsker Rebbe *shlit"a*, among others, "*Zechor Yemos Olam*" (ZYO) was created, initially under the direction of Rabbi Yoseph Elias *shlit"a*, the eminent *menahel* of Bais Yaakov of Washington Heights.

Of important note is the mission statement that emerged from the new pedagogical blueprint of ZYO: the objective of study is not to impart the horrors of the Holocaust per se, but something that is far more crucial – a mindset steeped in Jewish fortitude and sanctity. Naturally, historical data is a prerequisite for the realization of this goal – but nevertheless a means to an end rather than an end in its own right.

Indeed, to discover that man is capable of unimaginable evil, one need not study the Holocaust; one need merely glance through the pages of a daily newspaper. In fact, from the very same source one may often derive that *sinas Yisrael* – anti-Semitism – continues to be a force that drives the nations of the world. Therefore, to focus on these themes while learning the Holocaust borders on the superfluous, or the pointless. It can therefore not be the purpose in studying *churban Europa*.

Moreover, an overly detailed and pictorial depiction of the horrors of Auschwitz and Majdanek would often serve to undermine the notion of *gadlus ha'adam*, human dignity and *kedushas Yisrael*. That surely is not the purpose of study!

The purpose, then, is to heighten the sense of Jewish identity in Jewish youth... to bolster the image of the Yid who acts with grace and faith, with self-sacrifice and *kedushah*... and with moral superiority in the face of the most sinister depravity the world ever saw. The purpose is to underscore the fact of *netzach Yisrael*, the Divine pledge that, notwithstanding the *middas hadin*, ours is an eternal people, outliving the foes who seek our demise. The purpose is to fashion a glorious tapestry of Jewish devotion to the Al-mighty, His Torah and His *mitzvos*... and of the resiliency of the Jewish spirit in the face of adversity. These components comprise the legacy we wish to impart – *must* impart – to the next generations of Jews.

Reb Dovid Hoffman has produced wonderful resources to advance this sacred agenda: now his second volume of stirring narratives, *Heroes of Faith*, is about to be released. These books are veritably brimming with accounts of spiritual giants whose actions during the Holocaust bespoke the highest spiritual plateau reachable from within the human condition.

In his commentary on *Bereishis*, the Sfas Emes offers a response to the famous question of R' Yitzchak: why did the Torah not begin with actual *mitzvos*, starting with "*Hachodesh hazeh lachem*"? Why was it important to read the narratives of *Sefer Bereishis*? His explanation: the Torah wished to teach that the actions of the *Avos* and of the *shevatim* created chapters of the Torah. The accounts of our holy forebears are the stuff of which Jewish legacy is made.

Albeit on a different plane, *Heroes of Faith* achieves the same goal. It is a text that substantiates the true legacy of the Holocaust years, a legacy that serves the ultimate purpose of Holocaust studies. Reading the stories of Rabbi Dr. Solomon Schonfeld, of the Radoshitzer Rebbe, of Rav Elchanan Wasserman, *zecher tzaddikim livrachah*, among many others – known *tzaddikim* and many who are unknown – infuses in one the most poignant sense of pride and self-esteem. Readers – young and old alike – cannot help but be inspired from the uplifting discovery they will make: the Jewish blood of these heroes of spirit was the same as that which flows through our own veins. The profound illumination with which they diffused a most profound darkness serves as our very own source of light.

Reb Dovid Hoffman, himself a grandson of survivors, an heir to a spiritual and emotional treasure, has offered students of *churban Europa* a manifesto of Jewish greatness. What he has compiled will help them bear the sacred torch of "*Mi k'amcha Yisrael, goy echad ba'aretz*." May Hashem shower this endeavor, as well as his future efforts, with *brachah* and success!

Shmuel Yaakov Klein

Foreword

Drawn from the original diary of Rabbi Yitzchak (Isaac) Avigdor *zt"l*, written while he was hospitalized in Wells, Austria, following his liberation from Mauthausen. Originally printed in the *Hartford Times* editorial, Saturday, May 8, 1965.

Survival and Revival

"We have survived – we are free," were the words I uttered, gasping with my fast waning breath, wavering between death and the suddenness of liberation.

It was May 5, 1945, as I lay weary and spent from a siege of typhoid fever, when before my befogged vision flickered a hazy silhouette of the white star on an American tank. It seemed like a dream and most of us didn't believe it.

I had to touch with my own hands and embrace the American tank to convince myself of the reality.

It may sound like a paradox, but today, many years later, when I review the memories of those days, I cannot believe that it was I who experienced the sufferings I had to undergo.

I asked myself, how did I survive? How did I escape death from the crematoria, concentration camps, ghettos, from hunger and whip lash and machine gun fire?

There were thousands of days, millions of minutes and seconds, each of which trembled on the delicate borderline between life and death.

Actually, thus far no vocabulary has been created in any language that could fittingly paint the colors of that horrendous inferno; no words that we currently possess can possibly explain that period of history, not even in a long series of articles or voluminous books.

We are still too close to the terrifying picture to sweep the horizon with one look and evaluate the degradation of the last holocaust.

There will arise poets and historians who will study and describe the epoch of gas chambers and crematoria; perhaps they will transcend our inadequacy.

But I can state that the simple secret of my own survival, and of many like myself, was the strong desire to live.

We had many known and unknown heroic fighters among the millions of martyrs. There were those of the Warsaw ghetto, who to the last breath tenaciously fought the cruel enemy.

But there were also those who died quietly and helplessly without militant resistance.

All of them died courageously and proudly. All of them stretched out with unwavering courage, their suffering the kind of which and the circumstances of which no other people could possibly withstand.

It required tremendous energy and faith to go on living. Historians will find an amazing fact that in the whole Hitler epoch of ghettos and camps, there was a small percentage of suicides amongst Jews.

No matter how much the enemy was scourging or torturing us, there was never any pessimism or despair of the kind that would bring about the thought of self-destruction.

So mightily were we all nerved, by our will to live, by the inner knowledge that eventual victory was on our side, that we considered living an extra day or even a few hours, the greatest heroism.

Not even for one moment did we lose faith that once more in the old history of our people will we be able to stand over the graves of the enemy.

There was no doubt in any of our minds about the indestructibility of our people; all we wanted was to witness the victorious emergence.

A German officer once told me that the thing he admired most in the Jewish people was their stubbornness in resisting an open revolt. We are waiting, he said, for you to attack any of the officers of the German army, and this would give us the best excuse to liquidate you all at once.

We knew that there were many towns and villages across Poland where individual Jews killed a German, spit at his face, or threw stones at him, and it always resulted in immediate bloodshed or slaughter of that entire Jewish community.

Heroically, we practiced the art of restraint, though it came to us at a high price of humiliation.

I joined a group of partisans who were hiding in the forest in underground bunkers. From time to time, we carried through acts of sabotage and other similar activities, but we always watched carefully never to leave any traces that would lead the Germans to think that the attack came from Jews.

We knew that once a Jew was identified with any such project the Germans would take it out on innocent women and children of the local ghetto.

It was very easy for them to do so, because they had all been incarcerated under wire fences. This was true in the ghettos and more so in the concentration camps. All the Jews were responsible and blamed for the faults of one individual.

Without help from the outside, without weapons, food and barest necessities, against the powerful forces of the Nazi military machine and the ruthless Nazi mentality, any reprisal or resistance was suicidal and doomed to failure.

I am positive, though a lot of people may disagree, that had we undertaken an open armed revolt against Hitler, there could not have been any Jews left in Europe at all. There were none left in the Warsaw ghetto.

We know now that in spite of the great historical value of the Warsaw ghetto uprising, as one of the most sublime deeds in our long and tragic history, it did not awaken the conscience of the world.

The Polish people of Warsaw stood by almost silently with their hands folded, and so did the powers of the Alliance. The desperate cry for help of the Warsaw fighters remained unanswered.

I learned two important lessons from my World War II experiences, and they both will stand out foremost in my mind as long as I live.

First, as a people, I learned that culture, civilization, progress – call it what you will – can raise the moral and ethical level of individuals, perhaps, but never of society as a whole.

Nations and countries will always remain primitive beasts in their human family relations. They will utilize culture and civilization only as a means of exterminating one another more efficiently and more speedily.

Secondly, I learned as an individual, how relative are the words "good fortune." In concentration camps and ghettos, yesterday's salvaged morsel of dried bread was the greatest treasure imaginable, far above the most extravagant comforts and luxuries of normal times. Devoid of a future, faced perpetually with a death warrant, our entire fate centered upon that infinitesimal fraction of time, that elementary fleeting moment in the present, revolving around that untouched morsel of bread.

{PREWAR:}
Rise of the Aggressor

Heroes of Faith

by Raize Guttman

Seventy souls went down to Egypt,
We were beaten by whip and by sword.
But the Jewish people are *"Heroes of Spirit"*
And with spirit so strong we endured.

For seventy years we were captives in Bavel,
But now Babylonia is gone.
For the Jewish people are *"Heroes of Courage"*
And with courage we still carry on.

The seventy gentile nations of the world,
Try to destroy our nation.
But the Jewish people are *"Heroes of Faith"*
And G-d saves us in each generation.

The galus is long, the pain is so deep,
There is only one way we survive.
It is Jewish spirit, courage and faith,
That has kept the Jewish people alive.

Hold onto your courage, hold tight to your faith,
Your greatness of spirit don't lose.
For so very soon, Mashiach will come,
In the merit of all heroic Jews.

| REB BORUCH FRANKEL |
An American Tale of Salvation

The American Dream; just the words alone seem to have a magical ring. For over two hundred years, through untold numbers of journeys by land and sea, millions of people left their families behind in Europe and other places and arrived in the United States in the hope of finding the streets "paved with gold," so that they may strike it rich and live the good life. Or, at the very least, earn enough money to send to their loved ones back home. For some it was a triumph; for others a dismal and abject failure. But for one individual, it was the difference between life and death for himself and his entire family.

In 1927, Reb Boruch Frankel left his wife and three children back in Poland and made the transatlantic journey by steamer to the New York harbor to try to make a living and support his family. It was quite a sacrifice. Reb Boruch was a scion of a great Chassidic lineage, and his roots were firmly planted back in the old country. Yet, he realized that there was greater opportunity in America, and together with a fellow immigrant he met in New York, he started an import business which did rather well. For three solid years, Reb Boruch and his partner labored in the business and, with Hashem's grace, they raised more than enough money for their families back home. Soon, they believed, they would head back to the old country and be hailed as champions of industry, the models of industrious success.

It was towards the end of his third year in New York when Reb Boruch received the telegram that would change his life. His father had passed away and he was required by Jewish law to sit *shivah* for seven days. Reb Boruch informed his partner that he would be unavailable for the next week due to his personal loss and his friend assured him that he could manage without him for those few days. Reb Boruch sat *shivah* in his small apartment on the Lower East Side, and his few acquaintances and associates came to pay their respects.

One day, in the middle of the *shivah*, his partner arrived and sat down opposite the mourner, as per Jewish custom. Reb Boruch was glad to see him and he spoke a bit about his father. At one point in the conversation, the partner excused himself and pulled a paper out of his pocket. He explained that an important matter had come up which required both partners' signatures. Reb Boruch nodded and without even glancing at the contents of the paper, signed it and handed it back. After a few more minutes, the partner stood up, intoned the customary words of consolation, and left.

After the week of *shivah* had concluded, Reb Boruch arrived at his office to find the place cleared out and his partner nowhere to be found. It took some time before Reb Boruch was able to learn the entire story: His "partner" had duped him into signing a paper that gave away his entire portion of the business! Knowing that Reb Boruch would not read the fine print on the document during his period of mourning, he came during the *shivah* and cheated his one-time friend and partner out of his life's savings! And during those very days that Reb Boruch was unavailable, he sold the entire business and ran away with the money, never to be heard from again.

Reb Boruch was left penniless, without enough money even to return to his family in Europe. Understandably, he was devastated over the situation. He could not understand how somebody could sink so low, and he walked around for days believing that this was the worst thing that could ever have happened. But the tides of destiny were coming in and they held the future salvation of the Frankel family.

With no place to go and no means to get there, Reb Boruch was forced to remain in New York. He took a job and earned some money. After two more years, someone suggested that he apply for American citizenship. Reb Boruch did so and in a short time, he became a naturalized American citizen. But he truly longed for home and he missed his family sorely, so after a few more months, Reb Boruch took whatever savings he had accumulated and returned to Poland, to the loving embrace of his family.

Years passed and by the summer of 1939, it was clear that war was imminent. The German army was poised to invade Poland, and the situation for millions of Polish Jews was becoming egregious. Many Jews wished to emigrate from Poland but most had nowhere to go. Boruch Frankel, on the other hand, was an American citizen and thus was able to procure a visa for himself with little difficulty. Securing visas for his family, however, was an entirely different matter. This was a huge deal which could take months, if not years, to complete. Nobody knew the future and nobody wished to wait years. It was decided that his best option was to return to America alone, and from there arrange for his family to escape the impending war in Europe and join him.

Upon his arrival in America, he worked day and night until he successfully arranged visas and tickets for his entire family. His wife and four children were scheduled to depart from the Italian port of Trieste on September 1, 1939, aboard the ocean-liner, Queen Elizabeth. To his chagrin and utter disappointment, he was informed by the shipping company that due to the outbreak of war, the voyage was canceled. His family was stranded in Italy for the time being, but with renewed efforts, Reb Boruch was able to secure them tickets aboard a second ship.

With the guiding hand of Providence, the Frankel family set sail on November 1, 1939, on the very last passenger ship leaving Italy. Traveling from Trieste, to Kosice in Czechoslovakia, to Ellis Island in New York, the Frankel family survived the war. And the dishonest partner who stole every penny, forcing Reb Boruch to remain in New York? Who knows... if it wasn't a Divine messenger sent from on High?

The Treasured Keepsake

Menachem (Manfred) Margulies was only eleven years old when the ominous thunderclouds of Germany's hatred began raining their vitriolic rainstorm on Germany's Jews. Many years earlier, his family had moved from Poland to Berlin to live the "better life" in the more cultured and tolerant Germany. But that was not to be. With Hitler's rise to power, Germany had turned into a boiling pot of hatred.

Like all Polish Jewish émigrés, Wolf and Rosa Margulies and their family were now considered *Ostjuden*. Germany wanted them out and Poland did not want them back. On October

28, 1938, the dreaded knock came. The Gestapo had come for Fred's father, Wolf Margulies. Germany had no need for him anymore and he was to be deported back to Poland. For some unknown reason, one of the officers looked at the list of names and asked, "By the way, does a Manfred Margulies live here?"

Rosa Margulies would not lie. "He does."

"Let me notify you that tomorrow the Gestapo will be having an *aktion* for the children. They will be coming for him." Then the officer shrugged slyly, "If he happens not to be here, I guess they won't take him." With that, he left.

Rosa immediately sprung into action. Together with her family, the Treffs, she arranged to hide Manfred along with his siblings and cousins until they would be able to escape Germany.

Less than two weeks later, on November 7, 1938, Herschel Grynszpan shot Ernst von Rath, a secretary in the German embassy in Paris. Von Rath's death two days later would indeed sound the death knell for European Jewry. The Nazis used the opportunity to inflict collective punishment on its Jewish citizens. They riled the masses into burning and destroying nearly three hundred synagogues, and vandalizing and looting 7,500 Jewish businesses, as police and fire brigades stood on the side. Indeed, that infamous night, well known as Kristallnacht, the night of the broken glass, was a turning point in history.

The pogroms marked an intensification of Nazi anti-Jewish policy that would culminate in the "Final Solution" – the systematic, state-sponsored murder of all Jews. It was clear to most Jews that their former lives as proud German citizens were to be no more. It was at that precise moment that Rosa Margulies knew that her son Manfred would have to make his escape from Germany with not much more than his life. Manfred, however, would not leave with just the shirt on his back. He needed something more. And he knew exactly where it was.

During Kristallnacht, virtually every shul in Berlin was torched with their windows smashed, *sefarim* and ritual books ripped to shreds and sacred Torah scrolls desecrated. Virtually every shul – all except one. It was a tiny little synagogue located on 37 Munschestrasse. The reason why it was spared was because it was wedged between two apartment buildings where high-ranking Nazi officers lived. A spreading blaze from that building would jeopardize their homes as well as their families, and as a result, the S.S. sent fire brigades and police specifically to that location to protect the Jewish sanctuary. If that wasn't ironic enough, the Nazis did not realize that they also were protecting something else. Something that young Manfred just had to retrieve before leaving his native land.

And so, with the unabashed recklessness of an eleven-year-old youth, he hurried back to the little synagogue on Munschestrasse, where he and his family would pray, in order to retrieve what was rightfully his. Although it wasn't burned and looted, the shul was boarded up and a young Nazi recruit in a brand-new uniform was posted outside. Manfred did not care. He may not have realized that he could have been asking for a one-way ticket to Buchenwald, where thirty thousand had been sent on November 11th – or worse – but he just had to get in.

"Herr Officer," he announced breathlessly, running up to the shul entrance, "I must enter this building. I left something very important inside!"

The officer was dumbfounded at the brazenness of the Jew. However, the boy had made the demand with such confidence and resolve that he simply did not know what to say. It was his first day on the job and he was not sure if he should turn down the request. Miraculously, he decided to let the boy in. Manfred dashed inside and in less than thirty seconds he came out holding a velvet bag tightly in his hands. Without waiting for the Nazi to comment or inspect his prize, he ran home as fast as his legs could carry him.

On December 6, 1938, together with his cousin Yanky Treff and some siblings and cousins, Manfred made his way on a kindertransport to Holland. He never saw his parents again and he never let that bag out of his sight.

A number of years ago, at the age of eighty-three, Fred Margulies died. His son related this story at the *shivah* and concluded that his father and cousins did escape to Holland; all except a sister were spared. But the story did not end there. In fact, the velvet bag that his dad had rescued from the shul that fateful day went with him wherever he went – during the hidings, the escapes, the misery, the deportations and displacements of the war and its aftermath. He never forsook it and was scrupulously careful not to lose it. It meant everything to him.

Suddenly, the *avel* stood up, amidst an incongruous mixture of tears and a wide smile, and picked up a small velvet bag from behind his chair. He lifted it up and showed all the visitors what his father, Fred, had risked his life for. The bag had a Magen David embroidered on it. From the bag, he removed a small *tallis*, worn in the tradition of German Jewish boys, and an even smaller siddur with a name neatly printed in Hebrew letters on the inside cover, Menachem ben Zev Margulies. And through the tears, in joyous tribute, the *avel* smiled as he thrust them forward and said, "He risked his life to retrieve these. And now they, and that moment, will be with us forever."

| RABBI DR. SOLOMON SCHONFELD |
Pure Humanity to the Rescue

It was the fall of 1938. Rabbi Dr. Solomon Schonfeld was a young rabbi of twenty-six who had taken over his late father's positions as rabbi of a small congregation and principal of a small day school – the first in England. News of the persecution of Jews in Germany and Austria began to filter in, especially the day after the terrible pogrom of Kristallnacht on November 9-10, 1938.

Sitting in his modest office, Dr. Schonfeld could not settle down to his daily work. A sensitive man, he understood the full impact of the tragedy. He had thought that such things could only happen in the Middle Ages, not in our age of progress. Here he sat, safe in his cozy room, while his fellow Jews on the other side of the Channel languished in concentration camps. What could he do to help them? He had no money. His father had never been money-minded. Whatever he had managed to save from his own modest salary he usually gave away when confronted with an emergency among his congregants. So the only thing left was compassion for his brethren, but this was clearly not enough.

Dr. Schonfeld's thoughts were interrupted by the sharp ring of the telephone. It was a Mr. Julius Steinfeld calling from Vienna. Dr. Schonfeld had talked to this man in Austria several times. Steinfeld, a courageous communal leader in Vienna, had been doing his utmost for his brethren in Austria without regard for his own safety. Briefly and carefully, so as not to run afoul of the censors, who he was sure were listening in on the telephone conversation, Mr. Steinfeld now told Dr. Schonfeld of hundreds of children whose parents had been arrested or killed in the pogrom and who were now left on their own. Could Dr. Schonfeld help them? His voice choked with emotion, Dr. Schonfeld promised to try.

A council of members of Dr. Schonfeld's congregation was hastily summoned to grapple with the problem. The gentlemen decided, for a start, to raise money to bring ten children over to England. Dr. Schonfeld left the meeting in a depressed mood. They were good men, but they didn't understand that it would take weeks, even months to raise the large amount they thought would be necessary to care adequately for the children. Meanwhile, hunger, sickness and the threat of further pogroms would take a heavy toll. Ten children indeed!

Something much more drastic had to be done. But Dr. Schonfeld did not dare spell out his plans. He was afraid he would be put into a straitjacket. He knew his congregation; they were a well-fed, well-housed community. The troubles on the Continent still seemed very far away. Bombs and war appeared highly unlikely. Perhaps the people of the congregation were a little too complacent. After a sleepless night, mulling everything over again and again, Dr. Schonfeld went to the British Home Office.

The impressive figure of a handsome six-footer with gleaming eyes and a winning smile gained ready access to one of the most important officials at the Home Office. Dr. Schonfeld told the official what had happened in Austria. This, of course, was no news to that gentleman. He, too, had read the newspapers. Then Dr. Schonfeld unfolded the details as he himself saw them, and reported what Mr. Steinfeld had told him on the telephone. The official muttered that he was very sorry but there was nothing he could do to help.

Then, for the first time, Dr. Schonfeld revealed his plan. He said he wanted to bring three hundred Jewish children from Vienna to London and care for them personally. The British official was stunned. How could one rabbi provide for so many children; to house, feed and clothe them? Dr. Schonfeld told him he had neighbors who would be willing to help; he personally would guarantee with whatever assets he himself possessed that the children would not become burdens to the British government. All that was necessary was that the children should be given permission to come to England.

The British official sized up his petitioner with growing admiration. This was a young man, not yet thirty years old, with a pure soul, a good heart and a tremendous will to help others. Could he send this man away? Would he ever be able to sleep peacefully again if he said no now? Thinking of his own children and his own home, he was ready to give his approval. But his duties as an official of the British government forced him to hold back. "Tell me, Rabbi, where will you put the children to sleep the first night they are here?" he asked.

Dr. Schonfeld fell silent, but suddenly he had an inspiration. "I have two schools of which I am principal. I will empty the school buildings. I will house the children there," he replied.

"I want to see for myself where there is room for three hundred children in your school," said the man behind the desk.

The rabbi and the British government official went out together, hailed a taxi and drove off to North London. Before the eyes of the startled pupils, the two men measured the length and width of each classroom. They began to figure in terms of so many children and so many square meters. It would have been barely enough, but there was one large room which could not be used. It had to be left clear as a dining room for the students.

Forty children would still be without shelter. "Well," said the official, "in view of the circumstances, I can give you passports for only 260 children."

But the official had not reckoned with Rabbi Schonfeld. "Wait! I own the house in which I live!" the rabbi exclaimed. "I will empty that out, too, In order to make room for the children."

Back Dr. Schonfeld went, the government official in tow, to his private home. Again, the yardstick came out. Defeated by the overwhelming humanity of this man, the official diffidently asked Dr. Schonfeld where he himself would sleep. Dr. Schonfeld took him upstairs to a tiny room in the attic filled with bric-a-brac. "I can sleep here," he said. The official had tears in his eyes as he shook the rabbi's hand and asked him to submit the names of the children to whom he should issue the permits to enter England.

Immediately, in the presence of the official, Rabbi Schonfeld telephoned the leaders of Vienna's Jewish community. He asked them to draw up a list of names and admonished them to see to it that the children on this list would be ready to travel as soon as possible. Two days later he was back at the Home Office with all the data about the children. A passport official began to prepare the individual papers. He was only halfway through when it was closing time at the office. He told Dr. Schonfeld to come back the next day; he would finish the remaining passports then. But on being reminded of the joy which these papers would bring to three hundred families in Europe, this kind man disregarded closing time and worked on the papers until midnight. Then he helped Dr. Schonfeld pack the papers and carry them to the post office to speed them on their way to Austria.

Now that the first step had been taken, the real worries began. Upon an urgent call from Dr. Schonfeld early in the morning, his friends assembled at his home. He told them what he had done and asked them to help him. A search for beds began. The local Boy Scout troop had a sufficient number of beds and blankets at their summer camp. They were only too willing to lend them for such a purpose. Several trucks were sent out to the scout camp to bring these, as well as many dishes and large pots and pans which were necessary to cook for the refugees.

Meanwhile, a cable reported that the children had left Vienna. Then disaster struck. A blizzard, the heaviest in eight years, blanketed London, and the schools were snowbound. But this did not deter Dr. Schonfeld. Together with a group of youngsters, he went out with shovels to clear the way for the trucks that would bring the refugee children. This accomplished, the school and his own home ready for the children, he hurried to the port of Harwich to greet his three hundred new charges.

What he saw moved him deeply. Here were ragged, starved, frightened youngsters, the remains of once proud families. He shepherded them into the hired trucks to bring them to their new shelters. Neighbors were waiting there. Everyone was willing and ready to help feed and wash the children and put them to bed on this, their first night in a new country.

The rabbi was close to exhaustion, but he stayed on duty until all the children had been settled. Only after that did he go home for his first good night's sleep in a week. Entering his house, he heard a little six-year-old refugee girl crying for her mother. He took the child in his arms, talked to her about her new country and promised to bring her mommy to join her soon. Then Dr. Schonfeld went up to his attic chamber for a well-earned rest.

| R' DOVID LEIBOWITZ |
No *Talmid* Left Behind

In 1933, seven years after coming to the United States, R' Dovid Leibowitz *zt"l*, one of the prime disciples of the Alter from Slabodka and nephew of the Chafetz Chaim, founded Yeshivas Rabbeinu Yisroel Meir Hakohen (better known today as Yeshivas Chafetz Chaim), named after his great uncle. As part of his quest to create a unique and high-level yeshivah, he searched for quality students whom he felt he could mold with his unique style of Talmud study as well as the Slabodka school of *mussar*.

One day, while sitting in the *beis medrash* of Yeshivah Torah Voda'ath in Williamsburg, New York, he noticed a young student of about fifteen years of age who was unusually studious and serious about his learning. R' Dovid invited him to come join him in his new yeshivah. Thus, a great *rebbi/talmid* relationship was born between the *rosh yeshivah* and one of his prime disciples; my grandfather, R' Yitzchak Hoffman.

For the ensuing five years, Yitzchak (affectionately known as Itzik) excelled in his studies and blossomed into a tremendous scholar, and R' Dovid nurtured him with pride and affection, even testing and granting him a rabbinic certificate of *semichah* when Yitzchak was only eighteen years old. Two years later, when Yitzchak became engaged to Rose Kamin, R' Dovid was only too happy to officiate under the *chuppah*.

Yitzchak Hoffman was a rare breed of Torah student and scholar. Although the drumbeats of war could already be heard as far away as the American shore, Yitzchak had his heart set on studying Torah overseas, in the great Lithuanian bastions of Torah. No amount of dissuasion could talk him out of his stated desire, and with the implicit support of his young wife, Rose, the two made arrangements to leave for Europe in the summer of 1938.

One of those who tried to convince the young couple to stay in New York was R' Dovid Leibowitz. On numerous occasions, he implored Yitzchak to reconsider; aside from the safety issue and advisability of moving to a continent on the brink of war, R' Dovid could not understand why Yitzchak needed to find a different place to study. Was he not getting all he needed from his *rebbi* back home? Did he think he would gain more from another of the Alter's *talmidim* in Europe? R' Dovid made his thoughts plain and clear, but Yitzchak could not be swayed. With single-minded focus and a persistence that was his trademark all throughout his colorful life, my grandfather put his relationship with his dear *rebbi* on the line, just so he could learn Torah in Europe.

Yitzchak and Rose arrived in Slabodka in 1938. Always the studious sort, Yitzchak took to the yeshivah like a fish to water. Rose, too, immersed herself in the quaint Lithuanian lifestyle. As an American, she was a curiosity to the locals and they held her and her husband in great esteem and affection. Nobody had much money in the small towns and villages of Lithuania, but life was so simple that nobody needed much money. This benefited the young couple as well, since they came with very little and spent even less. Life was indeed quite glorious for that short period of time.

The Second World War broke out in 1939, but in the early stages of the conflict, Slabodka was little affected by the raging battles. Although anti-Semitism did see an uptick even in Lithuania, the students and married fellows continued their learning schedules as before. The newspapers were continuously scrutinized for daily information, but the idyllic village life changed little. The Hoffmans were constantly receiving letters from family and friends back home, urging them to leave Slabodka immediately, but they always responded that they were not being affected and felt no reason to run away. Besides, although everyone was sending them letters to leave, no one was sending them money for safe passage out of Europe – and without money they weren't going anywhere.

One day, in mid-May of 1940, a message from the American embassy in Kovno arrived, telling the Hoffmans that it was urgent for them to report to the embassy immediately. Yitzchak and Rose knew better than to take this message lightly. The town of Slabodka neighbored with the larger city of Kaunas (Kovno) and was situated directly across the Neris River opposite the heart of central Kovno. It didn't take them long to get to the embassy. They identified themselves and were immediately whisked into an inner office. An embassy official came right to the point.

"Mr. and Mrs. Hoffman, you are American citizens. We at the American embassy feel it is our duty to warn all American citizens in this area of the impending danger. Therefore, we urge you to make immediate arrangements to go back to the States, where you will be safe. Here, in Europe, we do not know how long we will be able to protect you."

Yitzchak and Rose looked at each other. They knew this was coming. Finally, Yitzchak spoke up. "Sir, even if we would want to return to New York, we cannot."

"Why is that?" asked the embassy official.

"Because we have no money," said Yitzchak, without the slightest hint of irony. "Just getting to a ship costs money – not to mention the ticket for the ship itself – money which we just don't have!"

The official was taken aback at the straightforwardness of the answer. "Well, what will you do when the war comes to Slabodka?" he asked.

"We will do whatever our people do! We will go wherever our people go!" was Yitzchak's clear and unequivocal answer.

Meanwhile, back in New York, developments of another sort were unfolding. In early 1940, R' Dovid Leibowitz suffered a massive heart attack, and his weakness was affecting his ability to run the Chafetz Chaim yeshivah. Bills were piling up and although he should have been taking it easy and seeing to his health, R' Dovid did not have a moment to spare. Teaching students, delivering *shiurim*, running the yeshivah affairs and traveling to raise funds were his constant duties and chores, and men half his age would have been hard-pressed to keep up with his rigorous schedule. The news out of Europe was not good, and this just made matters all the more worse.

Late one night, R' Dovid sent a message that he would like to speak with one of his *talmidim*. Aba Zalka Gewirtz (Zalky) was extremely close to his *rebbi* and hastened to R' Dovid's small apartment, situated in the yeshivah building above the main *beis medrash*. As soon as he walked into the room, he read the expression on his *rebbi's* face and knew something was wrong.

"What is it, Rebbi?" asked Zalky, concerned.

"Aba Zalka," said R' Dovid, "do you have any money left from your wedding gifts?" A strange question indeed.

"Well, I do have a little bit left," said Zalky.

"Good," said R' Dovid. "This is a matter of *pikuach nefesh* (saving lives). I want you to take whatever money you have and send it to Slabodka, to your brother-in-law, Yitzchak Hoffman. (Yitzchak and Zalky had married sisters, Rose and

Libby Kamin.) Don't delay! We have to get them out of Europe before it is too late!"

Zalky marveled at his *rebbi's* far-reaching concern. R' Dovid was ill and his yeshivah was going through a rough spell. And yet, R' Dovid was able to pinpoint a former *talmid* in need, thousands of miles away, who had left him years earlier, and focus on rescuing him from the jaws of danger! Of course, Zalky agreed to help, but he wondered aloud how he would send the money. Lithuania was an occupied country, and American law strictly forbade the transfer of funds to unauthorized countries. "You'll think of something," said R' Dovid, and urged Zalky to hurry, for this was not a matter to be taken lightly.

Turning to another brother-in-law, Alter Chaim (Hy) Kamin, who was more proficient in American law and procedure, Zalky learned that the only way to transfer funds was through the State Department in Washington, D.C. Zalky gave whatever money he had to Hy, and Hy made the four-hour train ride down to Washington to wire the funds to the American embassy in Kovno.

A mere two weeks after their first encounter in the American embassy, Yitzchak and Rose were once again summoned to the embassy with an urgent message. When Yitzchak walked in, he found the same official and told him, "I told you already, we cannot go anywhere since we have no money!"

Wordlessly, the official handed him the wire transfer, showing how a sizable sum of money was sent from a Mr. Hy Kamin in Washington, D.C., for the benefit of Irving and Rose Hoffman! He handed them their money and informed them that their best bet – possibly their only hope – to secure safe passage across the Atlantic was aboard an American troopship which was designated on a special mission to Europe, the USS American Legion.

President Franklin D. Roosevelt had directed the USS American Legion, a converted ocean-liner, to leave New York and proceed to Petsamo, in northern Finland. There, she was to embark the Crown Princess Martha of Norway and her party to bring them to the United States, their homeland having fallen to the Germans the previous spring.

On the fifteenth of July, 1940, the USS American Legion embarked Crown Princess Martha and her three children. The Army troopship also embarked a host of American nationals and refugees from a variety of countries: Finland, Estonia, Latvia, Lithuania, Sweden, Norway, Denmark, Germany, and the Netherlands, the total number of people being 897. Among the passengers was a young Danish comedian and musician, Victor Borge, as well as fifteen prominent nationals of American republics, including the Mexican foreign minister.

Yitzchak and Rose wasted no time in arranging their affairs in Slabodka. Then, they traveled by train for one week straight – even on Shabbos – until they reached Finland and procured passage aboard the American Legion. Rose was in the second month of pregnancy, and she became violently ill on board. Thankfully, the trained army medical staff aboard the ship made it their mission to treat the sole pregnant woman on board, and they waited on her hand and foot. Crown Princess Martha could not have received better or more royal treatment than Rose did on the American Legion!

The ship sailed for the United States on August 16, 1940, and reached New York twelve days later, escorted on the final leg of the voyage by several American destroyers.

| R' MICHEL MUNK |

An Indestructible People

On November 10, 1938, the day after the infamous Kristallnacht riots all throughout Germany, over thirty thousand German Jewish men were arrested for the "crime" of being Jewish and sent to concentration camps, where hundreds of them perished. Some Jewish women were also arrested and sent to local jails. Businesses owned by Jews were not allowed to reopen unless they were managed by non-Jews. Curfews were placed on Jews, limiting the hours of the day that they could leave their homes. The Nazi state imposed a fine of one billion *Reichsmarks* ($400 million) on the Jewish community in Germany for being the "cause of the German nation's rightful outrage." Jews were ordered to clean up their shops and make repairs after the pogrom. They were barred from collecting insurance for the damages. Instead, the state confiscated payments owed by insurers to Jewish property holders. In the aftermath of the pogrom, Jews were systematically excluded from all areas of public life in Germany.

The morning after the pogroms, a group of truncheon-wielding Gestapo agents burst into the home of R' Michel Munk *zt"l, rav* of the K'hal Adath Israel Synagogue in Berlin. Brutally, they dragged him outside and forced him into the street. A number of other communal leaders had been similarly rounded up and the Nazis efficiently marched the men through the streets of Berlin, to the ruins of the once magnificent Adath Israel Synagogue, which had been set aflame and burnt to destruction.

The Jewish leaders stood inside the great building and were shocked. What they saw was utter devastation. The *aron hakodesh* was incinerated, there were gaping holes in the walls, and the entire electrical system of the synagogue was destroyed in the fire.

Some of the men began sobbing quietly, and the Nazis smiled with satisfaction. Suddenly, and all at once, they saw a glow at one end of the destruction. It was hard to make out, but after moving away some of the wooden pews and overturned bookshelves, they were able to make their way up to the front of the sanctuary. There they saw an unmistakable light. It was the *ner tamid*, the Eternal Light that hangs above the ark in every synagogue. The Eternal Lights are never extinguished or turned off, and in the Adath Israel Synagogue, it had its own battery. Somehow, miraculously, it had escaped the looting and fire of the previous night, and it cast a glow over the sanctuary.

The Nazis who were standing around were confused – and amazed. One of them turned to R' Munk and asked what the light was. R' Munk was silent for a while before intoning in a quiet voice, "This is our *ner tamid* – Eternal Light. It is the symbol of G-d's eternal and imminent Presence in the Jewish people."

The German looked at him with hatred in his eyes. "You accursed Jews. *Ihr Juden seit ein unverustliches volk* – You Jews are an indestructible people!"

| LEIZER COHEN |

Lighting Up

After the United States entered World War II, an amended Selective Service Act signed by President Roosevelt required that all men between the ages of eighteen and sixty-four register for the draft. The local draft board of the Selective Service System conducted the registration. A lottery based on birthdays determined the order in which registered men were called up by Selective Service. The first to be called, in a sequence determined by the lottery, were men whose twentieth birthday fell out during that year, followed, if needed, by those aged twenty-one, twenty-two, twenty-three, twenty-four and so on.

It was unusual, therefore, but not alarming to Leizer Cohen, a Chicago native who was born and grew up in the Midwest, when an official-looking letter from the United States army appeared in the mail one day in March 1944. Leizer was thirty-six years old, married with three children. As prescribed by law, he had registered for the draft years earlier, but he was never selected. Now, with the war turning against the Axis, Leizer didn't even consider the possibility that he would be needed to serve.

But, of course, he was curious. Leizer opened the letter, wondering what the army could possibly want from him. When he read the contents, his face slowly lost its color until it matched the white paper in his hand. Indeed – it was a draft notice! Leizer was overage, but apparently the army was understaffed. In fact, this call-up was due to the impending Normandy invasion on June 6, 1944 – the famed D-Day campaign. Leizer read the letter with dismay: He was to report to the downtown Chicago induction center the following

Saturday morning at 8:00 a.m. An ominous line at the end of the letter made him blanch: "Anyone who fails to respond to this summons will be arrested."

"On Shabbos?" Leizer whispered to himself. "What will I do there? Even if I arrive Friday eve before nightfall, how will I *daven* with a *minyan*? There are no Jews downtown!" But there was no getting out of it. He knew how serious this matter was, and if he was selected, he would summarily be inducted to serve in any one of the theaters of war. And this was just the beginning! How could he keep Shabbos, as well as observe all the *mitzvos*, if he was drafted into the army?

Despite his misgivings, Leizer had no choice but to gather his belongings on Friday afternoon and prepare to spend Shabbos in a downtown Chicago hotel. He brought along Shabbos provisions; candles, wine, challah, a siddur and a *Chumash*. As the sun set over the Chicago skyline, Leizer found himself chanting the Friday night prayers slowly and meaningfully, but in total solitude.

After his lonely Friday night meal, Leizer took out his *Chumash* to review the weekly Torah portion, *Parshas Vayakhel*. He was tired from the long week. He reached the verse, *Do not kindle a fire in all your dwellings on the Shabbos day* (*Shemos* 35:3). He repeated the words of the verse over and over, but his eyes soon began to flutter, and then close. His mind, though, continued to dwell on the verse even in his dreams. *Do not kindle a fire...*

Leizer awoke the next morning, his heart heavy with dread. After *davening* alone in his hotel room, he joined the thousands of people in the induction center waiting to be examined by the army doctors. Leizer responded dutifully to each question he was asked. It was a long day and he was examined by doctor after doctor. For the first time in his life, he wished he wasn't in the best of health, but as luck would have it, he passed every examination with flying colors.

Late in the afternoon, Leizer was seated opposite an obviously Jewish psychiatrist, Dr. Schwartz. After some routine questioning, Leizer voiced his misgivings about joining the army. "Doctor, I am an Orthodox Jew, and I'm very worried about how I will be able to observe the Sabbath and all the other commandments in the army." Leizer attempted to appeal to the man's sense of propriety. "And besides, who's going to take care of my wife and three children?"

Leizer waited for a response, but the doctor just shrugged, unmoved. Leizer watched him reach into his pocket to pull out a cigarette. As the match flared in the doctor's hand, the words of the *Chumash* from the night before flashed through his mind: *Do not kindle a fire...*

"Hey, Doctor, you are Jewish, right? Why are you smoking on Shabbos?" Leizer admonished him.

The doctor stopped writing in mid-sentence. Then he looked up slowly and rolled his eyes. "Listen, it's been a long day. Will you give me a break?"

But Leizer did not give him a break. He continued to expound on the prohibition of lighting a fire on Shabbos, that it was absolutely forbidden, and how could a Jew dare do such a thing?

As Leizer ranted on, the doctor furiously scribbled a few notes on the file in front of him. "Here," he said, interrupting Leizer mid-sentence. "Take this to the doctor in the next room."

It was another Jewish doctor, it seemed. Leizer handed him the file and sat down. The doctor looked down at the note, then peered up at the man standing before him. "What is your name?" he began. Leizer responded dutifully to each question until suddenly, this doctor, too, took out a cigarette and lit up. The verse flashed again in Leizer's mind. *Do not kindle a fire...*

Leizer couldn't hold himself back. "Doctor, you look Jewish. Why do you smoke on Shabbos?"

The doctor looked up suddenly from the file and stared at Leizer. "What?" he asked, incredulously.

"Why do you smoke on Shabbos?" Leizer repeated. "Surely you know it's forbidden for a Jew to light a fire?"

The doctor shook his head in disbelief. "Oh, boy! You're too nervous for the United States Armed Forces. We don't need guys like you. Go home."

Relieved, Leizer left the army induction center. He was so excited to be exempt that he ran all the way back home, where he told everyone about the miracle he had experienced.

Leizer Cohen was a fortunate man. He went on to raise his family to light up the world with Torah, *mitzvos* and *chessed*... but never, ever to "light up" on Shabbos!

| MAX SCHMELING |
Righteous Gentile

In a time when the world had literally gone mad, not that many years ago, the world was thrown into a darkness the likes of which mankind has never experienced since the times of Noach and the Biblical Flood. The rise of the Third Reich, and with it, the brutality of Nazi Germany, is a chapter in the history of the world that reflects the depths of barbarism, sadism and pure unadulterated evil on a national, and even global, level.

Although Nazi power increased in Germany day by day from as early as 1933, it wasn't until the night of November 9, 1938 – Kristallnacht: the night of broken glass – when all inhibitions were released and the facade of normal policy was hideously cast aside. On that infamous night, in a coordinated attack on Jewish people and their property all throughout Germany, Hitler Youth, Gestapo, S.S. and S.A. murdered ninety-one Jews; arrested twenty-five to thirty thousand and sent them to concentration camps; destroyed 267 synagogues; and ransacked thousands of homes and businesses. The S.A. shattered the storefronts of about 7,500 Jewish stores and businesses, hence the appellation "Kristallnacht" (Crystal Night). Jewish homes were vandalized and many unfortunate Jews were beaten and assaulted.

There was one man, a famous German sports hero by the name of Max Schmeling, who did not sit idly by and watch the carnage unfold. The fading memories of this well-known German from the Nazi era, World Heavyweight Champion from 1930 to 1932, usually have it that he was a willing model for Adolf Hitler and the Third Reich, a self-proclaimed Aryan Superman. Schmeling may indeed have lunched with Hitler and had lengthy conversations with Goebbels, master propagandist of the Nazi regime, but his tale is far more complex than it first appears. He was a decent man in conflict with the Nazi regime and racial policies of the Third Reich – and a man who demonstrated generosity, righteousness and humanitarianism.

Max Schmeling was a shy man of humble origins who came of age amidst the glitter and turbulence of Berlin's 'Golden Twenties.' As the heavyweight champion of Europe, his career inevitably brought him to America, where he defended his title numerous times, until he soon lost it in a blatantly unfair decision. Four years later, he was imported as a sacrificial lamb for the invincible Joe Louis. Although a 10-1 underdog, Max Schmeling scored what some consider the upset of the century. Joe Louis won the rematch on June 22, 1938, in one of the most discussed fights of all time. The fight was portrayed as the battle of the Aryan versus the Black, a struggle of evil against good.

During the 1936 Olympics in Berlin, Max Schmeling exacted a promise from Hitler that all U.S. athletes would be protected. On several occasions Hitler tried to cajole the respected boxer into joining the Nazi Party, but Schmeling vigorously refused to join the Nazi Party or to publicize the Nazi propaganda line. Over Goebbels's personal protest, he refused to stop associating with German Jews or to fire his American Jewish manager, Joe Jacobs.

The story of Max Schmeling is the story of a hero, who during the Kristallnacht pogrom of November 1938, saved the lives of two young Jewish brothers named Lewin.

On that fateful November night, the two brothers, Henry and Werner Lewin, found themselves out on the streets of Berlin while the vicious mobs raged, pillaged and burned anything that looked or seemed even remotely Jewish. Realizing the severity of their situation and the danger to their personal safety if they were caught and identified, they ran through the streets of Berlin looking for a safe place to hide. One of the brothers recalled that their father, David Lewin, was a friendly associate of the renowned boxer, Max Schmeling, and without any other options at their disposal, they decided that they had to take a chance on his hospitality.

Schmeling lived in a suite in the ritzy Excelsior Hotel in the center of Berlin. The Lewin brothers ran as fast as their legs could carry them to the hotel and urgently rang his bell. When he responded, they identified themselves and begged him to have mercy on them. Immediately, Schmeling agreed to hide the two teenage boys in his apartment and even went so far as to leave word at the front desk that he was ill and no one was to visit him. For two days, the Lewin boys remained under Schmeling's personal care and he did not let them leave his home until it was safe to go outside once again. He requested no remuneration or acknowledgment for his kind act and at a later date, he even helped the brothers get out of Germany.

They escaped and came to the United States where one of them, Henry Lewin, became a prominent hotel owner. This episode remained under shrouds until 1989, when Henry Lewin invited Schmeling to the States to thank him for saving his life. To this day, Henry Lewin believes that he and his brother owe their lives to Max Schmeling and he is convinced that Schmeling himself could have died or faced severe consequences for his humanitarian gesture.

Hitler never forgave Schmeling for refusing to join the Nazi Party, so he had him drafted into the Paratroops and sent him on suicide missions. Miraculously, he survived each one and after the war made enough money through boxing to purchase a Coca-Cola dealership. He was known as one of the most generous philanthropists in Germany until the day he died on February 2, 2005, at age ninety-nine, in Hollenstadt.

Max Schmeling became one of Germany's most revered sports figures, not only for his singular athletic accomplishments, but for his humility, discipline and character. In a world gone mad, he was one man who demonstrated extraordinary generosity and humanitarianism.

| SATMAR REBBE |

"We Are All Alive"

In 5703 (1943), a thirteen-year-old boy traveled with his father from his tiny Hungarian village to the city of Satmar, to celebrate his bar mitzvah in the presence of the great Satmar Rebbe, R' Yoel Teitelbaum *zt"l*. It was Shabbos *Parshas Va'eschanan*, and as was the custom in Satmar, the rebbe would read from the Torah and also receive the sixth *aliyah*. The *gabba'im* would arrange the *aliyos* so that the *Aseres Hadibros* (Ten Commandments) would be read by *Shishi* (sixth *aliyah*) and the bar mitzvah boy was to be honored with *Chamishi* (fifth *aliyah*).

When his turn came, the boy stood at the *bimah* and peered into the Torah as the holy Satmar Rebbe *leined*. He felt a great charge of excitement and holiness as he recognized the importance of the moment. He was no longer a child – he was a man, with responsibilities to G-d, his family and himself. It was a stirring emotion.

Suddenly, the rebbe's voice rose to a thunderous roar as he finished off the verse he was reading, with the words: *Anachnu eileh poh hayom kulanu* **chaim** – "All of us here today, we are all alive." It was as if a bolt of lightning had come down and pierced the hearts of all those standing around while the rebbe shouted these words. In those trying and soon-to-be awful days of the coming war, these words would be a protective shield that would surround all those who were blessed to be standing up at the *bimah* at that moment.

Indeed, there were five men present: the Satmar Rebbe; his personal *gabbai*, R' Yosef Ashkenazy *z"l*; the *gabbai*; and the bar mitzvah boy and his father. A sixth man, the usual *gabbai*,

R' Feivish, had not been present and missed the blessing. They all survived the war while R' Feivish *Hy"d* did not.

{ WAR BEGINS: }
Oppression

by Raize Guttman

I stand
Trapped
In the midst of horror
Hanging in the balance
Am I really here?

We have been standing
Crammed together
For hours
For days?
I have lost track of time.

I try to grasp the hand of my son
Who is next to me.
I gasp for air
There is none in this cattle car
On the way to... a place
That we heard about
But didn't believe existed.

I don't know how much longer
I can hold on
I don't think much longer
But I will...

You see me now
In pictures
On the walls of museums.
You look at me in books
That describe what we went through.
But you can't understand
Even I don't understand or believe
What we went through,
And I was there.

I died in Auschwitz
As they opened the doors
And we all fell out in one heap
The living, the half dead, the dead
And me.
I was there — I wanted to make it
To be able to live to tell the tale.

But you — my beloved children
Are telling my story.
Always remember us
We, who were murdered by the Nazis.
And we will remember you
And beg Hashem from on High
To have mercy on His people.
We will ask Hashem to finally bring
us all together again
So that we could proclaim in unison,
With perfect clarity and faith,
"HASHEM HU HA'ELOKIM."

| REMA – R' MOSHE ISSERLES |
The Merit of a *Tzaddik*

The German army occupied Krakow in the first week of September 1939. The German military authorities initiated immediate measures aimed at isolating, exploiting and persecuting the Jews of the city. On October 26, 1939, the part of German-occupied Poland which the Germans did not annex directly came under the rule of civilian occupation authorities under the leadership of Hans Frank, the former legal counsel to the Nazi Party. Appointed Governor General by Adolf Hitler, Frank established his headquarters in the Wawel Castle in Krakow, which the Germans designated as the capital of the *Generalgouvernement*. Numerous other office and government buildings were seized by the S.S. and adopted for their nefarious purposes, including Gestapo headquarters and police stations and prisons run by the German Security Police, who established their headquarters near the Montelupich Prison.

On certain occasions, the Germans would only occupy a portion of a building, leaving the rest of the building – usually the upper floors – to the residents. Needless to say, Jews who lived in buildings that were partially occupied by the Nazis lived in constant fear of a Nazi barging into their home, looting their valuables, and arresting their family members.

R' Yitzchak Isaac Klingberg, son of the late Zolishetzer Rebbe, R' Shem Klingberg *zt"l*, was one of those who was displaced from his home when the Nazis transformed his apartment into an office, although he was fortunate to be allowed to sleep in the hallway of the building.

On one occasion, a German officer woke him from a fitful sleep and yelled, "*Zhid*! Get into the office! The commandant wants to see you."

R' Yitzchak scrambled to obey the man's orders. He followed the German into the office and stood at attention, while the drunken commandant managed to stumble around his desk and sprawl into his chair.

R' Yitzchak's eyes widened in terror as the commandant pulled his revolver out of his belt and flung it on the desk between them. "You see this revolver?" he barked at his shivering victim. "I'm going to ask you a question. If you don't answer me truthfully, I'll kill you."

R' Yitzchak managed to nod, but his heart sank. The commandant was so drunk that he would probably shoot him with the slightest provocation – even if he did speak the truth.

"*Waas es das Rema* – Who was the Rema?" the commandant demanded.

What sort of question was this? R' Yitzchak stared, speechless. Why would a German commandant want to know about the Rema, R' Moshe Isserles *zt"l*, the sixteenth-century Torah leader whose works are among the foundations of Torah law? R' Yitzchak was formulating a befitting reply, but before he could say a word, the commandant abruptly stood from his chair.

"I have an order from the High Command in Berlin to destroy the cemetery here in Krakow!" he shouted. "But then they sent us a telegram, telling us not to touch the Rema's shul, or his grave."

R' Yitzchak blinked in surprise. Could this really be true?

The German's bloodshot eyes bore into R' Yitzchak as he raised his voice. "*Waas es das Rema* – Who was the Rema?" the commandant asked again, with drunken urgency.

R' Yitzchak didn't know where to begin. Should he talk about the Rema's life, or simply mention his great written contributions to Torah Jewry? Or perhaps his many books on Torah law, or the fact that his gravesite was a pilgrimage for thousands of Jews for hundreds of years?

But before R' Yitzchak could utter a word, the commandant suddenly swayed and slid to the floor, passing out right at R' Yitzchak's feet. Looking around, R' Yitzchak let out his breath with words of thanks to Hashem, before beating a hasty retreat from the commandant's office.

• • •

After the war, R' Yitzchak learned what happened to the Rema's grave and the incredible miracle that prevented it from being destroyed, from a cousin of his who had returned to Krakow to see what remained of the once vibrant Jewish community. His cousin, Shimon Spira, was among the paltry two thousand survivors of the Krakow ghetto who had managed to escape the hands of the Nazis. At war's end, it was natural for him to return to the city where he had spent his entire life, but there was not much to see in postwar

Krakow. Where were the sixty thousand Jews who had made Krakow their home before the war?

As his feet led him through the deserted streets, his recollections were interrupted by a tap on his shoulder. "Excuse me, sir."

Shimon turned to see a shabbily dressed young man, accompanied by two friends of about the same age. "We're looking for the grave of the Rema. Could you show us the way?"

Shimon raised his eyebrows in surprise at the sound of the holy Rema's name passing through this young man's lips. The three men standing before him were bareheaded and did not appear to be religious, or even Jewish, for that matter. What interest would these men have with the Rema's grave?

"Why do you want to go there?" he asked warily.

"My friend, despite the way we look, we really are Jewish. We were quite young when the Nazis took over, and we were forced to work for them. Our assignment was to knock down the tombstones in all the Jewish cemeteries across town."

The man's voice grew hushed. "When we reached the Rema's gravestone and prepared to knock it down, the air-raid sirens went off, and we ran to take shelter in the nearest bunker. When the all-clear sounded, we came back out and were about to try again – and again the sirens went off! This happened time and again. Every time we went back to knock down the gravestone of the Rema, the sirens would go off, and we were forced to run away."

"In the end, we never did knock down the stone," said a second man, with a sheepish shrug, "but we did manage to chip off a small chunk from the gravestone. It bothered us immensely and we have come back here today to ask forgiveness from the great *tzaddik*."

With the world completely shattered by war, three secular young men sought atonement for chipping a stone. Shimon was visibly moved and he immediately led them toward the famous shul and the adjoining cemetery.

"See that beautiful building?" R' Shimon gestured to the high archway that marked the entrance to the old shul. "The Rema's father built it in his honor, four hundred years ago. The Rema himself is buried out back, in the cemetery."

Shimon fell silent for a moment. "On the Rema's *yahrtzeit*, Lag B'Omer," he continued quietly, "so many Jews would come here to *daven*... And now there is no one left... no one left..."

• • •

"I showed them the grave," Shimon later told his cousin, R' Yitzchak Isaac Klingberg, "and just like they said, the Rema's gravestone was still standing tall and straight. I listened as the three men asked the Rema for forgiveness, and then they vowed to change their way of life."

"All in the merit of the Rema," R' Yitzchak concluded. "It's amazing what protection a righteous person can provide so many years after his death."

| BELZER REBBE |

"Organizing" the Blessing of a *Tzaddik*

During the early part of the Second World War, the Belzer Rebbe, R' Aharon Rokeach *zt"l*, along with his distinguished brother, R' Mordechai *zt"l*, the Bilgoray

Rav, found themselves in the Bochnia ghetto, before their dramatic escape to Hungary. Many of the ghetto inhabitants came to ask for a blessing and to seek the rebbe's advice. R' Aharon, who slept no more than two hours a night and survived on a mere few sips of coffee and a glass of milk smuggled into the ghetto by his ardent followers, did not turn away even a single soul. He offered comfort and solace to all those who came to him, never mentioning his own great tragedy – the loss of his entire family.

Incredibly, even the chief Nazi, a sadistic tyrant by the name of Muller, went so far as to visit the *"wunder rabbiner"* to receive a blessing from him and offer to double his rations! Such was the esteem that everyone – even the accursed *resha'im* – held for the Belzer Rebbe. They believed that keeping him contained within their midst was some sort of "good-luck charm."

Among those who came to the Belzer Rebbe's crowded apartment in the ghetto were Bronia Koczicki and her two little sons; Tzvi, age six; and Yitzchak, age three. At this stage in the war, they had all seen numerous miracles and salvation, especially little Tzvi, who was thrown from a speeding railcar on his way to Auschwitz, and lived to tell about it.

After the rebbe blessed her and her two children with a heartfelt but general blessing – *"Di Eibishter vet helfen"* (G-d will help) – Bronia did not leave the rebbe's presence. The attendants attempted to move her along, but she refused to budge. Finally, she looked at the holy countenance of the rebbe and begged, "Please, rebbe, please bless my sons with fine generations in the future."

There was a commotion in the back of the room. "Poor woman," someone whispered, "she probably lost her mind in these troubled times. Every day, children's *aktions* take place. Hundreds of children are constantly being murdered and this woman is asking not only that her children remain safe, but that they live to bear a future with fine generations, a future of living Jews!"

But the Belzer Rebbe understood the deep implication of what she was asking. Slowly, he motioned to the young boys to come close to him. He placed his hands on their heads and blessed them with generations upon generations of fine Jews. His hands rested on their heads as his words seemed to shake the very foundation of the world. When he was finished, he smiled brightly at the two young boys.

"We will live through this war, we will live through this war!" Bronia kept telling her bewildered children as she walked out of the rebbe's presence and back to her own apartment. She was so convinced of the fulfillment of the holy Belzer Rebbe's blessing that she infused her children with tremendous hope and faith.

Many years later, when Bronia (who married the Bluzhever Rebbe, R' Yisroel Spira *zt"l*) would tell over this story, surrounded by grandchildren and great-grandchildren, she would smile conspiratorially and say, "At times, one has to be aggressive when it comes to blessings." Then she would add as if in an afterthought, in a manner of good-natured advice, "In times of war, one has to organize everything – even a blessing from a *tzaddik*!"

The Boy Who Saw the Glass Eye of the Nazi

The misery of ghetto life is well documented. Food was scarce and overcrowding was prevalent. Disease ravaged the downtrodden Jews who moved about trance-like from place to place, with little or nothing to do to pass the time. And the stench of death was everywhere. Death lurked in every corner of the ghetto and touched everyone, from elderly Jews who simply gave up on life to young, innocent babes who languished in the streets, eventually succumbing to the lack of food. Death swirled about the streets – the proverbial "*mashchis*" (destroyer) who roamed the streets looking for victims. Unfortunately, he didn't have to search very hard and his victims practically came to him.

Then there were the children. As with children everywhere, the sinister side of life may often be concealed by their overarching need to act like children. Ghetto children also roamed the streets but they were looking for games to play. They created heroes and villains and chased each other, squealing and yelping as they played their games. Bombed-out buildings became fortresses and pockmarked streets were used to simulate army maneuvers. It may have been the only normal aspect of life that could be found in the ghetto.

One child was different, though. He wasn't into games – at least not the innocent kind. He was a young boy, short in years but long in life experiences. He had witnessed the death of his parents and had watched his siblings being taken away. It was only due to his innate resourcefulness and ability to survive that he wasn't taken with them. He had no place to call home, and no relatives or adults to look after him. He did this all for himself. And he was good at it. He knew where to find bread and water, he knew how to "work" the shopkeepers to give him morsels of food. And he slept... wherever.

So what did he do for fun? He became a vigilante. He was a natural leader and other children cleaved to him. He began fighting back. He had scouts who told him where the Nazi soldiers were positioned and others who would provide him with ammunition. But it was he – only he – who would conduct the "operations." Stealthily, he would creep up behind the enemy's "position" and pelt the hapless soldiers with stones. It wasn't about hurting the Nazis; it was a measure of revenge that he felt he was accomplishing. The Germans would cry out in surprise and begin searching for the "attacker" – but they were always too slow.

The boy would conduct his "operations" day after day, until his reputation began to spread. The adults would marvel at the young tyke's ingenuity and the children would utter his name in tones of reverence. At first, the Germans shrugged it off as a childish prank. What could they do already? They were fighting a war; this was child's play. What they neglected to take into consideration was that the boy was also fighting a "war" – his own personal war – and he would not stop fighting at any cost.

Eventually, their indifference turned into concern. The boy was becoming something of a folk hero. People were talking about him and he was making the Nazis look foolish. It was time to do something about it. Issuing a reward for the capture of the child or collective punishment for a child's prank would make them look weak and justify their fears in front of the ghetto's population. So they began their own "operation" to catch the boy. They monitored packs of kids and tracked their movements until they were reasonably sure that they had their boy. And the next time he struck, they were ready. The boy was caught!

A larger than necessary group of soldiers hauled the boy away, as he began yelling, crying and proclaiming his innocence. Every person in the street stopped in his tracks to watch as the young vigilante, the hero of the ghetto, was dragged to the Gestapo headquarters to await his punishment. No one needed to say out loud what they all knew he was slated to receive.

Victoriously, the soldiers entered the Gestapo building and dumped the still crying boy on the floor in front of the chief. He immediately jumped up and began pleading for his life in front of the Nazi. Gone were his confident attitude and courageous demeanor – a demeanor that he became legendary for these past few weeks. Now he played the part of a young child who had lost his entire family, who had not eaten in days and thought the whole thing was just a game. Surely, the Nazis could not think that he was a danger to them in any way?

The Gestapo chief smiled throughout the child's monologue. This was the child that had caused his soldiers to panic? This boy was dangerous? He was nothing more than a pathetic kid. But to the Nazi way of thinking, a victim is a victim, and if it was a Jewish victim, that made it all the more worth meting out a cruel and inhuman punishment. The chief thought for a moment and decided that he needed a bit of amusement himself.

"A game? That's all this was?" he barked to the young child, who had practically cried himself out. "Well, then, if it's games that you seek, how about we play a game of my own?"

The boy shifted nervously in place. A Nazi game was unlike a normal game and he didn't believe it was a game he wished to play. But what choice did he have?

The Gestapo chief pulled off his cap. Then he bent down and looked the boy directly in the eye. "I will tell you a little secret," he began, with a conspiratorial smile on his lips. "At the beginning of this accursed war, I was a soldier battling on the front lines. During one skirmish, I was hit by shrapnel and it damaged one of my eyes. The eye was lost but I was rushed to the best medical facility in Berlin and the doctors gave me a glass eye. It is the most perfect eye ever invented and the doctors told me that no one would ever be able to tell the difference between my good eye and my glass eye."

The boy's gaze shifted upwards as he looked into the Nazi's eyes. The German quickly straightened up and said, "You like games, yes? So here's my game. If you can tell me which eye is my real eye and which is my glass eye, I will let you live. If you cannot... I will shoot you myself."

The soldiers standing around burst into howls of laughter. Indeed, this was a great game and they knew that the boy had as much a chance to live as he did to die. But the boy understood that this was no game and he gazed intently at the Gestapo chief's eyes. It took him no longer than ten seconds before he pointed to one side of the German's face and said, "That one. That's the glass eye."

Instantly, the smile vanished off the chief's face and was quickly replaced with a scowl. He grabbed the boy by his shirt and screamed, "How did you know? How can you tell so quickly? If you tell me that it was just a guess, I will kill you right now!"

The boy was now composed, much more than he was just a few moments before when he played the part of an innocent child. His gaze was even as he looked into the face of the German. "It was not hard to tell," said the boy. "I looked into your eyes and I saw that one eye was cold, deadly cold. It had an expression that was totally devoid of humanity; it bespoke murder and an animalistic impulse to kill."

The boy paused for a moment. "When I saw that eye, I knew that the other one was the glass eye!"

R' BORUCH HALEVI LEIZEROVSKI
It's All in G-d's Hands

When World War II broke out, R' Boruch Halevi Leizerovski *zt"l*, the *rav* of the Lithuanian shul in the Polish city of Lodz, was shipped to Auschwitz and became another nondescript prisoner in that most blood-soaked of all human habitats. Upon arrival at Auschwitz, all inmates underwent the *"selektzia"* – selection – by the inhuman beast, Dr. Mengele. With a minor indication of his finger, this "elegant monster" indicated who would live and who would die. Like hundreds of thousands before him, R' Boruch passed by and, as a healthy young man, was directed to the right – the work brigade – rather than to the gas chambers. Close to three horrifying years followed, years of backbreaking labor and starvation, years of indescribable pain and anguish.

At a later date in the war, R' Boruch was ordered to pass by Dr. Mengele again. Of course, he understood its meaning, having been educated with blood and tears in the definition of that most dreadful word in the entire dictionary, *selektzia*: the weak would perish, while the fate of those who appeared to be in better health would be postponed until the next *selektzia*.

At the time, R' Boruch had contracted an abscessed wound at the heel of his foot, causing extreme pain with every step he took. When his turn came to pass the beast, he controlled himself with an iron will from displaying any pain, making his passage with a normal stride. Mengele did not discern R' Boruch's agony and motioned him to the right.

Not a moment passed before R' Boruch realized what a terrible mistake he had made and was overcome with deep remorse. Memory flashes came back to him from the first moment the Nazis marched into Lodz and the atrocities they carried out, acts that are simply unfathomable to a normal human mind. Why, thought R' Boruch, would he want to continue to experience this pain, this torture? For what: a few more days of pain and torture?

"Have I suddenly become clever, deciding my own destiny?" R' Boruch said to himself. "No," he made up his mind firmly. "Let Hashem decide. He Who has guided me these last three years without the slightest planning on my part, will follow me through to wherever I'm destined to be, either among the survivors or among the *kedoshim* – martyrs."

Without another thought, R' Boruch slipped out of the group of men he was in, eluded the guards milling about and sneaked back into the line of people about to pass Mengele. He wanted to pass by one more time, with his true pain showing. This time around, when he passed by, he did not camouflage any of his symptoms, not even the facial contortions associated with his painful walk. Mengele motioned him to the left, together with a group of sick and infirm inmates.

They didn't need to be told where they were headed. The brutal facts of life in Auschwitz and all Nazi concentration camps had taught them all too well what to expect. R' Boruch, like the other religious members in the group, began to prepare for his final passage, the imminent crossing of that fateful bridge into eternity.

But Hashem had other plans; He doesn't follow a human script. *How great are Your deeds, Hashem; exceedingly profound are Your thoughts.... A boor cannot know, nor can a fool understand this.* The infirm were not taken to the gas chambers. Rather, they were loaded onto trucks and taken to a modern hospital facility in the Auschwitz compound that the Nazis had built for one specific purpose: to dupe the International Red

Cross into believing that the Germans provided outstanding medical attention to their prisoners!

R' Boruch spent close to two weeks in the hospital in the care of world-class physicians. They attended to his foot and largely restored his general well-being. Some time later, he found out that the entire group that was directed to the right side was ordered to participate in a "death march." These marches were so named since the objective was to cause as much death as possible. At the final stage of the war, when the Nazis realized that the end was nearing, they ordered the last remnants of the concentration camps, including Auschwitz and Birkenau, to march tens of kilometers aimlessly, with almost no food or drink. To our great misfortune, the vast majority perished, may Hashem avenge their blood.

"Imagine what would have happened to me," said R' Boruch later, "had I ended up on the right side, with the healthy ones. My ailing foot could have never survived even half a day of those marches. Reclassifying me as sick was Hashem's method of saving my life."

| R' ELCHANAN WASSERMAN |
"We Are the *Korbanos* of Klal Yisrael"

R' Elchanan Wasserman *Hy"d* was in his mid-sixties when the war broke out. He had spent a great deal of time in America raising much needed funds for his yeshivah in Baranovitch. Although he became quite fond of the *bnei Torah* he met in America and held out great hope and promise for their future, he resisted their pleas to remain in America and chose to return to a Europe that was about to be engulfed in flames. As a *rosh yeshivah* and a leader who acted as the conscience of the Lithuanian yeshivah world, he felt a personal and public responsibility to be with his flock in their time of need, come what may.

R' Elchanan held fast to the principles he had declared while traveling in London when he announced that he would return to Lithuania. "A captain does not abandon his ship in the middle of a storm," he told his friends who were begging him to remain in England where he would be safe.

Unfortunately, a year later the ship had sunk. The yeshivah was destroyed and the students had scattered to the four winds. The community was disintegrating. There was no more that R' Elchanan could do, so he prepared for his flight from certain death. Through the benevolence of American benefactors, an airplane stood ready in Kovno to fly the Wasserman family to Sweden. But at the last moment, R' Naftali Beinush, R' Elchanan's son, broke his leg while loading the suitcases onto the wagon to Kovno. Now that they were unable to reach the airfield, the family was trapped.

Tragically, R' Elchanan fell victim to the Nazi collaborators on July 6, 1941/11 Tammuz, 5701. In those days of terror, R' Elchanan spent most of the day on the ground floor of the building, studying Torah. People were constantly coming in, seeking shelter, shaking with fear over what was happening. But when they looked at R' Elchanan's face, they drew strength from its angelic glow. "Not a trace of fear or worry ever showed on his face," a survivor testified.

R' Elchanan had recently taught his son, R' Naftali Beinush, how to say the blessing over the mitzvah of giving one's life for the sanctification of the Holy Name. He was constantly reminding those around him that those who are about to sanctify Hashem's Name must beware of any unworthy thoughts, so as to be a pure sacrifice, without blemishes.

The armed Lithuanian murderers came bursting into the house where R' Elchanan was lodging, hunting for rabbis, whom they called Communist sympathizers. R' Elchanan stood over his open volume of Talmud, completely absorbed in what he was learning. He knew perfectly well what his fate would be: his burning face reflected the knowledge in a look that struck awe into all who saw it.

Even one of the murderers was stricken with fear. He mumbled, "Maybe we should leave him," but the others refused and insisted on taking him to the Ninth Fort, literally the valley of death. Thousands of victims waited there. All throughout that day and most of the next, R' Elchanan strove to focus his mind on being a pure and holy sacrifice, so as to ascend to Heaven unstained.

The final moments of the life of the great *tzaddik*, R' Elchanan Wasserman, are described in the introduction written by his son, R' Simcha, for the *sefer Kovetz Shiurim*. It is based upon the eyewitness testimony of R' Ephraim Oshry *zt"l*, one of the few survivors of the Kovno ghetto. The introduction recounts the last words that R' Elchanan spoke to the group of thirteen Torah scholars who were being led to their deaths together with him. They had been interrupted in the midst of their study in order to be sacrificed on the altar of G-d.

R' Elchanan spoke quietly and calmly. His face was serious but serene. His final words did not include any personal references; he didn't even include a personal parting to his son, R' Naftali Beinush. His words were directed towards all of Klal Yisrael.

"In the Heavens, we must be viewed as righteous, because we have been selected to atone for Klal Yisrael with our bodies. Despite this, here and now, we must do a full and complete *teshuvah*. Time is short; the trip to the Ninth Fort will not take long. We must keep in mind that our sacrifice will be better accepted by Hashem if we do *teshuvah*, and through this we will save the lives of our brothers and sisters in America.

"Let no foreign thought enter our minds, as that will make us *pigul*, an unfit *korban*. We are preparing ourselves to perform the greatest mitzvah of all, as it says, *The Beis Hamikdash was destroyed by fire; by fire it will be rebuilt.* The fire that burns our bodies is the very fire that will help rebuild the House of Israel."

R' Elchanan's unwitting prophecy came true for him. It was he who had written: "These are the birth pangs of Mashiach.... No man can escape from the part that has been assigned him in this process."

| KEDUSHAS ZION |

The Best Way to Fulfill a Mitzvah

Soon after the war broke out, R' Benzion Halberstam *Hy"d*, the previous Bobover Rebbe, fled his hometown of Bobov for the relative safety of Lemberg. En route, he stopped in Lutzk, where he spent the holiday of Sukkos. Due to war conditions, it was impossible to obtain an *esrog*; the only one available was a dried one from the previous year. The Bobover Rebbe sat together with other *rabbanim* who had fled to Lutzk, all of them despondent at the thought that they could not fulfill the mitzvah of taking the *arba'ah minim* that year. Seeking to allay their sorrow, the Bobover Rebbe proceeded to tell the following story which his grandfather, R' Chaim Sanzer *zt"l*, had related on Sukkos.

Once, *sheker* (falsehood) was walking down the street when he met the *yetzer hara* (evil inclination), who was looking very ill. "What is the matter?" *sheker* asked him.

The *yetzer hara* replied, "Don't you realize that it is now the month of Elul, and the Jewish people are all occupied with doing *teshuvah* (repentance) wholeheartedly? No matter how hard I try to get them to sin or prevent them from repenting, I cannot succeed! They're putting me out of business!

"And then comes Sukkos," the evil inclination continued to lament, "when the people will rejoice in their sukkah and fulfill the mitzvah of taking the *lulav* and *esrog* – that will finish me off!"

After thinking for a moment, *sheker* told his friend that he had a wonderful idea which would solve the problem: "The *esrogim* are imported by boat from Greece. Why not sink the ship? That way there will be no *esrogim* available, and the Jews will not be able to fulfill the mitzvah!"

Delighted with this nefarious plan, the *yetzer hara* hurried off to immediately implement it.

Some time after Sukkos, *sheker* again encountered the *yetzer hara* on the street. This time he looked even worse than he had the last time. When they met, the *yetzer hara* shouted, "You're no friend of mine! The advice you gave me backfired – it had the exact opposite effect!"

"Calm down," soothed *sheker*. "Tell me what happened."

"Well, in previous years, when the Jews had their *esrogim* for Sukkos, they fulfilled the mitzvah, but I was still able to score the occasional victory. There were some people who only had in mind that everyone should notice what a beautiful, expensive *esrog* they had; others wanted those around them to notice with what great *kavanah* (intent) they were performing the mitzvah. However, this year, since there were no *esrogim*, they were all heartbroken at being unable to fulfill the mitzvah, and they cried out to Hashem, repenting wholeheartedly, remorseful that they did not merit performing this important mitzvah.

"Under such circumstances, Hashem considered it as if they had fulfilled the mitzvah. As the Sages determine: *When a person is prevented from doing a mitzvah, Hashem considers it as if he had indeed fulfilled it.* So you see," lamented the *yetzer hara*, "your plan totally backfired on me!"

The Kedushas Zion (title of the Bobover Rebbe's famous *sefer*) finished his story and looked at the determined faces all around him. "This story is very relevant to our situation today. We are unable to properly fulfill the mitzvah of *esrog* because we are in the category of 'One who is prevented from fulfilling the commandment.' Thus, Hashem will perform the mitzvah for us in heaven, and it will be considered as if we had fulfilled it in the best possible way!"

Later, the Stutchiner Rebbe would recount this episode and say, "The Bobover Rebbe's story comforted us, for we were shattered that we could not fulfill the mitzvah of taking the *arba'ah minim*. Thanks to him we were able, despite the terrible circumstances, to feel a measure of joy on Yom Tov."

| BOYANER REBBE |
Keeping His Word

It was tax season. Papers were piled high on the desk of Louis Septimus, to be checked and processed in his office on Lower Broadway, where he and his brothers ran a CPA firm. Suddenly, the phone rang. "Who is it?" he asked, not even raising his head from the worksheet he was checking.

"The Boyaner Rebbe wants to talk to you," came the voice of the rebbe's secretary. Anyone else would have to call back. But no one could refuse to talk to the saintly rebbe who, in those early years, contributed so much of his time and efforts to enlist the help and resources of his followers and acquaintances on behalf of the Hatzalah work. "Please forgive me, Mr. Septimus, I must see you as soon as possible. It is a matter of life and death," said the gentle voice fraught with urgency.

"I'll be over as soon as possible," responded Louis. He shoved a pile of papers into his briefcase, rushed out of his office, and took a cab to the rebbe's modest house on East Broadway.

Unusually agitated, the Boyaner Rebbe, whose near-blinded eyes behind the thick, steel-framed glasses saw so much more and deeper than most, sparkled when he warmly greeted the young accountant. He invited him into his sparsely furnished study where a large shelf was filled with books. An open *sefer*, a well-worn Tehillim, lay in front of him on the bare table.

"Reb Elimelech Tress told me that only you have contact with people who have the means to sign papers for this group of our friends that must get out of Europe if there is to be a chance to save them."

Louis, who knew very well why he had been summoned, looked at the batch of freshly prepared affidavits that the rebbe handed him. He shook his head.

"Please, please, do not turn me down," pleaded the rebbe. "This may be the last chance to get them out. Letters, telegrams, and phone calls have been pouring in almost every hour. Hashem will help you find someone who will sign these papers," the rebbe said, his voice choking with suppressed tears.

Louis looked at the heavy batch of affidavits and frantically searched his mind for someone among his clients and friends whom he could possibly approach. "There is only one person that I know who has the means and the heart to sign these papers - Irving Bunim. But he has already signed too many. And I promised not to bother him again so soon."

The rebbe got up from his chair, walked over to Louis and pressed the affidavits into his hands. "Please, try; the *Eibishter* will be with you. We must do something before it is too late."

Though skeptical, the young accountant placed the precious papers into his briefcase and left after bidding the rebbe farewell. The rebbe walked him to the door. "Hashem will be with you and you will be *matzliach*," he said softly.

A cab brought Louis to the Manhattan office of Eden Textiles, where Irving Bunim, as usual, was caught in a maelstrom of work - not all of it related to his business.

"Louis, why didn't you make an appointment?" he asked the young accountant when he entered his office, while a secretary was piling a batch of letters on his desk, waiting for his approval and signature. "Anyone but you, I would have asked to come back another time."

Prepared for this, Louis put on his most persuasive manner that so often had helped him enlist the help of reluctant men of means to lend a hand to the rescue work.

"Irving, when the *Eibishter* calls and gives us a chance to save lives, there is no time to wait for an appointment. The Boyaner Rebbe himself has given me these affidavits with tears in his eyes. It's a matter of life and death, a last chance for his people to get out of the living hell in Poland. There is no one else I know who can sign these affidavits but you."

The busy, usually gentle philanthropist, on whom so many called for help, frowned and looked at the batch of affidavits, his face set. He shook his head. "Louis, I have never said no to you. But I am afraid this time. I have already signed far too many. I don't think they will even accept them anymore in Washington."

All of Louis's most cogent, most effective arguments failed to sway his friend this time. Finally, with a sigh, he gathered up the affidavits and put them back into his briefcase, trying frantically to think of someone else in Bunim's class to whom he could appeal, when the kind businessman, who had turned to the batch of letters before him, suddenly looked up.

"Louis, I'll tell you what I'll do. If the rebbe himself signs a note that he personally will take care of the people when they get to the U.S., then I'll sign their affidavits."

With an expression of hope and relief on his face, Louis warmly shook the tall burly man's hand. "Thanks, Irving," he said affectionately. He took the briefcase and rushed out onto Broadway, grabbed another cab, and a short while later walked into the house of the rebbe.

The rebbe, who had been eagerly awaiting his return, opened the door himself, looking hopefully at the young man. Louis took the affidavits out of his briefcase and put them before the rebbe, on the bare table next to the open Tehillim. Slightly more stooped than usual, the rebbe peered down at the papers again and again. They were unsigned.

Louis told the rebbe that it was up to him to get them signed. "Mr. Bunim promised that he would sign these affidavits if the rebbe personally signed a note to him that you would take care of the people for whom they have been made out, if and when they come to America."

The rebbe looked up in surprise. Then he bent down to stare at the affidavits in front of him, silently swaying convulsively back and forth over the frayed, yellowed Tehillim. A tear rolled into his gray beard from behind the thick glasses. He raised his head, looked around at the bare walls of the sparsely furnished study, and began to quietly moan in anguish.

"The rebbe must know that it is only a formality. You just sign the note to Bunim and I assure you that no one will hold you to it," Louis said over and over to him, breaking into his agonizingly suppressed moans.

"How can I sign such a personal promise?" the rebbe asked, inner torture breaking through his choked voice. A few more minutes passed in silence. The rebbe's head sank ever lower onto the Tehillim, as if seeking strength and an answer. Suddenly he rose, picked up the affidavits, and walked over to the young accountant who was too startled to say anything. He gave Louis the affidavits, shook his hand fervently, and said, "Please, take these back to Mr. Bunim. And if he will not sign them, Hashem will guide you to someone else with a heart and soul big enough to provide the affidavits in this hour of need. But I cannot sign something for which I cannot possibly be responsible."

The rebbe put his trembling arm around the young man's shoulder as he walked him to the door. "Hashem will help you," he said prayerfully, over and over again as Louis went down the steps.

His soul wrenched and not very hopeful, but somehow strengthened by the rebbe's arm around his shoulder, Louis rushed out to find a cab. A short while later, he strode once again into the front office of Eden Textiles. Irving Bunim was in the midst of an important business conference when Louis Septimus was announced. He excused himself and walked out into the front office. One look at the crestfallen face of the accountant told him the story.

"The rebbe will not sign a promise he cannot possibly keep," he said. "But the rebbe hopes you will change your mind."

A few long, hard moments of what seemed like a silent dialogue and prayer passed as these two kindred souls looked into each other's eyes. Louis again took the affidavits out of his briefcase and put them on the desk before the businessman. Irving Bunim stared down at them. Suddenly, his head straightened up and the usual, kind smile slowly crept out of the creased corners of his eyes and spread over his genial face.

"It is only out of sheer respect for the integrity of the rebbe who will not sign the note that I will sign his affidavits," he said firmly and with great *bitachon*.

A half hour later, a cab brought Louis to the office at 616 Bedford Avenue with the signed affidavits. There was no time to lose. Tomorrow might be too late. Perhaps a few more embers might be saved from the raging fires that destroyed everything in their path. The rebbe's tears had not been shed in vain.

| RADOSHITZER REBBE |
The Shofar of Eternity

How does one go about fashioning a shofar and blowing it on Rosh Hashanah in a Nazi concentration camp? Where does one even find a shofar in the depths of gehinnom? Who has the presence of mind to even consider attaining a shofar in that place of death and madness?

To the holy Rebbe of Radoshitz, R' Yitzchak'l Finkler *Hy"d*, the question was not how one blows a shofar, but rather, how does one not blow a shofar on Rosh Hashanah?

The year was 1943. Rosh Hashanah was rapidly approaching and R' Yitzchak'l of Radoshitz had decided that he would definitely fulfill the mitzvah of blowing the shofar on Rosh Hashanah, even under the horrible conditions in the Skarszysko concentration camp. When he told this to his fellow inmates, they looked at him incredulously. "Blow the shofar? Here, in a concentration camp? It can't be done. Besides, Rebbe, we don't have a shofar!"

The rebbe replied calmly, "It can be done, and it will be done! I ask only for your help and cooperation."

The men who were close to R' Yitzchak'l and revered him as a *tzaddik*, agreed to gather a small sum of money, whatever they had with them in the camp. With this, they bribed a Polish worker who lived outside the camp to bring them the head of a horned animal. Unfortunately, the gentile didn't follow directions precisely and to their great distress, he brought the head of an ox, whose horns may not be used for a shofar.

The inmates were crushed; they had used up most of their resources and had nothing to show for it. But the rebbe was undaunted. Disregarding their strong protests due to the dangers involved, he encouraged them to try again. This time, for a second fee, a sum they barely scraped together, the Polish worker got it right and smuggled in the head of a ram. The rebbe was overjoyed.

But who would know how to make a shofar from the ram's horn? And who would undertake such a dangerous assignment? And where would he get the necessary tools? The task seemed impossible in the slave labor camp.

The rebbe remembered a former Chassid of his, Moshe Naichatchitsky, who used to *daven* in his *shtiebel* and who now worked in the metal workshop of the Skarszysko camp. When the rebbe spoke to Moshe and outlined his plan, Moshe began to tremble and tears came to his eyes, for every step of the way, he knew, would be filled with grave peril. Nor did he have the faintest idea of how to fashion a ram's horn into a shofar. But when he saw R' Yitzchak'l standing in front of him, with tears in his eyes, begging him to enable the poor Jews to fulfill this holy mitzvah, how could he possibly refuse? The rebbe promised him that if he accepted this perilous assignment, he would survive the war.

Somehow, Moshe was indeed successful. Shortly before Rosh Hashanah, he presented R' Yitzchak'l with a finished, completely kosher shofar. The rebbe's joy knew no bounds. On the morning of Rosh Hashanah of 5704, the rebbe's barracks was filled with Jews who wanted to join with him in his *minyan*, to *daven* with him and to hear him blow shofar. The rebbe recited *"Min Hameitzar"* in a choking voice, and then sounded his precious shofar.

One of those present in the barracks at that time, Reb Avraham Altman, later gave his impression of these events. "What shall I say? For me it was like the assembly at Mount Sinai at the time of *Mattan Torah*. Don't laugh or ridicule me. This is how I felt then and this is how many people who participated in that holy gathering also felt."

Moshe Naichatchitsky did indeed survive the war. He moved to Israel, where he married the rebbe's youngest daughter, the only member of that great *tzaddik's* family to survive the Holocaust. After a tireless search, he located his precious shofar which had been lost for many years. The shofar today resides in the Yad Vashem Archives in Jerusalem.

| R' CHAIM KREISWIRTH |
"One Mitzvah Follows Another Mitzvah"

On August 23, 1939, the Molotov-Ribbentrop Pact was signed. It effectively divided the once proud country of Poland into two provinces: one of Germany and the other of Russia. On September 1, 1939, the German invasion of its agreed upon portion of western Poland started World War II, while the Red Army waited until September 17 to invade eastern Poland and occupy the Polish territory assigned to it. Eleven days later, the secret protocol of the Molotov-Ribbentrop Pact was modified, allotting Germany a larger part of Poland, while ceding most of Lithuania to the Soviet Union. Under the terms of the pact, Vilna, along with the rest of eastern Poland, was occupied by Soviet forces in late September 1939.

In an effort to stay one step ahead of the Nazi plan to destroy European Judaism, R' Chaim Kreiswirth *zt"l*, as well as thousands of other Jews, fled from Poland to the newly independent capital city of Vilna, which the Soviet Union transferred to the Lithuanian authorities in October of 1939.

Their independence was short-lived, however, as the Soviets occupied Lithuania, and in August 1940 incorporated Vilna, along with the rest of Lithuania, into the Soviet Union. On June 22, 1941, Germany attacked Soviet forces in eastern Poland and captured Vilna. R' Chaim fell into the hands of the accursed Nazis and was shipped off to one of the notorious labor camps.

R' Chaim was young and energetic and was always looking out for his fellow Jew. Although there were many sick and decrepit individuals in the camp, there was one man whose condition had become utterly appalling. He was stricken with numerous diseases, including leprosy with boils all over his body, and had been blinded when the Germans thought it would be a good sport to poke out his eyes. He was a miserable, wretched sight to behold and consequently was shunned by his fellow inmates, left to die in misery and filth. R' Chaim would not allow this to happen and he befriended the young man and attempted to assist him and nurse him back to health. He gave up his own meager rations to feed him and washed and dressed his wounds. He never considered his own frail health and the chance that he might contract a disease as well. All he cared about was seeing this man healthy once again. Miraculously, he succeeded beyond any and all expectations, and although the man remained blind, he regained his health and beat the diseases. Eventually, he was able to rejoin a work battalion.

R' Chaim's actions became legendary and wherever he walked, people would talk to him and discuss their issues. R' Chaim was a "people person" and would speak energetically to everyone, providing hope and encouragement even in the midst of pain and misery.

Apparently, R' Chaim was a bit too energetic, for he was noticed by a passing S.S. overseer who felt that perhaps this popular young man was enjoying himself too much in the "care" of the Nazi labor camp. Clicking his heels, the S.S. lieutenant issued an order to haul him away for questioning and punishment. Guards grabbed R' Chaim and stood him in front of the S.S. man, who called him a spy and ordered him to be shot on the spot.

As R' Chaim was being prepared for execution, he closed his eyes and offered a silent prayer to Heaven. "Master of the World, I just acted above and beyond to care for an unfortunate Jew who was sick and dying. It was with great *mesiras nefesh* that he became well again. Now, I ask that You give me my reward for that act here in this world, and allow me to live in order to care for others for the rest of my life. *Chazal* tell us: *One mitzvah follows another mitzvah*, but if I die now, all my future good deeds will die with me." R' Chaim's thoughts centered on survival, rather than surrender, and he prayed with every fiber of his being.

"Not right here," shouted the S.S. lieutenant, waking R' Chaim from his reverie. The guard was ordered to take the prisoner away and shoot him outside the gates of the camp, so that no German would have to waste valuable time and energy removing the body and burying it in the camp. "Shoot the Jew and leave him to rot in the forest," was the direct order.

The guard marched R' Chaim outside the camp's gates and stood him up against a tree. All the while, R' Chaim continued praying, begging the Al-mighty to allow him to live in order to help others. Suddenly, the guard's demeanor changed and he spoke in a low conspiratorial voice. "Listen, I will shoot into the air and you run away from this place. Do you hear me?"

R' Chaim nodded in shock and when the German guard inexplicably shot his pistol into the air, R' Chaim took off in a dead run. He ran for days and days, hiding out until he somehow managed to reach safety. He lost no time in escaping the continent of Europe, and within a short time, he landed on the shores of the Holy Land.

| R' YISROEL ZEV GUSTMAN |
Overcoming All Obstacles

R' Yisroel Zev Gustman *zt"l* had succeeded his father-in-law as a member of the Vilna *beis din* (Halachic Court) at twenty-two years of age. How did such a young man secure such a coveted position? As it were, the day prior to his appointment, R' Yisroel Zev spent an entire day engaged in Torah discussion with none other than R' Chaim Ozer Grodzenski *zt"l*, head of the Rabbinical Court and a worldwide leader of Torah Jewry. The two enjoyed a particularly close relationship. Obviously impressed by the Torah knowledge and ability of his young charge, R' Chaim Ozer recognized the opportunity and had him appointed to the court.

The ominous clouds of the Second World War were overspreading the European continent and everyone was searching for a way to ride out the impending storm in safety and security. In 1940, when R' Gustman came for what would be his final visit to his mentor, R' Chaim Ozer, the great *rav*, already in the throes of his final illness told him something that he did not tell anyone else: "*Du vest zei iburkumen – idi v'idi* – You will overcome them, both them and them," and he motioned towards east and west. At the time, R' Gustman did not understand the importance of these words. The meaning would only become clear later.

July 13, 1941 will go down in infamy as "Rabbi's Day" in Vilna. On that horrible and shocking day, German officers and Nazi S.S., with the assistance of bloodthirsty collaborating Lithuanians, attacked *rabbanim* and *roshei yeshivah* – anyone they perceived to be of rabbinic intent – throughout the city. R' Gustman himself was attacked in his home and beaten mercilessly. Somehow, he managed to pull himself free of his attackers and hide in the courtyard outside.

Someone brought him a workman's cap and a hair clipper. He shaved his beard, donned the cap, and hid in a neighbor's house for one day. But he knew that he could not remain there for long. Surely the Nazis would not give up the search for him. But where could he hide?

Then he remembered an experience with R' Chaim Ozer that had taken place some time earlier, in the good days.

As per doctor's orders, it had been R' Chaim Ozer's practice to go for a wagon ride each afternoon for some fresh air. On most days, he would ask someone, usually a younger *talmid chacham*, to accompany him so that he would have someone with whom to discuss Torah topics. Often, R' Gustman accompanied R' Chaim Ozer on these wagon rides and the two would focus on intricate Talmudic discourses. One day, as they were riding through the outskirts of the city, R' Chaim Ozer halted in the middle of a specific Torah point and motioned to the side of a wooded area. "Right there is a cave," said the *rav* cryptically. "Remember where that cave is." He also pointed out various types of vegetation that were edible and other plants that were poisonous – with no explanation as to why he was deviating from their Torah discussion.

R' Gustman listened with obedient attentiveness but didn't feel it was proper to question R' Chaim Ozer on why he felt the need to point out these things. He just nodded and followed R' Chaim Ozer's gaze. He had never forgotten that incident. Now, years later, under Nazi occupation and on the run, R' Gustman understood the significance of R' Chaim Ozer's words. With his wife and young daughter, he headed for the wooded outskirts of Vilna, to the same cave R' Chaim Ozer had pointed out years earlier. They hid there for a while and were safe from their pursuers. They ate the edible plants and avoided the poisonous vegetation. No doubt, they would have had no idea which to eat and which not to eat were it not for that unusual and impromptu lesson in vegetation. At times, the Gustman family even sucked out the moisture from clumps of earth to stay alive.

They later fled deeper into the forest and met a group of partisans, Lithuanians who had banded together to fight the Germans. Though they were not known for their love of Jews, the partisans permitted the Gustmans to join their group.

When the war ended, the Gustman family returned to Vilna where they remained for some time, along with fewer than two hundred Jewish survivors. At that time, the city was under Russian control. One of the local government officials was a Jewish Communist who took a liking to R' Gustman. One day, he came secretly with a warning. He had learned that R' Gustman was to be arrested and sent to Siberia the next day. That very day, the family left Vilna and escaped the Russian authorities. R' Gustman, along with his wife and child, succeeded in crossing the border to freedom. They made their way to the United States and later, finally settled in Jerusalem.

R' Chaim Ozer's parting words were indeed prophetic. Russia is in Eastern Europe. Germany is in Western Europe. First the Russians controlled Vilna; later, the Nazis would invade Lithuania and the Jews of Vilna would be subjected to typical Nazi barbarism. And after that, the Russians once again took over the city and the Gustmans fled for their lives.

"You will overcome them," R' Chaim Ozer had said, "both them (the Germans) and them (the Russians)."

The "Chief Physician" of the Warsaw Ghetto

Umschlagplatz was a dreaded word among the ghetto Jews. It meant "transfer point" for deportation, usually located near a railroad siding. Huge throngs of people were pushed toward the barbed wires that divided the area in two. On the ground lay hundreds of men, women and children, valises, all kinds of possessions, bedding, prayer shawls, food packages, and single shoes lost by some who were caught in the latest round-up. Jewish police officers ran back and forth following orders from the Gestapo or the *Platz-Kommandant*. On the roofs of nearby buildings were machine guns manned by the S.S. and gendarmes. Bullets would swish by and wounded victims would fall to the ground. People would pass them by, step over the fallen, and step on each other. From the *umschlagplatz*, everyone knew, there was only one place to go – into the cattle cars. And when these were crowded to suffocation, the train left for what the Germans called "resettlement in the east." Though the Jews did not yet know that they were heading for an extermination camp, they were full of dark forebodings about their unknown destination.

But one Jew from the Warsaw ghetto attempted the impossible and succeeded in rescuing hundreds, if not thousands, of Jews already on the *umschlagplatz*, hours, and sometimes even minutes, before they were pushed into cattle cars. His name was Nachum Remba, a modest and scholarly man, described by those who knew him as a "saintly figure." He embarked on a rescue operation worthy of the most daring adventurer.

He set up a pretend First Aid Station right next to the *umschlagplatz*. This "hospital" was staffed with trustworthy doctors and nurses. Remba donned a long white doctor's coat and entered the *umschlagplatz* as head of the "hospital." With great authority, he pointed out to the German officers the Jews he claimed were too weak to make the journey east, and demanded that he be permitted to take them into the "hospital." Nachum hurriedly walked from one side of the *platz* to the other, from one German to another, rescuing Jews, pulling them out of the *umschlagplatz* and sending them back to the ghetto. Always calm, always smiling good-naturedly, he would appear where no one dared set foot, where one could get shot for merely standing there. Fearlessly and with dignity, he faced the German henchmen on the *umschlagplatz* and demanded that they free this very sick one or this malnourished young one, who were unable to make the difficult journey east. And the Germans, who valued authority and those in position of authority above all else, began to refer to him as "Haupt-Artzt Remba" – Chief Physician Remba – and acceded to his requests.

The new "patients" were quickly taken to the hospital, where the deception continued. In the "hospital," the rescued were ordered to lie down on cots. Some were "bandaged" while others were treated with "medicine." As soon as the path was clear, they were taken by "ambulance" back to the ghetto and reunited with their families. The nurses wore especially wide coats under which they were able to hide the rescued children. It was frequently necessary to put them to sleep to make their rescue possible.

Remba kept a diary of life in the Warsaw ghetto, but it was lost. A few passages, however, are extant, thanks to the ghetto historian, Emmanuel Ringelblum. "At night," Remba noted in his diary, "I imagined that I was hearing the thump of children's feet, marching in cadence under the leadership of their teacher. I heard the measured steps, tramping on and on without interruption to an unknown destination. And to this day I see that scene in my mind. I see clearly the figures, and I see the fists of hundreds of thousands that will come raining down on the heads of the henchmen."

How was Remba able to deceive the ever-vigilant Germans? "This is the irony of it," writes one eyewitness, "that even the Germans, with their refined system of punctuality, were capable of being fooled, at least for a while. They never suspected that a Jew could pull off such a daring act. And until they caught on to the 'Jewish trick,' many a Jew was rescued." Who knows how many more Jews Nachum Remba might have saved had he not been betrayed by members of the Jewish police, who saw in him a dangerous rival because he rescued Jews for nothing while they demanded heavy bribes from the victims.

In the spring of 1943, Remba was again on the *umschlagplatz*, this time not in his white doctor's coat in the role of savior, but as victim. The Germans caught him during the Warsaw ghetto uprising and deported him to the Majdanek death camp. There, too, Remba did everything he could to alleviate the suffering of his fellow prisoners, according to witnesses. He was especially close to the children, telling them stories, taking them for walks, making them forget, if even for a while, their horrible surroundings. In the end, he went to the gas chambers with them.

| BELZER REBBE |
The Great Escape (1)

It was a cold, dark night in the Tarnow ghetto. Someone was impatiently knocking on Dr. Joshua (Isaiah) Hendler's window. "I am a Jew, a friend. Please, open the door, doctor."

Dr. Hendler rushed to the door. In the doorway stood a Belzer Chassid he had known from better times, a man by the name of Goldfarb. His distress was obvious and he spoke in great haste. "Doctor Hendler, we need your help. Money is no object; we will pay you as much as you ask. The Rebbe of Belz has been injured trying to escape the Nazis and his life is in danger. He is not far from here, in a small village near Tarnow, and he needs immediate medical attention."

Dr. Hendler knew well the risk of leaving the ghetto without a permit: the punishment was death. But he had also heard of the great "*wunder rabbiner*" – the Belzer Rebbe – and in a matter of minutes he was dressed. With his doctor's satchel in hand, he followed Goldfarb. They climbed over fences and crawled in the mud until they were finally outside the ghetto limits. There, a Polish farmer with a horse and buggy was waiting for them. Once they were in the carriage and on their way, the Chassid briefly sketched the plight of the Belzer Rebbe since his escape from Belz. He had suffered through the death of his family and his beloved son, R' Moshe'le, and now he had had a serious accident. The Belzer Rebbe; his brother, R' Mordechai of Bilgoray; and two of their ardent followers had hired a taxi with a Polish driver for an astronomical sum of money to drive them to a tiny inconspicuous village called Wisnicz. This village was so far under the radar of the Nazis that it was barely affected by the German occupation. It was the general hope that Wisnicz might provide a safe haven for the Belzer entourage until the end of the war. However, during the late-night drive, the car missed the road and turned over into a ditch, and the frail rebbe was badly hurt.

After a drive of close to an hour in the pitch-black Polish countryside, the doctor and his escort reached the village where the rebbe was waiting. The Polish driver led them to a barn. There, seated on a bundle of straw in the pale light of a hanging kerosene lamp, was the world-renowned Belzer *tzaddik*. The rebbe's face was bandaged with a red kerchief, as if he suffered from a toothache. His beard and *peyos* were shaven and his hands and clothes were covered with blood. Dr. Hendler attended to the rebbe, treating his injury and bandaging the large gash on his leg, all the while finding it difficult to take his eyes off the *tzaddik*. The rebbe's holy gaze, in spite of all the pain, was calm, as if he were totally removed from the pressing problems of the mundane world. After he finished with the rebbe, he tended to the other, more fortunate passengers, who had escaped the accident with only mild injuries.

When the doctor was finished, the Belzer Rebbe asked what his fee would be. "Not even a broken penny," replied Dr. Hendler. He told the rebbe that he had simply done his human and professional duty; there was no limit to his joy that he was privileged to help the great rebbe, his brother, and their companions in such a moment of distress.

The Belzer Rebbe was very moved by the doctor's reply. Before they parted, he blessed Dr. Hendler that he and the close members of his family would survive the war. He then gave the doctor a twenty-zloty coin, not as a payment, but rather as an amulet. The rebbe told the doctor to watch over the amulet, for its merit would always protect him.

On the way back to the ghetto, Goldfarb, the Belzer Chassid, asked Dr. Hendler to sell him the amulet. "Doctor, why do you need such an amulet? You are a Jew who does not observe tradition and law. As such, an amulet from a Chassidic rabbi is meaningless to you."

He offered the doctor two thousand zloty for the twenty-zloty coin. Hendler did not respond. Goldfarb raised his bid to twenty thousand zloty. The doctor still remained silent. Goldfarb continued to bargain for the amulet. "I will pay any amount you wish," he pleaded.

Finally the doctor responded, "Listen here, no matter what price you are going to offer, I am not going to part with the twenty-zloty coin given to me by the Rebbe of Belz. To me this coin is priceless; it is worth *mein gantze leben* (my very life)!" The subject was dropped, and the two men returned to the ghetto before dawn.

When the Tarnow ghetto was liquidated in September 1943, Dr. Hendler, together with other able-bodied young people, was deported to Plaszow. He took with him his most precious possessions, the amulet and a medical manuscript he had been writing in the ghetto. When the doctor faced deportation again, this time from Plaszow to a concentration camp in Germany, he buried the amulet and his manuscript near his barracks in Plaszow.

Just as was promised by the Belzer Rebbe on that dark night in a remote Polish village, Dr. Hendler survived the war. After liberation, he returned to Plaszow and began to search for his amulet and manuscript. His barracks was no longer in existence and the search was a tiresome one. But eventually he did locate the site and retrieved both the amulet and the manuscript.

Much later, Dr. Hendler recalled, "I must confess that I experienced miracles and wonders. When the Tarnow ghetto was liquidated, tens of thousands were massacred. Only a few Jews were transferred to the Plaszow ghetto, near Krakow, and I was among them! There, the great majority of Jewish slave workers fell like flies from exhaustion, torment and mass murder. Yet I survived all the tortures and left that terrible place alive, with my health intact. Even that respectable Chassid, Mr. Goldfarb, fell among the innumerable victims, while I was saved. Later, my sister and I survived deportation to Germany. Who knows? Perhaps the rebbe's emotional blessing and amulet helped me survive."

For the rest of his life, Dr. Hendler proudly displayed in his Tel Aviv apartment the twenty-zloty coin, the amulet that saved his life.

| BELZER REBBE |
The Great Escape (2)

The stopover in Wisnicz was short-lived. An informant had sniffed out the hiding place of the Belzer Rebbe and his brother, R' Mottel (Rokeach) of Bilgoray, and measures were taken by leading Belzer Chassidim to have them brought to the Bochnia ghetto. But the international network of Belz was hard at work and secret plans were hatched to extricate the rebbe and his brother from Poland. In May 1943, the plan was brought to fruition and a brave officer by the name of Captain Shtaier was hired to carry out the details of the rescue. The captain was really a resourceful Polish officer who had joined Hungarian counterintelligence. As part of his duties, he made weekly expeditions into and out of Poland to gather intelligence. He was put in charge of the rescue operation and was handsomely rewarded – to the tune of a half a million pengos (about $20,000 on the black market in those days) – for his bold plan.

According to the plan, Captain Shtaier would be traveling in the service of the Hungarian army. His stated mission was to bring two prominent generals who were captured on the eastern front, back to Hungary from Poland for interrogation. The two captured generals would be none other than the Belzer Rebbe and the Bilgoray Rav.

The captain made all the necessary arrangements at the various border checkpoints both in Poland and Hungary. All the forged documents were in perfect order, as were the various license plates he prepared for his car. The only possible problem was the fact that he had forgotten to bring along two sets of Russian uniforms. When he realized his error, it was too late to go back. However, he had confidence in his plan and did not foresee any major difficulties.

After long months of preparation, the journey to freedom began. The first step was the dramatic escape from the Bochnia ghetto. Among many bold and heroic deeds was that of the Chassid, Reuven Walkin, who played the "body double" of the Belzer Rebbe for a few days so that the ghetto administration, and especially the ghetto commandant, Muller, would not become aware that the rebbe was missing.

With the two "generals" in his back seat, both clean-shaven and dressed in civilian clothing, Captain Shtaier successfully passed the first checkpoint. As he passed each additional checkpoint, his confidence grew and he merrily sang Polish and Hungarian songs. At one point in the journey, he even left his two illustrious passengers alone in the parked car while he entered a bar to have a few drinks.

When he returned he could not find the car. He began to search frantically for the vanished car only to discover that the car was parked in precisely the same spot where he had left it. But it was shrouded in a heavy mist as if to conceal it from eyes that were not supposed to see it. He crossed himself, for now he was sure that all he had been told about his two passengers was indeed true.

Finally they reached the Hungarian border, the last leg of their dangerous journey. The good captain was in especially high spirits, for at last he was completing his mission and would receive the balance of his payment. He changed the license plates on the car and discarded the old ones in a nearby potato field where he buried them deep in the ground.

As they approached the first major checkpoint in Hungary, the officer did not foresee any mishaps. When they stopped at the barrier, he presented all the necessary papers to the young border guard. The guard looked at the pictures in the documents, carefully compared them to the two passengers in the back seat, and then checked their names against a list in his possession. "Sorry, I can't let you pass. I have no order from my superiors to expect the arrival of two captive generals," the young soldier said.

"Well, then, check with your superior officer," Captain Shtaier commanded in a strident voice. The superior appeared moments later. He apologized for the inconvenience, but he confirmed the young soldier's statement. He had no instructions to allow the passage of two captured Russian generals. Then, as if to reinforce his importance, he looked into the car and asked the two men in the back seat, "Where are your uniforms?"

They, of course, remained silent. Captain Shtaier spoke up. "They are under strict orders to speak to no one except at headquarters back in Budapest. We must leave immediately!

How long do you expect us to wait here at this godforsaken place?" The Hungarian officer continued speaking loudly and in a confident tone while he tried to figure out what had gone wrong and to work out an alternative plan.

Just then, a vision appeared from down the road. Three men on horseback were riding towards the car. Their Hungarian uniforms and the stars on their lapels indicated that they were superior officers, generals, and not to be taken lightly. Without even inquiring why the car was stopped, they ordered the border guards, both the junior officer and senior officer, to let the car pass with the captive generals. Captain Shtaier didn't wait for a second invitation. He quickly put the car into gear and sped away. As the car crossed the border, the three mounted Hungarian generals watched them go and seemed to salute the two "generals" in the car. Once more, the car was on its way to freedom with its two prominent passengers.

The awed stillness in the car was shattered a few minutes after they crossed the border as the good captain, bewildered and perplexed, blurted out, "I have no idea who those men were. I have connections with many of the high officers in the Hungarian army, but frankly I must admit that I did not recognize those three high-ranking military men who came to our rescue at the border."

R' Mottel spoke up and with a smile replied, "We did. They were the three previous Belzer Rebbes; our father (R' Yissacher Dov Ber), our grandfather (R' Yeshayah), and our great-grandfather (the Sar Shalom) – all top-ranking generals in the Al-mighty's army!"

| BLUZHEVER REBBE |
A Time for Blessing

In Bergen-Belsen, on the eve of Chanukah, a *selektion* took place. Many Jews were randomly taken out of the barracks and shot. The Nazis were enjoying this game and Jewish bodies were piling up on the ground. S.S. men with rubber truncheons and iron prods kicked, beat, and tortured the innocent victims. When the tortured body no longer responded, the revolver was used...

The random *selektions* went on inside the barracks and the brutal massacre continued until sundown. When the black angels of death departed, they left behind heaps of tortured and twisted bodies.

Then Chanukah came to Bergen-Belsen. Amidst the pain and grief, a few devoted Jews banded together and decided that they must do something for the Festival of Lights. A jug of pure olive oil was not to be found, no candle was in sight, and a menorah belonged to the distant past. Instead, a wooden clog, the shoe of one of the inmates, became the menorah; a string pulled from a concentration camp uniform was the wick; and the black camp shoe polish served as oil. The men hurriedly prepared the materials necessary for the mitzvah and asked the Bluzhever Rebbe, R' Yisroel Spira *zt"l*, to light the extraordinary "menorah" and recite the blessings.

Not far from the heaps of dead bodies, the living skeletons assembled to participate in the kindling of Chanukah lights.

With tears in his eyes, the Bluzhever Rebbe lit the first light and recited the blessing: "To kindle the Chanukah candle." Then he made the second blessing: "Who has performed miracles for our ancestors in those days, at this time." Each blessing was declared with tremendous import and concentration, and answered with a resounding "amen" by all those present.

The rebbe then came to the third blessing: "Who has kept us alive and sustained us and brought us to this occasion." Before he could utter a word, he paused and hesitated. Looking around, he studied his surroundings and the intense feelings displayed on the faces of the men gathered there. Finally, he turned back, closed his eyes, and made the blessing, lighting the single wick. Not one eye remained dry from tears as together they sang the Yom Tov melodies and stared heavily at the small flame burning defiantly in the middle of that Nazi hell.

There was an assimilated Jew who witnessed this scene with a mixture of bitterness and apathy. Mr. Zamietchkowski, one of the leaders of the Warsaw Bund, was a clever man with a passion for debating matters of religion, faith and truth. Even here in Bergen-Belsen, his passion for discussion did not abate. He never missed an opportunity to engage in all manner of conversation.

As soon as the rebbe had finished the ceremony of kindling the lights, Zamietchkowski elbowed his way to the rebbe and said, "Spira, you are a decent and honest person. I can understand your need to light Chanukah candles in these wretched times. I can even understand the historical note of the second blessing, 'Who did miracles for our fathers in days of old, at this season.' But what I don't understand is, how can a person in this terrible place with dead Jews lying all around us, make the *Shehecheyanu* blessing, thanking G-d for keeping us alive and bringing us to this time? I mean, is this such a 'wonderful time' that G-d deserves to be thanked for all that He's done? For this you are thankful to G-d? For this you praise the L-rd for 'keeping us alive'?" His voice was wretched and anguished as he stared at the Bluzhever intently.

"Zamietchkowski, you are one hundred percent right," answered the rebbe. "When I reached the third blessing, I also hesitated and asked myself, what should I do with this blessing? I turned my head in order to ask the rabbi of Zaner and other distinguished rabbis who were standing near me, if indeed I should skip the blessing. But just as I was turning my head, I noticed that behind me stood a throng of men, a huge crowd of living and breathing Jews, their collective faces expressing faith, devotion, and concentration as they listened to the rite of the kindling of Chanukah lights.

"I said to myself, if the Al-mighty has such a nation that at times like these, when the bodies of their beloved fathers, brothers and sons are heaped about, and death is staring them in the face from every corner; if despite all this, they stand with devotion and listen to the blessing, 'Who did miracles for our fathers in days of old, at this season,' then indeed, I am under a special obligation to recite the third blessing."

| KOVNO RAV |

"A G-d-fearing Jew Can Never Be a Slave!"

In the waning days of the Kovno ghetto, the remaining Jews were made to undergo torturous suffering at the hands of the Germans and their bloodthirsty Lithuanian cohorts. Each day, the Jews were marched outside the city and forced to labor in the fields, laying the foundation for a new airport that was to be used by the Nazis. From morning to night, the ragged Jews were beaten into submission and it wasn't long before the entire ghetto was liquidated and the Jews killed.

Each morning, before they were marched off to work, a *minyan* for Shacharis was held clandestinely. One day, as the *ba'al tefillah* (one leading the prayers) was saying the *Birchos Hashachar* (morning blessings) out loud, he suddenly paused by the blessing, "Blessed are You Hashem... Who has not made me a slave."

The people waited for him to continue but instead, with a terrible anguish in his voice, he cried out, "Is this a joke? Can a person who is beaten daily and forced into oppressive labor at the hands of a merciless master really give thanks that he is not a slave? What is he if not a slave? How can I say these words when I really don't believe in them?"

His outburst caused an uproar in the small *minyan*. Fortunately, the Kovno Rav, R' Avraham Kahana-Shapira *Hy"d* was present at the *minyan* and he immediately calmed the situation down. Walking over to the angry man, he shook his head.

"You are making a mistake, my friend," he said. "This blessing is not talking about physical slavery – but rather spiritual bondage. It is true that the Germans wish to crush and destroy us by means of false hopes and deception and that all of us who are imprisoned in the ghetto exist under the sentence of death. And yet, no matter what dreary situation a Jew finds himself in, he must never lose his faith. In his mind and heart, he is a free man and always will be. So, of course you should make this blessing – for a G-d-fearing Jew can never be a slave!"

| PONEVEZHER RAV |
Dedication

Two brothers, members of the wealthy Solomon family, formerly of Kovno, traveled to Bnei Brak in the summer of 1942 to consult with the Ponevezher Rav, who had escaped Europe after losing his entire family. The threat hovering over the Jewish community of Palestine was imminent. Informed sources reckoned that within ten days, German Field Marshal Rommel would invade the Holy Land and take full control of the country. How were they to respond to such an outcome?

The Ponevezher Rav listened to them carefully, his serious demeanor attesting that he fully comprehended the gravity of the situation. Yet his response was swift and startling. He was suddenly gripped by strong emotion and said, "Ten days? In ten days the enemy will be here? So, then we still have ten days! In that case, I will get on with building a yeshivah! And if I succeed, it will endure!"

In the midst of the general fear, R' Yosef Shlomo Kahaneman *zt"l*, the Ponevezher Rav, laid the foundation cornerstone of the planned new Ponevezh Yeshivah in Bnei Brak. Indeed, events vindicated his trust. The British victory over Rommel's Afrika Corps at El Alamein ended the direct threat to the Jews living in Palestine. And the cornerstone that was laid on that fateful day is still the cornerstone of the yeshivah that thrives to this very day!

The yeshivah took some time to build but the *rav* never lost sight of his vision. In 1944, as the war raged on in Europe and the Pacific, and European Jewry was being systematically crushed under the weight of Nazi tyranny and oppression, the Jews of the Holy Land lived in relative security. Nevertheless, their anguish and grief over the plight of their European brethren was always at the forefront of their thoughts and prayers.

Two yeshivah students from Petach Tikvah had been visiting Bnei Brak and were returning late in the day to their yeshivah. They decided to stand on the main road and hitch a ride. After waiting for a few minutes, one of the boys noticed a light in the distance. The two began walking towards the light but as they got closer they stopped. What they saw amazed them. Straight ahead, on the crest of a looming mountain laid out before them, was the Ponevezher Rav, R' Yosef Shlomo Kahaneman, carrying a lantern and walking around and around the mountaintop as if searching for something.

They quickly approached and asked concernedly, "Rebbi, can we help you? Have you lost something?"

The Ponevezher Rav looked up in surprise. He was so absorbed in his thoughts that he hadn't even heard them coming. He turned to them and smiled, "I need no help, thank you. I have not lost anything."

"But, Rebbi," they persisted, "what are you doing with a lantern in the evening on top of an empty mountain?"

R' Yosef Shlomo gazed across the slope. His eyes were wide with childish enthusiasm and anticipation. Once again, he smiled at the boys and said, "I am looking at something. Don't you see what I see? Over there is the main yeshivah building with a thousand students toiling in intense Torah study. On that side are the dormitories with three hundred *bachurim* in this building, and three hundred in that building. Look at the grand dining hall and the yeshivah library that we have built here. Is it not a beautiful sight to behold?"

The boys followed the gaze of the Ponevezher Rav but all they could see was a barren mountain and an old man living in a world of dreams. He had lost everything in the Holocaust – his wife, his children, everything he had built. There was no yeshivah building, no dormitories and no libraries. A thousand students? Whom was he kidding? The two boys came to the conclusion that the Ponevezher Rav was not dealing with reality and quietly and sadly, slipped away.

It took a few years, but eventually the dream of the *rav* became a reality. The grand yeshivah building, which rests majestically on a mountaintop overlooking the sprawling city of Bnei Brak, is home to over one thousand students, *avreichim*, and Torah scholars. The dormitories and libraries are all in existence and put to good use.

Many years later, one of the two students who had been on that mountain with the Ponevezher Rav on that late afternoon came to Bnei Brak to speak with him about an unrelated matter. He introduced himself by saying, "Rebbi, if you will recall, I met you many years ago on top of the mountain as you held a lantern..."

The Ponevezher Rav peered at him carefully and said excitedly, "You are one of the *bachurim*? If yes, then come with me!"

Although the *rav* was many decades older than the young man, he proudly served as a tour guide, taking him on a grand tour of the entire Ponevezh campus. It was a majestic tour. At one point in the tour, the *rav* stopped and said, "Young man, I want you to teach future generations how an old, sick man was able to build an empire like this. Let me ask you: Do you think I built it by myself? Could one man really build all of this? No! What it takes is dedication, and *Hakadosh Baruch Hu* will help you succeed."

One man changed the face of Jewry when he could have remained a broken man, embittered by the tragedies that had befallen him and our nation. He was over sixty-five years old when he began building the greatest empire of Torah in our day. He had reason to give up and let others take over. Instead, he changed the face of the Jewish nation in general, and the yeshivah world in particular, for all eternity.

Saved by a Pendant

When a train pulled up at one of the main Nazi killing centers, filled with a large group of Jewish women prisoners, many Polish villagers came out to watch as this latest batch was taken away. As the Jewish women were gathering their possessions to take them along into the camp, the Nazi officer in charge called out to the villagers standing in the vicinity, "Anything that these Jews leave behind you may take for yourselves, because for sure they will not be coming back to collect them!"

Two Polish women who were standing nearby saw a woman towards the back of the group who was wearing a heavy, expensive coat. Not wanting to wait and see if others got the coat before them, they ran to the woman and knocked her to the ground, grabbed her coat and walked away.

As the Jewish women were being led away, these two Polish women lay down the coat to divide the spoils hiding inside of it. As they rummaged through the pockets, they discovered gold jewelry, silver candlesticks and other heirlooms. They were quite pleased, but still, as they lifted the coat it seemed heavier than it should be. After further inspection they found a secret pocket, and hidden inside was a little baby girl!

Shocked at their discovery, one of the Polish women insisted to the other, "I don't have any children, and I'm too old to give birth anymore. How about you take the majority of the gold and silver and let me have the baby." The other woman agreed to the deal and the Polish woman took her new "daughter" home to her delighted husband. They raised the Jewish girl as their own, treating her very well, and never told her anything of her history. The girl excelled in her studies and became a successful pediatrician, working in a top hospital in Poland.

After some years, the girl's "mother" passed away. A week later, she heard a knock at the door. An old woman invited herself in and said, "I want you to know that the woman who passed away last week was not your real mother..." and she proceeded to tell her the whole story.

The girl did not believe her at first, but the old woman said to her, "When we found you, you were wearing a beautiful gold pendant with strange writing on it, which must be Hebrew. I am sure that your mother kept the necklace. Go and look." And with that parting advice she left.

The girl went into her deceased mother's jewelry box and found the necklace, just as the woman described. It was hard to believe that she had been of Jewish descent, but the proof was right there in her hand. As this was her only link to a previous life, she cherished the necklace. She had it enlarged to fit her neck and wore it every day, although she thought nothing more of her Jewish roots.

A number of years later, she traveled abroad on vacation and came upon two Chassidic-looking boys on the main street, trying to interest Jewish passersby to wrap *tefillin* on their arms (for the males) or accept Shabbos candles to light on Friday afternoon (for the females). Seizing the opportunity, she told them her entire story and showed them the necklace. The boys confirmed that a Jewish name was inscribed on the necklace but did not know what to say about her status. They recommended that she send a detailed letter to their mentor, the Lubavitcher Rebbe. If anyone would know what to do, it would be him.

She took their advice and sent off a letter that very same day. She received a speedy reply saying that it was clear from the facts that she was a Jewish girl. The letter also suggested that perhaps she would consider using her medical skills in Israel, a place in desperate need of talented pediatricians.

By now her curiosity was piqued. She decided to go to Israel where she consulted a *beis din* (Rabbinical Court), who declared her Jewish. She moved there permanently, was accepted into a hospital to work, and eventually met her husband and raised a family.

Some years later, in August 2001, when there was a terrorist attack at the Sbarro cafe in the center of Jerusalem, this woman was walking nearby with her husband. She told her husband to return home to the kids and she proceeded to rush to the scene where she helped treat the wounded and get the injured into ambulances and to hospitals.

When she herself arrived at the hospital, she met an elderly man who was in a state of shock. He was searching everywhere for his granddaughter who had become separated from him. She calmed him down and went with him to search amongst all the patients in order to find his granddaughter. When she asked how she could recognize her, the frantic grandfather gave a rough description of a gold pendant necklace that his granddaughter was wearing. After searching amongst the injured, they finally found the granddaughter, who was wearing the necklace.

At the sight of this necklace, the pediatrician froze. She turned to the old man and said, "Where did you buy this necklace?"

"You can't buy such a necklace," he responded. "I am a goldsmith and I made this necklace. Actually, I made two identical ones for each of my daughters. This is my granddaughter from one of them, and my other daughter did not survive the war."

And this is how a Jewish girl, brutally torn away from her mother on a concentration camp platform nearly sixty years before, was reunited with her father.

| R' AHARON KOTLER |

Knowing Who Is a Friend and Who Is Not

From September 1943 until the war ended, the demands on Irving Bunim as a speaker, translator, advocate, fundraiser, *shtadlan* (community leader) and diplomat were endless. He traveled across the United States numerous times, speaking to Jewish groups, informing them of events in Europe, making appeals and lobbying for federal intervention.

Despite the strain, Bunim felt privileged to accompany the esteemed *rosh yeshivah* and head of the Va'ad Hatzalah organization in New York, R' Aharon Kotler *zt"l*, on many of these trips. He marveled at the great sage's uncanny insight into psychology and politics and with true *emunas chachamim* – total devotion and belief in the words and deeds of Torah scholars – had no compunctions carrying out his every request. On one occasion in late 1944, R' Aharon was informed by Yitzchak Sternbuch in Switzerland, via Dr. Julius Kuhl's Polish diplomatic cable, that the Nazis intended to separate the captured Jewish American soldiers, those Jewish prisoners of war not in concentration camps, from other Allied POWs – a certain death sentence.

It didn't take long before R' Aharon called Irving Bunim and announced in his characteristically peremptory way, "Bunim, we're going to Washington!"

As the great man had issued a directive, Bunim immediately packed his bag and headed to R' Aharon's house. However, when he arrived at the Kotler home, he discovered that his *rebbi* was ill – so ill, in fact, that he could hardly walk. Bunim begged R' Aharon to stay home and let him go alone. The *rosh yeshivah* flatly refused. Bunim was familiar with R' Aharon's tenacious nature and knew that to argue was futile. Together, they took the first train to Washington, D.C., where Bunim surmised that R' Aharon hoped to see President Roosevelt and bring him his petition – something they had never accomplished before.

As the train left Penn Station in New York, Bunim began drafting a memorandum calling for an Allied protest against Nazi intentions. He wrote and rewrote the text. It had to be just right. As they arrived in the Washington station, he had completed all but the last paragraph. R' Aharon, sick as he was, rested on the train with a Gemara in hand.

Accompanied by Bunim, the ill Rabbi Kotler made his way to the home of a close friend, Rabbi Yehoshua Klavan. Immediately, Bunim sat down to finish the memorandum. When it was finished, Bunim read it to the two men. "It's a sad story," Bunim began, holding the paper aloft, "that after twenty centuries of oppression, murder and pogroms, you will allow what the Nazis are planning, the destruction of the Jewish prisoners of war..."

"No, no, no!" R' Aharon suddenly shouted, waving his arms. Startled, Bunim looked up. R' Aharon shook his head vehemently. "That part you don't need! Some gentiles will say that if we suffered like that for two thousand years, let it go on for one more."

Bunim ran his pencil through the last lines. He had thought he was writing a personal memorandum to Roosevelt himself. "I really believed we had a true friend in the president," Bunim remembered later, "but Rabbi Kotler knew differently." Indeed, R' Aharon grasped what others ignored: with Roosevelt's reluctance to support relief, rescue and immigration of Jews, the Va'ad Hatzalah had to find a real Washington ally, one who could bring effective pressure on the German government at that difficult time.

After much discussion, R' Aharon chose to deliver the memorandum written by Bunim to David Niles Jr., Roosevelt's Jewish personal assistant. It was a brilliant stroke, for the shocked Niles immediately passed the information on – not to the president, for that would have accomplished nothing – but to General Dwight Eisenhower, then Allied Commander of the European Theater of War. General Eisenhower was so incensed by the Germans' insidious plan that he quickly prepared a special message to be broadcast by radio and loudspeakers along the front lines. The protest was strongly worded and effectively presented, stating that the Allies were fully aware of the Germans' intentions and planned to hold them responsible at the International Court of Justice. It worked: the Jewish POWs were spared.

R' Aharon's assessment of Roosevelt was painfully accurate. In October 1944, a Va'ad-Agudah delegation (including R' Avraham Kalmanowitz, Elimelech [Mike] Tress, R' Jacob Rosenheim and Meir Schenkolewski) spent an entire Shabbos at the White House, waiting, hoping to put the case for saving Europe's Jews before the president. However, Roosevelt had no intention of ever meeting them. Finally, they were permitted to see the First Lady, Eleanor Roosevelt, who promised that her husband "would do his utmost to save the camp inmates."

In the end, the president rejected a plan by which the Allies would recognize captive Jews as prisoners of war. If approved, the plan would have enabled the Allies to carry out reprisals against German POWs if the Jews were harmed. But Roosevelt, as R' Aharon knew all along, was not interested in helping Jews. Such a position, Roosevelt argued, would lead to a "chain of violence without end on both sides."

| VYELIPOLIER REBBE |
Survival of the Five Minzer Brothers (1)

The small town of Gdiv (Gdow) in southern Poland (Galicia) was located on the main trade route, at the crossroads of the Krakow and Imperial routes. Many Jewish-owned inns and taverns were established there, resulting in the growth of the Jewish settlement in this area. In the mid-nineteenth century, the Jewish population was 376, constituting 25 percent of the total population. By 1939, Jews were the clear majority in Gdiv, controlling most areas of trade with stores and shops in the market square, while the number of shops run by Poles was very small.

One of the most prominent and memorable establishments in Gdiv was the bakery owned and operated by the Minzer family. Yisroel, Blima, and their six sons and two daughters were well-known in the community, not just for the mouth-watering rolls and baked goods that were produced in their shop, but even more so for the kindness and open-heartedness that allowed them to charitably hand out more of the rolls and baked goods than they actually sold. Blima herself was a bastion of charity and goodness. She literally couldn't help herself from giving away freshly baked bread and pastries to any indigent individual that stepped through her door. Naturally, the indigent made sure to frequent the Minzer bakery – sometimes to get free food, and other times to rest and even sleep near the warm ovens – and no one was ever turned away. Yisroel would often joke that if not for Blima, they would be wealthy; she literally gave away all of their profits!

After the German invasion of Poland, the already difficult times became even more so, and more and more people found themselves with little or nothing to eat. Thus, an early-morning stop at the Minzer bakery, at the strategically located corner of Krakowska and Bochenska streets, was more of a daily necessity than an actual luxury. Blima couldn't give out the bread fast enough and she refused to allow the lines to extend out of her shop. People from all walks of Gdiv society found themselves in her bakery, and even the most proud and prominent community members were treated with respect and quick efficiency, ensuring that they would receive a fair share of bread and rolls before they left.

One morning, in the early days of the war, a commotion arose outside the Minzer bakery. One of the leading Chassidic rebbes of Galicia had appeared in person, requesting a bit of food to eat. Yisroel hurriedly ran out to greet the Rebbe of Vyelipole (Wielipole), R' Yitzchak Lipshutz *Hy"d*, and honorably escort him and his attendant inside their establishment. In the village of Vyelipole, approximately sixty miles to the east of Gdiv, the Jews were literally starving. The Germans had halted all local commerce, and restrictions against Jews were mounting day by day. The Vyelipolier Rebbe, like all Chassidic rebbes and rabbinic leaders under the German occupation, was a prime target of the Gestapo and he was forced to run away, looking for a place to stay and a bite to eat.

Of course, Yisroel and Blima treated the rebbe with the utmost respect, taking him into their home and providing accommodations and provisions for as long as the rebbe stayed in Gdiv. R' Yitzchak, for his part, was exceptionally appreciative of the Minzers' efforts on his behalf and showered the family with blessings upon blessings. The Vyelipolier Rebbe did not stay long in Gdiv, but when he departed, he warmly blessed the entire Minzer family with continued success and the wherewithal to live through the trying days of war. The surviving members of the Minzer family, until this day, remember the warmth of the Vyelipolier Rebbe's blessing and credit their amazing survival during the war to this blessing.

The process of concentrating the Jewish population of the region started as early as March 1941. All the Jews from small villages were ordered to move to ghettos in the nearest towns. They had to leave behind almost all their property. The Jews of Gdiv, as well as all the local villages and towns in the southern Krakow district, were herded together like cattle in mid-1942, and transported to the city of Wieleczka, famous for its salt mines. In Wieleczka, Yisroel and Blima underwent the infamous *"selektion,"* where they, with their daughters and their eldest son, were separated from the rest of the family and transported off to an unknown concentration camp, never to be heard from again.

The other five brothers, Herzka, Michael, Yossel (Joe), Shmiel and Froyim (Ephraim), might have shared their parents' fate if not for Michael's quick thinking. At one point during the selection process, a German commandant by the name of Kunda announced that the German Luftwaffe (air force) was looking for skilled steel workers and "*blechors*" (aluminum roofers). All those with experience, shouted Kunda, should step forward. Michael, not even knowing exactly what a "*blechor*" was, immediately stepped forward and urged his brothers to do the same. There weren't many Jews who were skilled in this field and thankfully, all five brothers were chosen and moved away from the rest of the Jews who were slated for deportation.

The small group of *blechors* were separated at the *appellplatz* (roll call area) in Wieleczka and transported by cattle car to an *arbeitslager* (work camp) in the industrial city of Stalowa Wola. Huta Stalowa Wola (HSW S.A.) is a steel mill and a major producer of military equipment in Poland. It was established in 1938-1939 in the Second Polish Republic, near the city of Rozwadov (Rzeszow). It was meant to be a group of factories built in an area in the middle of the country, away from the borders shared with Germany and the USSR, and designed to provide a secure location for the production of armaments, high alloy steel and weapons – artillery, heavy machine guns, fighter plane parts, and the like. A city quickly grew around the mill, and took its name from it. Today, the mill is still the major employer in the town of Stalowa Wola, and a major producer of military equipment in Poland.

In 1940, the German army appropriated the steel mills and converted them into factories, building armaments and other war materials for the army and Luftwaffe. They imported Jews as slave laborers to do the necessary work. When the five Minzer brothers arrived in 1942, they were sent to the infamous Rozwadov ghetto, which was later split into two distinct concentration camps. "Camp A" became a *Judisches Zwangsarbeitslager* (forced labor camp for Jews). "Camp B" housed the families of the forced laborers. In "Camp A" men and women were separated and the camp was organized as a concentration camp. Some of the two thousand prisoners worked outside of the camp for different German army workshops. The Minzer brothers were forced to walk four kilometers each day from "Camp A" in Rozwadov to the factories and steel mills of Stalowa Wola.

The group of prisoners which included the Minzer brothers was placed under the care of a veteran Polish steel worker by the name of Alois Slezhak. Slezhak had been the foreman in this particular factory before the war, when it was under Polish control, and was indispensable to the operation. The Germans recognized his value and kept him on to oversee the new laborers and their work. What the Germans did not know, and surely would have resented had they found out, was that Slezhak was a kindhearted Pole who hated the Germans and was actually quite fond of the Jews. He immediately took a liking to the Minzer boys, especially Froyim, who was shielded from all harm and never worked a day in the mills. Slezhak went out of his way to provide extra rations of bread for all the Minzers and, according to Froyim, "kept a cauldron of soup bubbling at all times on a large flame meant for aluminum welding purposes." The Jewish inmates under his care were treated to hot soup on a daily basis and whenever a German overseer would come into the factory to do a spot check, Slezhak would simply remove the pot of soup and replace it with some metal sheeting that actually belonged on the fire. However, the moment the German was gone, the soup was quickly and efficiently returned to its place on the flame.

The Minzers were glad to be under Slezhak's watch and when the Germans eventually liquidated "Camp A" in Rozwadov and transferred the prisoners to a barracks within the Stalowa Wola complex, it made their lives that much more manageable.

However, the war was churning on and by the summer of 1944, the Russian Red Army was advancing deep into southern Poland. The Germans knew it, the Poles knew it, and even the Jewish inmates were well aware that the closer the Russians came to Rozwadov, the sooner the Germans would liquidate the remaining prisoners in all the area camps and transfer them to the death camps of Auschwitz and Buchenwald. Slezhak always had his trusty transistor radio handy and he would report news from the war front. He would also report any news he heard from the S.S. and Gestapo, and in July 1944, when he found out that in a few short days "his" Jewish inmates would be shipped away to their final destinations, he knew he had to act.

Slezhak sat down with Herzka and Michael, the two oldest of the Minzer brothers, and drew for them a map of the local countryside. He diagrammed all the villages, farms and roads in the immediate area outside of Stalowa Wola, and explained where the densest parts of the forest were. He was even able to give a fairly accurate report on which direction the Russian soldiers would be arriving from and where the retreating German forces would be headed. It was important, he explained, that one stay out of sight from both the Russians and the Germans, for both armies were known to shoot on sight when they came across stray individuals, the Germans believing them to be Polish spies, Russian soldiers, or worse - Jewish fugitives, while the Russians trusted no one and in their eyes, everyone was a German spy. Thanks to his "intelligence" reports, Slezhak knew where all the armies were at any given time.

The kind Pole urged them to escape at their earliest possible opportunity, and showed Michael how and where to use the sledgehammer he so conveniently afforded him. There was one weak and vulnerable area of the chain-link and wooden fence that surrounded the labor camp, and the very next night, in the midst of a torrential downpour, Michael silently located the spot and prepared to smash his way through the fence. His four brothers and numerous others noiselessly followed him and were grateful to note that the two German guards in the watchtower had either fallen asleep or were totally not paying attention to what was about to happen.

Michael lifted the sledgehammer and delivered a mighty blow that rang out through the pouring rain and otherwise stillness of night. In what could only have been a miracle of sorts, the entire portion of the fence gave way with that one powerful blow, and a gaping hole opened up as if by magic. This alerted the guards and they scrambled to retrieve their weapons and shoot at the escaping prisoners. Again, the guiding hand of Hashem was ever-present that night and not one of the eighty-five inmates of the Stalowa Wola labor camp that escaped that fateful night was harmed. The five Minzer brothers, together with another eighty courageous Jewish souls, fled into the rain and darkness, never to be incarcerated again.

Unfortunately, all those who remained in the camp that night and were too afraid to run were deported the very next day to Auschwitz.

The "Mad Priest" of Dachau

For the Jews, the Warsaw ghetto was unbearable; illness, starvation, forced labor and overcrowding was the norm. To German industrialists, the Warsaw ghetto represented an opportunity to make great profit employing Jews as slave laborers and becoming sensationally rich. Fritz Schultz was one such German industrialist who appropriated a group of factories in the ghetto that provided various staples and supplies to the German army. The work performed in the numerous factories was considered essential to the war effort, so the lives of the Jewish workers were temporarily spared. One of the factories manufactured shoes and Fritz Schultz was wise enough to maintain the previous owner of the factory, a Jew by the name of Avraham Hendel, as the manager and foreman, to run his entire operation.

Avraham Hendel was not a typical factory manager. A Gerrer Chassid who had done well for himself before the war with his shoe factory in Warsaw, he saved some of Polish Orthodoxy's greatest Jewish leaders by assigning them to positions in the factory he once owned. He hid rabbis and supported the underground, aiding every suffering Jew he could. He secretly allowed the rabbis, many of them outstanding Torah scholars, to study in peace in his factory, only performing perfunctory tasks for the benefit of German inspectors. With the help of his non-Jewish employer, the German Fritz Schultz, Hendel could warn Jews of upcoming selections and raids. Through a combination of business acumen and hard work, Avraham Hendel successfully filled his production quotas.

Among the *tzaddikim* who were protected in the Schultz workshop were: R' Moshe Betzalel Alter *zt"l* (brother of the Gerrer Rebbe); the Piaseczener Rebbe, R' Kalonymus Kalman Shapira *zt"l*; the Sosnowiecer Rebbe, R' Duvid Halberstadt *zt"l*; R' Alexander Zisha Frydman *zt"l*; and the Rapaport brothers from Bielec, Mendele, Simcha, Aharon and Yaakov. The Alexander Rebbe, R' Yitzchak Menachem Danziger *Hy"d*, one of the oldest and most revered rebbes in all of Poland, also worked in the Schultz workshop. As the Nazis were constantly on the search for him, his only protection was an assumed name, and eventually the Nazis discovered who he really was. They sent him to the gas chambers of Treblinka, together with R' Mendel Pabianicer *Hy"d*.

The atmosphere in the factory has been described by an eyewitness, Hillel Seidman, in his Warsaw ghetto diary: "Now I am in the Schultz factory; I have come at the time when people are both hammering in nails and reciting *Hoshana* prayers. Here are gathered, thanks to one of the directors, Mr. Avraham Hendel, the elite of the Orthodox community; Chassidic masters, rabbis, scholars, religious community organizers, well-known Chassidim. Sitting behind the anvil for shoe repair is the Koziglover Rav, Yehuda Aryeh Frimer, once dean of Yeshivas Chachmei Lublin. He is sitting here but his spirit is sailing in other worlds. He continues his studies from memory, without interruption, his lips moving constantly. From time to time he addresses a word to the Piaseczener Rebbe, the author of *Chovos Hatalmidim*, who is sitting opposite him, and a subdued discussion on a Torah topic ensues. Talmudic and Rabbinic quotations fly back and forth; soon there appears on the anvil – or, to be precise, on the minds and lips of these brilliant scholars – the words of the Rambam and Ra'avad, the author of the Tur, the Rema, and earlier and later authorities. The atmosphere in the factory is filled with the opinions of eminent scholars, so who cares about the S.S., the German overseers, the hunger, suffering, persecution and fear of death? They are really sailing in the upper worlds; they're not sitting in a factory on Nowolopie 46, but rather in the Hall of the Sanhedrin."

Hillel Seidman further testifies in the Warsaw ghetto diary that on August 26, 1942, Avraham Hendel delivered eight thousand gold coins to the Gestapo, in order to remove

R' Moshe Betzalel Alter from the *umschlagplatz* (from where the Jews were deported). Avraham Hendel did indeed succeed in having him returned to the Schultz factory.

What ever became of this great and righteous man? What ultimately happened to him and how did he manage to escape and live out the rest of war, after the Warsaw ghetto was burned and razed to the ground in the spring of 1943?

Avraham Hendel escaped the ghetto and became "Yozef Tulcszak" – a Catholic monk, who was considered "insane" and a person to stay away from. As the ghetto was burning down, the Piaseczener Rebbe called Hendel and ordered him to leave. The day had come for him to use the Aryan identity papers he had held ready for a long time. The rebbe gave him his blessing. R' Moshe Betzalel Alter, too, took his hand and blessed him with great emotion. Their blessings were fulfilled.

By literally dodging shells, explosives and the constant rain of bullets in the air, Avraham worked his way through the streets of the ghetto, and eventually beyond its walls. Immediately, he took up residence in a different part of town, and became known as Yozef Tulcszak. He wore the clothes of a Catholic clergyman, and he was visible to all in his distinct clothing and mannerism. It was said that he hid his *tefillin* under his clothes and, during one raid by the Gestapo as they were looking for Polish spies and rebels, the *tefillin* were actually discovered in his building. The Nazis searched for the owner of the *tefillin*, sure that they had found a Jew hiding out in the building, but they never thought to accuse the monk living there.

When the Poles of Warsaw rose up against the German occupation and attempted to fight back, Yozef Tulcszak was captured and consigned to the Dachau concentration camp. Due to his position as a member of the cloth, Yozef Tulcszak was inevitably drawn into the conflict, getting involved in the ill-fated revolt. The Nazis came down hard on these rebels and wiped most of them out. When the surviving rebels were sent to Dachau, the monk was among them. He got his nickname from one of the other rebel prisoners, who sarcastically called him "the mad priest" because his lips never stopped whispering prayers, though no one could hear the words. And in fact, Avraham was constantly whispering prayers, Torah, and pages of Gemara that he knew by heart.

He kept to himself in the camp, just him, his prayers and his Torah, and even the most cruel of the S.S. officers left him alone, due to the reverence with which most of the Polish prisoners regarded him. It was good luck that the nickname "the mad priest" stuck to him, because he regularly expressed sympathy for the Jewish prisoners and even showed willingness to help them, which to the Germans and Poles alike, was insanity.

Avraham Hendel survived the war and settled in Tel Aviv.

| R' YEHOSHUA NEUWIRTH |
The Protective Effect of Shabbos

All it took was eight days for the German blitzkrieg to overpower Holland. The Dutch thought that they were safe; their neutrality would keep them in the good graces of their war-mongering neighbor to the east. So when the Germans attacked on May 10, 1940, the Dutch mounted very little in the way of resistance, and their inevitable surrender came quickly.

The Neuwirth family was fortunate to have escaped from Germany in 1939, arriving in Holland soon after the devastation of Kristallnacht, on account of a special permit signed by Queen Wilhelmina of the Netherlands, allowing forty-two German rabbis to escape the menacing Nazis. Rabbi Aharon Neuwirth was among the lucky ones chosen. His son, Yehoshua Yeshaya Neuwirth (future author of the famed book on the laws of Shabbos, *Shemiras Shabbos K'hilchasah*), and his two brothers left Germany on a kindertransport and were reunited with their family when they arrived in Amsterdam. Amazingly, the family managed to stay together and they all survived the war.

With the capture of Holland in 1940, the Nazis tightened the noose around the Jewish citizens of that country. As they did in every country they invaded and subdued, they rounded up the Jews and forced them into ghettos. From there, they transported them to labor and death camps. From November 1941 until the end of 1942, thousands of Dutch Jews were shipped off to work camps and later to concentration camps like Westbork and Vught, from where they were ultimately taken to Auschwitz.

It took a series of "close calls" and amazing acts of Divine providence before R' Aharon decided that it was time for him and his entire family to go into hiding. He had searched far and wide for a suitable location. The suitcases were long packed and now it was time to climb up to the attic of an adjacent house – a narrow and confined space that was well concealed from the street and the prying eyes of neighbors and Nazis alike. It was late October and with the advance of an early winter in Amsterdam, the attic was cold – frigid at times – and the family suffered terribly from the harsh climate.

Yehoshua's mother could not handle the cold and wished to descend to a lower apartment, to live again like a normal human being, but his father held firm and explained that although it may have been cold up in the attic, it was certainly safer than down below where the Germans were eager to capture and deport any remaining Jews they found.

Indeed, the Germans were always on the lookout for Jews. Quite often over the next few weeks, they could hear German soldiers walking around downstairs, calling out, "Where are you, Jews?" as their jackboots pounded on the wooden floors down below. The Neuwirth family sat in perfect silence, petrified, not daring to move a muscle. Time and time again, Nazis and their Dutch accomplices came through the house, searching, listening and hoping for the chance to expose a concealed hiding spot containing Jews.

But the Neuwirth family was never found. A Jewish underground organization knew of the family's whereabouts, and would leave food parcels near their hideout. If not for these parcels, the family would have starved to death, for they had no other means to obtain provisions. In fact, the underground continued to provide for them until the conclusion of the war.

For close to two months, the Neuwirth family remained in the freezing attic. When it was clear that the Germans had given up searching in their area, the family cautiously and stealthily crept back down into their home, and began to live again. For the next three years, until war's end, they remained in their apartment without ever walking outside, or even walking near a window. For three whole years, they did not look out the window! Can one even imagine today how an entire family could sit in an apartment for such a long period of time without the ability to leave – or even look outside – and never be seen, heard or caught?

How did they spend their time? Much of the day was devoted to *tefillah*, reciting Tehillim, and silent learning sessions with their father. They had brought one tome of the Talmud with them – *Maseches Kesubos* – which father and sons studied over and over in silent whispers. Young Yehoshua had brought with him the third volume of *Mishnah Berurah*, dealing with the complex and multi-faceted laws of Shabbos. It was also at this time that Yehoshua studied the mechanics of the Jewish calendar and how one might set one up for the future. He took on the challenge of committing it to writing. A look at his calendar shows a precisely worked traditional calendar in all respects: the festivals and fast days are marked, weekly Torah readings listed, the time of each Rosh Chodesh is given, as well as candle-lighting times and all other necessary information. This was prepared by a fifteen-year-old boy – all done while in hiding! He managed to get his calendar to the underground, who were able to make copies and distribute them to various individuals they knew hiding throughout the country.

Yehoshua had one sister who was blond and could pass for a gentile. Believing that it was important for at least one member of the family to live in the outside world – in case they were caught, at least one family member would remain alive – Rabbi Aharon Neuwirth sent her out into the world where she was able to find work as a maid in the home of a prominent Dutch Supreme Court judge.

The family was happy but she was miserable. She would write letters and have them delivered through the underground, describing how the judge's family mistreated her and forced her to work like a slave, especially on Saturday, the day before the Christian day of rest, cleaning and preparing the large house for their holiday. If nothing else, just the thought of working on Shabbos caused her a great amount of grief and depression, and these sentiments were reflected in her letters.

Rabbi Neuwirth was beside himself. Of course, it was important for his daughter to survive, but at what cost? Her physical and spiritual health and security were in jeopardy and he refused to allow her to remain in the gentile's home. He was able to pass her a message telling her to run away and come back home as soon as it was safe to do so. They would find her another job, somewhere safe, somewhere where she was not forced to desecrate the holy Shabbos.

The following Friday afternoon, just a few short hours before Shabbos was to begin, a soft knock was heard on the door. When Rabbi Neuwirth cautiously opened it, his daughter fell into the arms of her grateful father, mother and brothers. They cried and cried – but in total silence.

What happened next was nothing short of a miracle. Allied bombing had become a frequent occurrence in Amsterdam, as the tide of the war was beginning to shift against the Germans. That very Saturday morning, the day after Yehoshua's sister managed to escape the home of her gentile employers, a bombing raid took place and the judge's house sustained a direct hit. The house was completely destroyed and the entire family living inside was wiped out!

| R' EPHRAIM OSHRY |

To Die as a Jew, Not as a Gentile

The Jewish community in Kovno (Kaunas) contained approximately forty thousand members and constituted a full 25 percent of the population in the city. Many of its members were professionals, including some of the country's leading doctors, lawyers and business people. Other members of the community were skilled artisans, merchants, small business owners and laborers. All major political sections within the Jewish community had organizations and youth clubs in the city, including the Zionists, the Socialists, and the various religious denominations.

When the Kovno ghetto was established by the Germans on July 10, 1941 in an underdeveloped suburb of the city known as Slabodka, all elements of the Jewish community were forced to relocate. At its peak, the ghetto held thirty thousand Jewish residents, most of whom were later sent to concentration camps, extermination camps, or were shot at the Ninth Fort. About five hundred Jews escaped on work detail and joined Soviet partisan forces in the surrounding forests. Of the almost forty thousand Jews in Kovno, less than three thousand survived the war.

One of the ranking families of the Kovno high society happened to be of Jewish descent, although one would never know it from the way they disassociated themselves from anything resembling Judaism and Jews. They only socialized with the upper-class Lithuanian aristocracy and made sure that no mention of their Jewish ancestry ever surfaced. They wouldn't be caught anywhere near a synagogue or entertain anyone that was Jewish or seemed even remotely Jewish. To this end, they refused to allow their sons to be circumcised in the manner of Jewish baby boys for thousands of years. They wished to have absolutely nothing to do with their ancestry, and made a point of relinquishing any semblance of their Jewish heritage.

However, Hitler and his marauding cohorts cared little for the level of observance or even association of those Jews who wished to have nothing to do with their religion. The Nuremberg Laws, which took effect in Germany in 1935 and eventually became Nazi doctrine in all its occupied territories, did not define a "Jew" as someone with particular religious beliefs. Instead, anyone who had three or four Jewish grandparents was defined as a Jew, regardless of whether that individual identified himself or herself as a Jew or belonged to the Jewish religious community. Even those who had not practiced Judaism for years found themselves caught in the grip of Nazi terror. Similarly, people with Jewish grandparents who had converted to Christianity were defined as Jews.

As a result, when the ghetto in Kovno was announced and every Jewish man, woman and child was forced to relocate into its cramped and confined area, this aristocratic family was swept along together with the Jewish community they so wished to divest themselves of, and found themselves stuck in the ghetto.

When the father of the household protested that he could nary be considered a Jew in any form or nature, a Nazi brute killed him on the spot for having the temerity to open his mouth. The mother and her two sons watched in anguished shock as their patriarch was hauled away like a piece of trash, and they followed the mass of cowering Jews into the narrow streets of the ghetto. As they walked, their thoughts never ceased to ponder the question that they couldn't understand: For all intent and purposes, they were gentiles. They were even more gentile than most gentiles! They despised Jews and never considered them to be their brethren. How, then, did the stroke of fate paint them as Jews, with the same brush as the other unfortunate victims of the Nazi onslaught?

For the duration of their stay in the ghetto, the members of this family did little to acknowledge their link to Judaism. However, one of the sons could not dismiss the questions that wreaked havoc in his mind day and night. He had never thought of himself as a Jew and yet here he was, suffering together with them. So then, what was it about these Jews – his blood relatives – and why were they so oppressed? He set out to find some clues in order to somehow make sense of his current predicament.

What he found was eye-opening. He observed the manner of Jews up close and he came to appreciate who they were. He recognized their spark of humanity, their kindness, their light among the persistent darkness and terror of the ghetto. And he developed a newfound love for these people, a fraternal bond that made him feel close to his "brothers."

He constantly asked himself: "If my lot is no different than them and if my fate is bound up in theirs, then why indeed must I be different than them? Why must I act and feel like a gentile, when I am a Jew? Why do I not have the symbol of my Jewishness forged into my skin like all other Jewish men? Why do I not have a circumcision?"

He expressed his intention to his mother, but she was too beaten and weary to put up any sort of opposition. He inquired and was directed to Rav Ephraim Oshry *zt"l*, one of the leading *rabbanim* of the Kovno rabbinate. Excitedly, he expressed his desire to be circumcised; it was his expression of the words of Dovid Hamelech: *I am with him in his suffering* (*Tehillim* 91:15). Rav Oshry was elated with the new penitent, and set out to make his quest into a reality. However, the impending circumcision encountered a snafu due to a technical consideration: There was no religious, G-d-fearing *mohel* left in the entire ghetto.

Thousands of Jews had already been deported and more were being liquidated on a daily basis. A real *mohel* could not be located and the only other alternative was to engage a Jewish surgeon to perform the procedure. The problem was that this surgeon lacked any basis in religious understanding, was an open violator of the Shabbos, and was certainly not worthy of acting as an emissary to such an important mitzvah. On the other hand, there was no one else, and there could be no greater *sha'as hadchak* (time of distress) than being incarcerated in the Kovno ghetto.

Rav Oshry discussed the question with other members of the rabbinate and finally issued his ruling that the circumcision may be performed by the irreverent surgeon. His final words state: "Each and every day, hundreds of our brothers are put to death at the hands of the accursed murderers, and here this young man is crying bitter tears, that if his fate is to die by the hand of the executioners, may he die a righteous death, like his pure and holy brethren, who give up their lives to sanctify the Divine Name. Now (with this circumcision) he will hereby be sealed with the covenant of the holy *bris* like his other holy brothers..."

| BOBOVER REBBE |
Last *Melaveh Malkah* in Bochnia

Finally, the gruesome message was sinking in. No matter how bribable their Gestapo was, no matter how sympathetic their Judenrat was, no matter how important their work was, in the end, they were all Jews and Hitler wanted all the Jews killed. The Bochnia ghetto was a temporary oasis where the indoor factory work was bearable and the ghetto authorities were better than most. The key word here was "temporary" and the question was "for how long."

Meanwhile, the Bobover *bachurim* in the ghetto were dreaming. They were dreaming of performing a certain mitzvah the way they had always done it back in Bobov. The Bobover Rebbe, R' Benzion *Hy"d*, and his father before him, had constantly stressed the importance of the mitzvah of *melaveh malkah*, eating a special meal after Shabbos in honor of Dovid Hamelech. In Bobov, the rebbe had presided over a glorious *tish*, infusing his *talmidim* with inspiring words of faith.

The Bobover *bachurim* in Bochnia felt an urge to continue this tradition, and so they sent word to the Bobover Rav, R' Shloime Halberstam *zt"l*, heir to the tradition of his fathers, asking him to consider their idea.

From his home outside the ghetto, R' Shloime weighed the proposition carefully. He had purposely chosen to reside outside the ghetto, hoping that it would allow him and his family to remain more anonymous – and thus less easily identifiable – to the S.S., the Gestapo and the Polish policemen. The consequences of being discovered inside the ghetto would be even more severe than being caught outside the ghetto, and to preside over the *seudah* would be doubly dangerous, for the Nazis treated any large gathering of Jews as a rebellion. The Jews of Bochnia did not even organize a daily *minyan* for this reason. But how could he say no to such a heartfelt request? His Chassidim were starving for spirituality and he knew it was up to him to satiate their souls.

The Bobover Rav decided to notify only sincere Chassidim who were willing to put themselves in danger. He recommended the slightly roomier home of a Bobover Chassid, R' Hersh Wagner, as the meeting place, assuring his Chassidim that he would slip into the ghetto to join them.

Late one Motza'ei Shabbos, the Bobover Rav called his son Naftuli to his side. Believing that the young boy had a better chance of surviving the war than he did, the *rav* wished his son to experience the *mesiras nefesh* of the Chassidim and the beauty of their enthusiasm for *mitzvos*.

"Come, Naftulche," he said, "we are going into the ghetto."

The boy's eyes widened. He knew the danger of being out in the streets, especially after working hours. His father's work permit would be useless at that time of night. And what if they were caught slipping into the ghetto? Naftuli left his questions unspoken. If this was his father's plan, he would not be afraid. Trustfully, he followed him out the door, through the streets of Bochnia, and to the infamous ghetto fence. A seemingly solid plank moved silently aside to admit both father and son. Minutes later, they arrived at R' Hersh Wagner's home.

The sight that greeted R' Shloime and his son stirred their souls. Forty young Chassidim stood respectfully, each with a *kezayis* of bread in his hand. Naftuli gaped. He had not seen such a gathering since he had left Bobov a lifetime ago.

For the next hour, the Bobover Rav addressed his Chassidim, filling them with strength and *emunah*, relating stories of the great Chassidic masters and words of Torah to reinforce his messages.

With tears in his eyes, he spoke of the never-ending killings and reminded them that whenever they took a bath, they should have in mind that this might be their *taharah*. He spoke of *kiddush Hashem* and how to properly perform this most difficult, yet most precious mitzvah. The Chassidim listened intently, hoping they would never be tested, praying that if they were, they would have the strength to do what was required.

In quiet camaraderie, they ate their bread and then they *bentched*. And then, to continue their tradition without compromising their safety, they rose, joined hands, and silently mouthed the timeless words of their *niggun*, poignantly symbolizing the singing and dancing they remembered from Bobov.

On the way out of the ghetto, the Bobover Rav urgently whispered to his son, "Never forget what you saw here. Never forget the *mesiras nefesh* for *mitzvos* – such *mesiras nefesh* performed with such love."

| R' CHAIM STEIN |
The Mysterious Horn Peddler

In June 1941, as the Nazi killing machine advanced toward the city of Telz, Lithuania, the famous Telzer Yeshivah was divided into a number of groups who fled in all different directions. One group of forty-eight students made it as far as the Lithuanian-Russian border, before a majority of them – thirty-two students in all – had a change of heart and turned back. The remaining sixteen boys continued onward and escaped over the border, hopping into the open boxcar of a freight train heading deep into Russia, with little more than the clothes on their backs and a prayer on their lips. Those who went back did not survive the war.

During the six years of their miraculous survival in the Siberian wilderness – quite often they were forced to flee from the pursuing Russian army and secret police – the group of sixteen made sure to set aside considerable time each day to study from a lone tractate of Talmud that they had with them. They also shared the one pair of *tefillin* that they had brought along.

Two of the leaders of the group, R' Chaim Stein *zt"l* and R' Meir Zelig Mann *zt"l* of Cleveland, Ohio, were young twenty-year-old *bachurim* at the time. Rabbi Mann kept a meticulous diary of the day-to-day events, struggles, and miracles – and even a log of which page of the Talmud they studied daily. R' Chaim also kept a diary in which he recounted the various Torah topics that the group studied each and every day, and exactly where and when they studied them. Both diaries are remarkable for their clear and precise detail, opening up a window into the lives of the yeshivah refugees on the run in the Siberian wasteland. Both diaries recount the following incident which occurred during their escape.

As Rosh Hashanah was quickly approaching, the group became anxious, desperately wanting to fulfill the mitzvah of hearing the shofar blown on the holy day. Realistically, though, they knew they had very little chance of obtaining such a prized object in the thick of the Siberian forest. Much prayer and Torah study, including reviewing *hilchos shofar* carefully, and readying themselves for the mitzvah, yielded results. Amazingly, on Erev Rosh Hashanah, a Russian vagabond, peddling, among other things, ram horns, suddenly appeared in the forest. The excited boys bartered some of their valued stash of tobacco and obtained a set of horns. They then proceeded to boil one of them to help loosen the bone that was attached to the inside of the horn. This would allow the bone to slide out, creating a usable shofar. To their utter dismay, the horn cracked during the procedure, thus invalidating the shofar's use for the upcoming holiday.

They still had the other horn to work on. However, it was getting late; sunset and the start of Rosh Hashanah was fast approaching and the stubborn bone would not budge!

It was a delicate procedure and it couldn't be rushed. They had already ruined one horn. Despair was setting in amongst some of the boys. They worked on the horn all afternoon, and finally, just mere moments before the holiday was to begin, Yisroel Meir Karnovitz, a member of the group, used a piercing iron to jar the bone loose. They hollowed out the inside of the horn, tested the shofar to see that it was in good condition, and thankfully found it to be working. These starving, deprived and forlorn teenagers spontaneously joined hands in the darkening Russian forest and began to joyously sing and dance, for they knew that wherever they were, Hashem would hear their shofar and answer their plea for life and survival.

The sequel to this story is told by R' Meir Zelig's son, Shmuel Yaakov. Sixty years later, in the Telzer Yeshivah in Cleveland, a young man approached R' Meir Zelig several minutes before the Yom Tov of Rosh Hashanah was to begin and introduced himself as the grandson of R' Yisroel Meir Karnovitz. R' Meir Zelig was so taken aback when he realized that it was precisely sixty years to the day, to the hour, and to the very few minutes before sunset since the fateful moment that this young man's grandfather had finished the procedure to ready the shofar for use in the Siberian wilderness.

Who was this mysterious horn peddler? It seems that he was the same mysterious individual who boarded a railroad car in which R' Chaim and R' Meir Zelig were riding to escape the Russian authorities, and without any explanation, offered to sell them candles on the night of Chanukah. They believed it was Eliyahu Hanavi, who comes to aid the Jewish people in mysterious ways and who will be the one to herald the future Redemption with the sounding of the great shofar of Mashiach; may that day come speedily.

R' SHLOMO ZALMAN HOROWITZ
A Sign of Heaven

In the winter of 1942, the Jews of Potek fled their city and ran to the forests around the Buczacz area to hide. This included the *rav* of Potek, R' Shlomo Zalman Horowitz *zt"l*, who continued to serve as a leader and role model while hidden away in caves, pits and tree hollows. The overwhelming fear of discovery led to arguments among the Jews. It was there that R' Shlomo Zalman stood revealed in all his strength and courage. He adjudicated the petty differences and guided his flock through serious malcontent. Although many hideouts were discovered by the enemy, the *rav's* hideout was never detected.

Around the time of the High Holidays, R' Shlomo Zalman emerged from his hideout, a deep pit, to breathe some fresh air among the trees. Walking along through the dense foliage, he discovered a broad clearing in the midst of the forest. It was amazing to see that in such a dense forest, there was a completely open field without a single tree in it. R' Shlomo Zalman decided that Heaven had caused it to be there in order for him to have a place to put up a sukkah. That was, no doubt, why he had discovered this spot – totally devoid of foliage that would impinge upon his ability to build a kosher sukkah – only now, just days before Sukkos.

The Jews in the forest had obtained some tarpaulins that the partisans had stolen from the Germans. R' Shlomo Zalman took them and made walls for the sukkah. Then, he put a roof over it, according to the halachah, with tree branches and leaves. There were plenty of those.

A few Jews among the group became angry when they saw the sukkah. They thought it might be spotted by

German aircraft, and then they would all be in danger. The *rav* maintained his position, though, that on the contrary, the merit of sitting in the sukkah would surely bring them Divine protection. Most of those hiding out in the forest were observant Jews, and they sided with R' Shlomo Zalman, turning the scales in favor of the *rav's* position to have a sukkah.

It was the third day of Chol Hamoed, and R' Shlomo Zalman was sitting with his son Shmuel in their sukkah in the midst of the forest. Suddenly, they heard a group of Nazi storm troopers marching in the area. All the Jews who were with them in the sukkah quickly hurried out and escaped back to their hiding places. R' Shlomo Zalman and his son, however, could not get away since their hideout was only a little ways from the sukkah, and if they ran back to their pit, they would easily be tracked and found by the searchers.

R' Shlomo Zalman decided that it would be best to stay in the sukkah and leave the rest to Hashem. He told Shmuel that if Hashem wished them to be revealed to the enemy and killed, they had no choice but to accept this. He only wished for one thing: that if they were killed, it did not happen right there, in the sukkah. What a *kiddush Hashem* it would be if he could tell his fellow Jews that the mitzvah of sitting in the sukkah had saved him and his son from death! The nonbelievers in the group would be convinced, too. They would all see that "one who keeps a mitzvah will come to no harm."

"Not for my sake, Hashem," prayed R' Shlomo Zalman. "Do it for Your sake, that Your Name may be sanctified before everyone." He recited Tehillim in a whisper and mentioned the names of his ancestors back to the holy Ba'al Shem Tov, which tradition says helps to draw down Divine protection.

Then they saw the evil ones approaching. The thud of their boots came closer and closer. They walked back and forth in front of the sukkah three times, but they did not seem to see anything. It was as if they had been struck blind. Father and son peeked out through the cracks in the walls of the sukkah. They saw soldiers standing right next to them. They could make out every detail of their uniforms. But for some inexplicable reason, the S.S. could not see the sukkah.

Suddenly, one of the evil ones pointed off to the distance, indicating that he had spotted something suspicious, perhaps a hiding place. Immediately, they all set off and disappeared into the forest. R' Shlomo Zalman took a deep breath, thanking Hashem for saving them, for taking them from death to life.

Later, when they met up with the other Jews again, they all wondered where father and son had hidden while the Germans were searching the area. When they heard that R' Shlomo Zalman and Shmuel had been sitting in the sukkah the entire time, they were truly astonished. Even the biggest skeptics had to agree that nothing short of a miracle had occurred and the hand of G-d had been at work. R' Shlomo Zalman would quote the words of Dovid Hamelech for many years to come: *He will hide me in His sukkah on the evil day.*

The Master Shoemaker

Hassag: It was called a labor camp, but it was a slaughterhouse. Many Jews from Czestochowa, from other Polish towns, and from Germany, Austria, Slovakia and Bohemia were forced to work for Germany's profit and to support the Nazi war effort. Forced labor camps were installed in the Hassag complex, with armament factories and workshops primarily in Hassag-Pelcery, a former textile factory near the train station which was converted into an ammunition factory. Hassag-Pelcery was the biggest forced labor camp in Czestochowa. By the end of June 1944, about five thousand Jews from Czestochowa and Lodz were forced to work there. By the end of 1944 it was one of the biggest work camps in the *Generalgouvernement* with about ten thousand Jewish prisoners.

The Jews lived in overcrowded barracks. Many died of starvation, cruel treatment, or from typhus. Their task was the manufacture of bullets, millions of bullets for the mighty Nazi armies. Day and night they stood over the machines as each sheet of metal went through its seven stages of preparation until it was perfected into its death-dealing form. One machine punched out disks from the sheets of metal. The next one drilled holes in them. Then they were flattened out. A fourth machine rounded them. The fifth polished the metal. At the sixth stop, the gun powder was inserted, and at the final stage, the sharp penetrating tip was attached to the missile. Similarly, the inmates also rode a conveyor belt through seven stages of hell, subjected to punches and reshaping of their bodies – pieces cut from their very being, crushed by an intolerable load, the marrow drained from their bones. They were only part of a vast mechanism of destruction – destroying and being destroyed at the same time.

The festival of Sukkos somehow found its way into Hassag. The Jewish prisoners discovered an unused corner between two factory buildings and co-opted the space for their use. Lumber was piled up, as if in storage, for the sukkah walls, and somewhat above these walls, branches were unobtrusively stacked for the *s'chach*. They slid in and out of this temporary dwelling with their treasured crusts of bread, thinking of the protective *sukkos* in the wilderness, and treasuring those stolen moments. They had no Torah scroll, and joy was absolutely foreign to those incarcerated in Hassag. Worse yet, on that date, just one year earlier, many of them were witness to the liquidation of the Chestochower ghetto and the demise of their loved ones. But the experience of eating in the sukkah, no matter how makeshift it was, was a genuine experience.

On one of the days of Chol Hamoed Sukkos, a whispered message flitted around the camp: the shoemaker had been delayed in his return from the ghetto. The shoemaker was one of the "fortunate Jews" in the camp who had W.W.J. status. As "skilled valuable Jews," these Jews had special talents and consequently enjoyed certain privileges, such as assignment to unguarded factories or performing various personal services for high-ranking German officers. Some of these privileged Jews were approached in secret before Rosh Hashanah and exhorted to search for a shofar among the ruins of the ghetto. Search they did, often endangering their lives, scrounging through the endless rubble; who would have believed that it was a coarse, rough-hewn man, an expert shoemaker, whom the Germans actually honored with the title "*Schuster Meister* – Master Shoemaker," who would come through in the end? Very little was known about him personally, but it was clear that he was unsurpassed in the craft of boot-making and, as a result, his talents were much in demand by the high-ranking German officers. It was this unassuming man, whose life was so assured (comparatively), who risked his life for a shofar for Rosh Hashanah. Yet beneath the humblest of surfaces lie deep reserves of self-sacrifice, especially when involving *kiddush Hashem.* In the end, the cobbler succeeded in smuggling in a shofar.

Some members of the *Aufraumungs Kommand* – the clean-up squad – guessed that he used his special status with the S.S. command to be allowed to search for special materials for his craft among the stores of ghetto plunder, which were kept under particularly heavy guard. Once inside, it was quite simple to slip the shofar under his loose clothing. It was simple, but risky, for had he been apprehended by the guard, few questions would have been asked, and little heed given to the answers. The sentence would have been swift - a rifle bullet on the spot or perhaps a prolonged torture followed by a public hanging. But the cobbler was not caught.

Now, during the holiday of Sukkos, he was looking to fulfill the dictum of the Sages: *One mitzvah brings on the fulfillment of another.* Fortified by the success of his first venture, the shoemaker was prepared to do much more to further the Yom Tov celebration. When he finally appeared, he did not head to the kitchen for his especially generous portion, but instead hurried into the depths of his hut. What had happened? The impossible - no - the incredible had come to pass for the second time in a month! He had successfully spirited a *Sefer Torah* out of the clutches of the dreaded Gestapo and smuggled it into the camp. He rolled it around and around his body, let his loose tunic hang over it, and then walked into the camp. He adamantly refused to reveal where he had gotten it from.

Once again, the clean-up squad advanced a theory that he had found it in the stores of Jewish property, where he had found the shofar, but they were wrong. It had not been nearly as easy to get the *Sefer Torah*. The S.S. maintained an extremely heavy guard on the holdings of Jewish plunder, and were particularly careful with *sefarim* and other religious objects, regardless of their value. The intrepid cobbler decided to bribe one of the guards but since he was not exactly solvent then, he offered the Nazi something that he could never have purchased for any sum: a pair of officers' boots! (The Germans seemed to have regarded handcrafted boots as a singular luxury and thus reserved for high-ranking officers. Hence, too, the cobbler's privileged status.)

It was later learned that he had literally saved the *Sefer Torah* from desecration because a short while later the Gestapo burned all the *Sifrei Torah*, *sefarim*, and various sacramental cloths and articles in one gigantic bonfire. This one *Sefer Torah* was the sole surviving remnant of the sacred articles of the ghetto. The cobbler selected it because of its small size, which made it feasible for him to wrap it around his stomach without causing a telltale bulge, and later, in camp, its size permitted easy concealment.

A regular *minyan* on Shabbos had already been instituted in one of the barracks, and it was there, on Shabbos Chol Hamoed Sukkos, that the heroic shoemaker turned to the inmates and demanded: "Who wants to hide the *Sefer Torah*?"

Two brave Jews decided to assume the responsibility. They immediately removed a board from the head of one of the wooden cots, and in the hollow underneath it, concealed the scroll.

The news of the *Sefer Torah's* arrival had naturally electrified the entire camp. On Simchas Torah night, they held crowded *hakafos* in the cramped run-down shack they called home. These *hakafos* would have been outlandish in any other situation. Carrying the *Sefer Torah* in their arms, as in conventional *hakafos*, was impossible, as they would have been running quite a risk. Being caught carrying the Torah would have meant sure death, but what value did their lives have, anyway? It would have been worth it! But the scroll would have also been destroyed, G-d forbid, and this was a loss they would not risk. The *Sefer Torah* remained safely ensconced in its hollow behind the board. The inmates stealthily walked around the wooden cot that contained its sacred treasure. As they passed, they leaned over and kissed the board that lay directly above the *Sefer*.

And so it went, far into the night. The silent "dancers" held themselves strenuously in check, as the joyous songs surged repeatedly to their lips. One song echoed softly in their ears. Because of its obvious relevance, they could not contain it inside. As they walked around the *Sefer*, they were almost deafened by the silent screaming that enveloped each and every one of them: "Rejoice on Simchas Torah, because it (the Torah) is our strength and our light!"

The *Sefer Torah* miraculously survived the war, although the whereabouts of the heroic shoemaker is unknown. Today, the *Sefer* is safely ensconced in the *aron kodesh* of the Gerrer *beis medrash* in Bnei Brak.

| BULGARIA |

German Ally, Jewish Savior

Of all the Slavic countries that came under German domination in World War II, Bulgaria stands alone in her concern for the safety of her Jewish citizens. With the exception of Denmark, Bulgaria was the only country allied with Nazi Germany that did not annihilate or turn over its Jewish population. History witnessed the resolute response of the patriotic army officers, the working class, craftsmen, peasantry, and intellectuals of every political shade - even the Bulgarian Orthodox Church played a heroic part - as well as the general population, who were all united in the single determination to protect Bulgarian Jewry from the fate that befell the Jewish people in other occupied countries. The anti-Jewish decrees had been issued and the cattle cars were already waiting to transport the victims to the extermination camp. But thanks to the Bulgarian people they remained empty.

This is the general background against which developed the dramatic struggle to save the Bulgarian Jews from annihilation. Acting under Nazi orders, the Bulgarian government, under the pro-German and anti-Semitic Prime Minister Bogdan Filov, who was appointed and controlled by King Boris III, consented to the annihilation of the Jewish population, and prepared the deportation of Bulgarian Jews to death camps in Eastern Europe. The first step came in the form of a "Law in Defense of the Nation," which factually outlawed Jews. The government intended the law to whip up ill feelings among business circles and suggest an easy way of eliminating commercial and industrial competition.

But the Bulgarian people immediately realized that the anti-Jewish legislation was only the initial step in a general attempt at their physical liquidation. They did not accept a "Law in Defense of the Nation," directed against compatriots with whom they had lived for centuries in friendship and understanding. The strong reaction of the people against the attempt to suppress the human rights of the Jewish population was expressed in floods of letters and telegrams addressed to parliament, cabinet ministers, statesmen, and social and political leaders. A wave of indignation surged throughout the country, demanding immediate cessation of the persecution against the Jews. Street demonstrations became common and had to be suppressed by the police with brutal force, imprisonment, and reprisals.

In spite of everything, in December 1940 the Fascist majority in parliament voted and passed the hateful racist law, which was approved by royal decree on January 21, 1941.

The law set up a Commissariat for the Jewish Problems, which daily issued orders tending to the complete plundering and ruination of the Jews, depriving them of elementary rights as citizens: the right to find employment, to education, to choice of place of domicile, to marry at choice, etc. All Jews were obliged to wear a yellow star in the streets, and their homes were marked with the inscription, "Jewish Home." The law provided for eviction of the Jewish populace from the capital to small provincial towns, and mobilization of the males into labor camps.

A number of parliamentary parties took the Bulgarian Jews under their protection, and many other progressive forces helped in every way they could. With clandestine propaganda, they explained to the Bulgarian people the real sinister designs behind these measures. The underground radio station was used to tell the Bulgarian people about the mass annihilation of Jews, Poles, Frenchmen, and others by the Nazis in Poland, the Ukraine, Byelorussia, and other territories, and the dangers threatening Bulgaria.

When the police started rounding up thousands of Jews within Bulgaria's prewar borders, the resulting public outcry and backlash stopped the government in its tracks. When Archbishop Stefan (recognized in 2001 by Yad Vashem as a "Righteous Gentile Among the Nations") learned that at least eight hundred Jews from Sofia were to be "evacuated," he rushed to the royal palace and refused to leave until the king finally agreed to hear him out. Another bishop, Kyril of Plovdiv, sent several telegrams to the monarch and, in a defiant act of civil disobedience, allowed local Jews to take refuge in his church and in his own home. He prevented the deportation of between 1,500 and 1,600 Jews from his diocese, who had been ordered to assemble at Plovdiv's train station during the night of March 9, 1943, by vowing to lie across the rails in the path of the first train transport taking them out of the country. He promised the thankful Jews, "Wherever you go, I'll go with you."

When about one thousand Jews from Kyustendil (a town about sixty-five miles southwest of Sofia) were ordered on March 7 to leave their homes with only a few belongings, the alarmed local citizenry formed a delegation of people to travel to Sofia and ask the authorities to rescind the evacuation order. In the end, a smaller delegation arrived in Sofia the next day and met with their parliamentary representative, Dimitar Peshev (awarded the title of "Righteous Gentile Among the Nations" by Yad Vashem in 1973), who happened to be the vice-chairman of the National Assembly. Upon hearing their urgent pleas, Peshev and nine other Assembly deputies tried in vain to speak to the prime minister but could only meet on March 9 with the minister of Internal Affairs, who at first denied any knowledge of the ongoing "evacuations." When pressured by his agitated visitors, who refused to leave his office until he agreed to intervene, the visibly shaken minister finally ordered, by telephone, the release of all Jews who had been detained. Incredibly, the new orders were not countermanded, so thousands of Jewish men, women and children, who had been waiting in school buildings and warehouses to board trains bound for the death camps in Poland, were allowed to return home.

Popular opposition and resistance continued, leaving little doubt that public opinion was decisively against the persecution of the Jews. On May 24, 1943, the traditional parade in the streets of Sofia to celebrate the National Holiday of Slavic Letters and Culture ("Cyril and Methodius' Day") turned into a demonstration against the government's evacuation and internment orders, which were forcing twenty thousand Jews to abandon their homes in the capital. The gathering was addressed by Rabbi Daniel Zion and several young men. The crowd started an impressive march, which was intended to join the demonstration of the university students and make its way to the royal palace to protest against the outrages to which the Jews were subjected. Clashes with the police were followed by numerous arrests. The police arrested over four hundred demonstrators during this mass protest, organized and led by leaders of the Jewish community (mainly Rabbi Daniel Zion).

When the government threatened to prosecute Archbishop Stefan for his appeals, letters, telegrams, telephone calls, and other public and private intercessions on behalf of the Jewish minority, Stefan responded by giving refuge at his home to Rabbi Zion and Bulgaria's Chief Rabbi Asher Chananel of Sofia, and declaring the doors of every church and monastery open to all Jews.

This mass demonstration alarmed the authorities and they did not carry out the second stage of their deportation plan - deportation to Poland, where the Jews of Europe found their deaths. Fearing internal unrest, the Fascist government and the king were forced to give up their plan to send the Jews of Bulgaria to their doom in the death camps.

Preparations began for an armed people's uprising. The partisan detachments inflicted telling losses on the German occupation forces. The rising tide of the partisan movement kept the government constantly engaged, and it found it impossible to send units of the Bulgarian army to the eastern front against the Soviet Union. Moreover, the resistance movement obliged the Germans to maintain armed forces in Bulgaria in order to protect their rear. It should be noted that in Bulgaria there was no separate Jewish resistance and partisan movement, as was the case in Poland and France. The Jews had for centuries shared the historic destinies of the

Bulgarian people, and during those eventful days they joined the partisan detachments and underground movement, fighting shoulder to shoulder for the freedom of their one common fatherland.

Bulgaria was officially thanked by the government of Israel, despite being an ally of Nazi Germany during the first part of World War II. This story was kept secret by the Soviet Union because the Fascist Bulgarian government, the king of Bulgaria, and the Church were responsible for the huge public outcry at the time, causing the majority of the country to defend its Jewish population. The Communist Soviet regime could not countenance credit to be given to the former authorities, the Church or the king, as all three were considered enemies of Communism. Thus, the documentation proving the saving of Bulgaria's Jews was suppressed until the end of the Cold War in 1989. Only then did the story come to light. The number of forty-eight thousand Bulgarian Jews was known to Hitler, yet not one was deported or murdered by the Nazis.

| R' MENASHE KLEIN |

Miraculous Savior

On one occasion, in the Buna-Auschwitz concentration camp, R' Menashe Klein *zt"l* underwent a terrible beating at the hands of a number of *kapos* who caught him committing the unspeakable "crime" of eating potato peels that he had found in a nearby trash dump. As his work detail was working outside the camp, R' Menashe noticed the peels and surreptitiously squeezed them into his pocket. Unfortunately, he was seen by another worker who reported him. Within minutes, two *kapos* grabbed him from behind and held him down, his face to the ground, while a third *kapo*, a notorious criminal named Willy (who had been in the midst of serving a twenty-one-year prison term for murder before he was released and put to work for the Nazi S.S.), beat him with a long, thick tree branch. R' Menashe recalled counting the amount of blows he received but he lost count after sixty-six or sixty-seven. He miraculously survived the ordeal but his body was so swollen that he could barely walk back into the camp when the work shift had ended.

As the entire commando entered the camp confines and headed for their barracks, R' Menashe decided that he had had enough. The starvation, the heavy labor, the beatings and the taunts had finally gotten to him and at that very moment, he didn't care anymore what would happen to him.

Near the entrance to the camp, there was an office where the Nazi guards, *kapos* and commandants would head after a full day's work to report the results of the day's labor. This was where the records were kept, and the official office staff monitored the various "commandos" from this location. Not surprisingly, very few Jews would ever walk in the vicinity of this "lion's den" for it was known that it didn't take much – just the sight of a Jewish inmate – to incite the wrath of the Nazis, and then, who knew what would happen?

But after such a terrible beating, R' Menashe didn't care anymore. With an audacity that even he did not know from where it came, he limped right into the office and began to scream that he was being mistreated and this was no way for a human being to have to live! He demanded that he be transferred to a different commando, one where he did not have to be under the control of Willy, who beat him so mercilessly.

R' Menashe was naturally dark-skinned and the pricks of his unshaven face were black. When he entered the office, one

Nazi called out, "Look what the *'shvartzer'* is asking for. He wants to be treated nicely." A number of S.S. men gathered around and lifted the Jewish prisoner off his feet, and then literally threw him face first out of the office, where he landed with a heavy thud. The laughter from inside the office was cacophonous.

R' Menashe didn't think it was funny – he was in too much pain. He crawled to a nearby tree and began to sob. Silently, he prayed to Heaven that he be released from his misery; the pain and abject degradation was too much. Suddenly, he sensed the presence of someone standing over him. He looked up – directly into the face of a high-ranking Nazi officer. Now he was terrified, but rather than yell and scream at him, the man spoke softly, almost kindly. "Young one, what happened? What is the problem?"

R' Menashe didn't think; he just let it all come out. Through a vale of tears and painful sighs, he cursed the *kapos* who tortured him day and night; who had no concept of mercy; who never thought twice about killing another human being. This place, he said, was merciless. He ranted on and on, in Yiddish, positive that the German had no clue as to what he was saying, and if he did understand, surely he would see to it that the Jew was punished. But the Nazi was silent throughout, and when R' Menashe finished his rant, the man turned and walked right into the office.

It wasn't more than a few short minutes before he emerged and walked over to the tree under which R' Menashe was sitting. In a friendly tone, wholly uncharacteristic of the Nazi S.S., he informed R' Menashe that he had nothing more to worry about from his *kapo* Willy; the man was being transferred to a different commando the very next day! A fresh burst of tears accompanied R' Menashe's unbelieving reply, but the

Nazi insisted that it was true, and he would see for himself that by tomorrow, things would get better.

Some way, somehow, these words were like a shot of cold water on a hot and dreary day; they literally revived his soul! Although he didn't think it would actually come to pass, this was the first time that he had been spoken to like a human being in a very long time, and it meant a lot to feel human again. R' Menashe returned to his barracks and even slept well that night. In the morning, he awoke and managed to put on the pair of *tefillin* he had hidden away, a practice he did every day in captivity. His *tefillos* (prayers) were also different that day – as if he felt something good was going to happen to him.

At the lineup, he stood at attention, watching and waiting. The entire commando was lined up and awaiting the morning roll call and orders. But for some reason, they were left standing outside for an unusually long period of time. Once again, hope crept into R' Menashe's mind, the good feelings lingering for a few extra moments.

And then, he saw him! Like a man possessed, the evil Willy came charging out of the work office, running up and down the rows, apparently looking for someone in particular. R' Menashe cringed. Undoubtedly, he was coming after him, after he had complained about the *kapo* the day before! Suddenly, there he was, huffing and puffing like a rabid dog. He ran up to R' Menashe and screamed, "You're not happy? Here? In this place? Don't worry – I'll already take care of you!"

R' Menashe almost fainted from fright. But then, another miracle occurred! A second *kapo* came over and with obvious authority informed R' Menashe that he was being transferred to a different work commando. Getting between the madman Willy and R' Menashe, the second *kapo* quietly winked at him and said, "Do not worry. He won't harm you. He's going away – far, far away!"

Indeed, that very day, R' Menashe was ordered to report to a different commando detail and Willy, the evil *kapo*, was shipped out of Buna. As for the kind Nazi officer who literally restored R' Menashe's life to him – he was never heard from ever again. In fact, no one ever saw him or remembered such a man – not before or after! It was highly unusual for a Nazi officer to show mercy to a Jewish prisoner, and even more so to get involved with other officers in an effort to help him. R' Menashe would later say that he firmly believed that this man was a messenger from Heaven – perhaps even Eliyahu Hanavi – sent down to this world to protect him from harm.

| REB ALTER KURZ |
Two for the Price of One

Each and every morning at 4:00 a.m. sharp, as well as every evening after a day of backbreaking labor, the inmates at Auschwitz-Birkenau were forced to line up outside their barracks and stand perfectly still, often for many hours on end. The *lagerkommandant* (camp commander), S.S. guards and *kapos* (prisoner supervisors) continuously walked between the rows of prisoners, swinging their batons and beating the captives mercilessly if they dared to even shiver in the freezing cold. The German overseers took their time checking and rechecking their lists, making sure every prisoner was accounted for. Meanwhile, the frozen and embittered men had to stand at attention through it all. It was always worse during the winter, when the stinging pain from the frozen snow would seep through their ragged shoes.

This daily torture was commonly known as the *"appell"* (line-up). The procedure never varied. The kommandant would stand at the front of every row and bark out the numbers that were branded on each inmate's arm. When that person's tattooed number was called, he had to run up to the front of the line and make his number visible to the guard. The guard would glance at the inmate's arm and confirm the number on his list. While doing so, he also evaluated the pace and spryness of the inmate, to determine his continued ability to work. The ones that did not meet his standards were sent to the crematorium.

In the barracks, after a nightly chorus of horrific cries and moans, those prisoners who managed to live through the night would identify their friends and neighbors who didn't make it and carry the poor souls to the front of the barracks where they would be picked up and carted away. Alter Kurz and his bunkmate Shloime Goldberg were kept busy on a daily basis with the unpleasant task of moving the corpses, and when they were finished, Shloime would quietly say Kaddish for the departed – the "lucky ones" by some estimations. Shloime's older brother, a veteran *gabbai* in his shul back in Hungary, had the job of saying Kaddish each morning, but since he had succumbed to the brutal conditions a few months earlier, the burden fell on his younger brother. After the Kaddish, it was time for *appell*, and the two would run quickly to the line-up.

One particular morning, as Alter prepared to leave the barracks for *appell*, he realized that Shloime hadn't moved from the bunk. "Shloime," Alter said in a hushed tone, "you must move quickly. We don't have much time."

"Alter," Shloime replied in a weak voice, "leave me here. I am sick and I cannot stand up. I won't make it through the line-up."

But Alter wasn't prepared to lose his friend. "Let me help you, Shloime; you must come now!" He tried, but Alter could not move his friend. No doubt he really was very sick, but like so many others, Alter suspected that Shloime had had enough. He had just given up and wanted to die. "Please, Shloime," Alter pleaded, "come with me; don't give up!" But Shloime didn't move.

There was no time left. Alter had no choice but to run to *appell* without Shloime. With a heavy heart and tears in his eyes, he looked back one last time at his friend. Then, he ran out of the barracks and took his spot at the end of the line, all the while thinking: "How could I have left him to die?"

Suddenly, Alter had a crazy thought: "I will run up to the front when they call Shloime's number and pretend to be him. Will the kommandant really notice? Is he that thorough?"

Alter whispered his plan to a friend, Hershel, who was standing to his left. "Alter," Hershel pleaded, "*Rachmana litzlan* (Heaven save you), you cannot help Shloime by getting yourself killed! You know what they'll do if they catch you? They will hang you for sure. Please, I beg you, don't do it!"

But Alter was headstrong and when he made up his mind about something, he didn't let it go. They waited anxiously and when the Nazi called Shloime's number, Alter didn't blink. He just ran up and held his arm out as was required. He kept his gaze fixed on the kommandant, looking him straight in the eyes, and kept moving quickly until he returned to his spot in the back of the line. Alter's heart was beating out of his chest. He just couldn't believe it. It worked! He pretended to be Shloime and the Nazis hadn't known. But Hershel was shaking with fear.

"Calm down, Hershel, it's over!" Alter said. But, of course, it wasn't over. Alter still had to run up again when his own number was called, and pray that the Nazi wouldn't recognize him.

It was surely a stroke of Divine providence, for Alter's actual number wasn't called for a very long time. When it finally was called, he ran up once again, but this time he made sure to keep his face down. Alter stuck out his arm, and then quickly withdrew it and ran back to his place in the row. Hershel was standing there, sweating in the cold frosty morning, his eyes shut tight. "Hershel," Alter whispered, "I'm back. I made it; I'm back." Relief flooded Hershel's features and Alter smiled triumphantly.

That evening, after a day of labor, when Alter and Hershel got back to the barracks, they found Shloime huddled in the corner of the bunk. Somehow, he managed to hide from the *kapos* and wasn't found all day. He was alive, and the day off from work had done him well. Shloime was feeling a bit better and Alter brought him some bread and hot soup that he had been able to trade for a piece of salami. Perhaps, Alter would later say, it was the fact that he had Hashem's Name, "Sha-lom," in his that kept Shloime alive during that day.

Shloime survived Auschwitz and went on to raise a fine family in Montreal. When Alter passed away some fifteen years ago, Shloime made a special trip to New York, specifically to be *menachem avel*, and told over the amazing story of how Alter Kurz saved his life.

| R' MORDECHAI FRIEDLAND |

Our Goal Is Eretz Yisrael

Our Sages teach us that when a person is sent to fulfill a Torah commandment, he will not be harmed. In this vein, when a father appoints his entire family of ten souls – mother, father and eight children – as "messengers in the fulfillment of a mitzvah," he literally spins a web of spiritual and physical protection around his family. This web is so strong that it allows his family to survive the tenuous years of World War II and ultimately regroup as a unified unit after the war, in the Land of Israel – whole in body and pure in religious spirit.

In the annals of Holocaust history, it is rare to come across a family that managed to elude the Germans, outmaneuver the Russians, and bypass the British – eventually regrouping in a joyous reunion at the port of Haifa, in the Holy Land. The story of the Friedland family is truly a remarkable one.

In the town of Kretchen, Poland, a small hamlet ten kilometers west of Lizhensk, the outbreak of the Second World War was greeted with gleeful chants and patriotic fervor. September 1, 1939 was the first day of school, and five-year-old Mordechai Friedland was not exactly keen on beginning his tenure in the Polish school system. Early that morning, as he waited on his front stoop for his older sister to escort him to school, he saw two airplanes fly over the neighboring village and drop bombs on an extension bridge that spanned the San River, which connected Congress Poland to Galicia. The planes then continued further east, attacking the armament factories in the industrial city of Stalowa Wola. The explosions were earth-shattering, but as a five-year-old child, he was less frightened by the military action and more excited by the sights and sounds of it all. Trucks and army vehicles were frantically driving to and fro and soldiers were scrambling all over the area, taking up positions. Soon an announcement was made by a local Polish official that the Polish national army was declaring war on Germany.

Of course, with the outbreak of war, school was canceled, and the young children were thrilled with the news. They marched with the soldiers in the streets of Kretchen, and followed behind the self-important Polish officials, closely following their every word and deed. That day was exciting, indeed!

It took only a few short days, however, before it became painfully obvious that the Polish army was no match for the overpowering German Wehrmacht. Polish forces were quickly routed and those quick-witted soldiers who refused to fight ran for their lives. The Germans conquered Poland with astonishing speed, and the cities and towns along the San River were soon occupied by German troops.

Reb Itche Duvid Friedland, Mordechai's father, was a man of action, not one to take a "wait and see" approach. He recognized the ominous storm clouds and could feel with every fiber of his being that the Jews of Poland were in for a rough time ahead. He knew it was time to go.

That very day, Reb Itche Duvid sent telegrams to his children – married and unmarried – who were living and learning in *yeshivos* and seminaries all over Poland. One son was a *rosh yeshivah*, and the other married ones were respected and prominent pillars of their respective communities. The message was urgent and it required that all the Friedland children, with their wives and families, immediately gather back at the family home in Kretchen. Reb Itche Duvid understood that with a family of more than ten souls (including spouses and children), it would be difficult to escape the advancing Nazi onslaught as one unified group. There would be many ideas and opinions of what to do, where to go, and how to escape. He knew his boys and respected their opinions. At this point, he wanted everyone's input, and then he would decide on a proper course of action.

Over the next week, the Friedland family regrouped, one by one, couple by couple, family by family, in the house they all grew up in. Mordechai was excited to see all his older brothers and sisters, and he reveled in their attention and their familiar smiles. But he could sense that all was not well. His father constantly wore a worried frown and the adults were usually conversing in low and urgent tones. Nevertheless, as a five-year-old and the youngest member of the family, he was showered with attention and he remembers it as a special time.

Finally, the day came when his father called the entire family together. He had heard their opinions and weighed their input. Now he had made up his mind and he was prepared to deliver his decision. Although Mordechai was only five years old at the time, his father's words still ring and reverberate in his mind as if it was yesterday.

"My dear children," he began, "we are facing a serious time in our lives. The war has started – it's going to be a bad war. The entire world is going to be involved in this war." Reb Itche Duvid had seen firsthand the effects of a world war; he had survived the First World War – the "Great War" – and clearly remembered its consequences. "We need to leave, to get out of this place, before it is too late. I know that it is late – the Germans have arrived and the danger is great. But I have a way for us to escape and I feel it's our only hope."

The entire Friedland family was standing in the backyard on that bright September afternoon, surrounding their father, hanging on to his every word. Reb Itche Duvid looked around at the faces of his sons and daughters and continued. "I have a tradition that's been passed down from the previous Radzyner Rebbe, that when a person makes up his mind that he is moving to Eretz Yisrael permanently - not like those fake *chalutzim* (pioneers) who go for a while and then come running back - but he lives there and stays in the Holy Land, such a person will be protected from harm."

Reb Itche Duvid Friedland suddenly stood and picked up a large stick he had placed next to him by the table. "Look here. This is my *shteken* - my walking stick. I swear that I will not abandon this walking stick until every one of us will arrive safe and sound in Eretz Yisrael! We are all *shluchei mitzvah* - messengers in the act of performing a mitzvah, and we all have a responsibility to make our way to Eretz Yisrael, no matter what happens to us in the coming weeks, months and years. We must all accept upon ourselves this *shlichus* - and no one has a right to cancel our mission!"

The impassioned words of Reb Itche Duvid made such an impression on his entire family that close to eighty years later, Mordechai Friedland still vividly recalls his father's words. Each and every member of the Friedland family accepted upon themselves right then and there that their ultimate destination would be the Land of Israel and that they would not rest or stop their efforts until they arrived there.

The meeting broke up and plans were accelerated. Within days, the family had packed up whatever they could and began to move eastward, to the relative safety of the larger city of Tarnograd. But the German presence there did not last long. Very soon, the Russians arrived and took over control of the city along with the entire eastern portion of Poland. This was in fulfillment of the terms of the infamous Molotov-Ribbentrop Pact, which insidiously divided the conquered country of Poland in half; Germany would control the western sector and Russia would receive the eastern sector. Tarnograd was in the east and was subject to the full authority of the Red Army of Russia.

What followed over the course of the next five-and-a-half years was nothing short of amazing. While in Tarnograd, the Friedland family was given a choice to become Russian citizens. When they refused, the family was deported to Novosibir, in Siberia, where they managed to stay together for close to two years under the harshest of weather conditions. From Novosibir, they went to Tampshich where the family split up yet again. Young Mordechai remained with his parents as they traveled from the northern regions of Russia to the western border town of Melkhay, where they lived on a *kolkhoz* (kibbutz) near the Iranian border.

From Melkhay, they came to Jambor, a transit town that saw many Jewish rabbis and dignitaries pass through it. These included R' Yankel Galinsky *shlit"a*, the Sadarvana Rav *shlit"a*, and R' Sekula *zt"l*. Their journey then took them through Lvov (after the war ended), Sosnowiec, Stetchin in Czechoslovakia, Bratislava, Aux Lemain and Marseille in France - where then thirteen-year-old Mordechai boarded the famous ship "Exodus" without his family, and attempted to land on the shores of the Eretz Yisrael.

Our Sages teach us: *Shluchei mitzvah einan nizokin* - literally translated as "Messengers in the performance of a mitzvah will not be harmed." For the Friedland family, this dictum proved to be more than a learned adage: It was the cause and effect of their ultimate salvation.

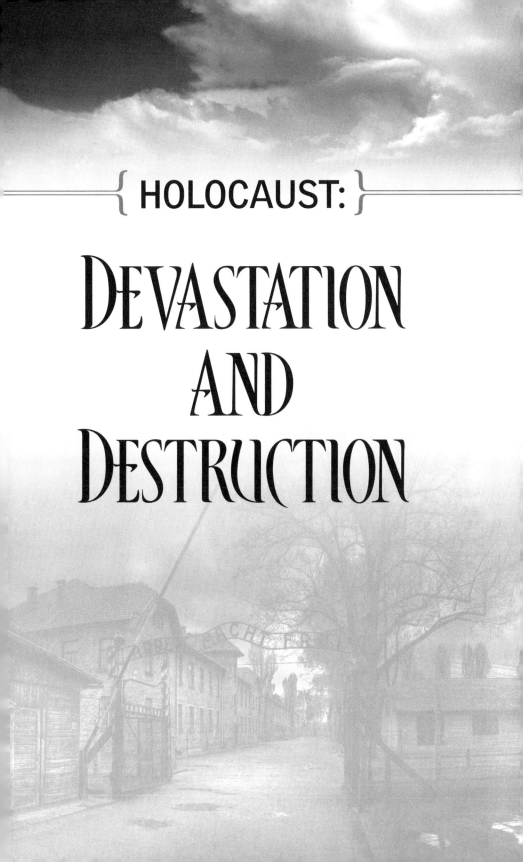

{ HOLOCAUST: }

Devastation and Destruction

by Raize Guttman

Frozen and shivering
He stood with the others,
At the open pit
With his fellow brothers.

The Nazis lined them up
And just for fun,
Had them immerse in kerosene
One by one.

Shmulik watched the men
As their skin began to burn,
And suddenly he realized
It was his turn.

He lowered himself
And tried to be strong,
But his brothers watched in horror,
He was down there too long.

With a sudden surge of power
He emerged with a glow,
There was something in his heart
That the others did not know.

Itzik turned to Shmulik
And asked him what transpired,
What happened in the pit
When they thought he had expired.

Shmulik, still quite shaken
Felt bold, no longer weak,
An inner strength he did awaken
And in a whisper, began to speak.

"They took away my clothing,
They took away my wife,
They took my precious children,
They wish to take my life.

"There's one thing even greater
The Nazis can't control,
My love for the Creator
That is etched inside my soul.

"And with my heart still yearning
I shall not fall nor fear,
With sparks of love still burning
We shall forever persevere."

| KLAUSENBERGER REBBE |

Anything but to Be a Nazi

The awful sights that accompanied the destruction of the Warsaw ghetto shook even the toughest of the tough. The Nazis were not content with displaying their destruction to the world; a slave labor group was brought from Auschwitz to Warsaw to dismantle the bombed-out buildings and cart away the mess. But even these hardened prisoners brought in from Auschwitz – even they, who were thought to have lost every speck of human emotion – were shocked by the destruction they beheld. The prisoners brought in from Auschwitz were given the task of clearing away every remnant that might remind future generations that 450,000 Jews had once been crammed into a few square city blocks.

R' Yekusiel Yehuda Halberstam *zt"l*, the Sanz-Klausenberger Rebbe, was among this group of prisoners; in fact, he was the supervisor. As the prisoners surveyed the desolate landscape, the rebbe suddenly fainted, appalled at the sight of a bulldozer ruthlessly scooping up an unrolled Torah scroll along with the building rubble. The scoop, filled with cement, plaster, and rolls of holy parchment all tangled together, rose high into the air, and the bulldozer rumbled over to a waste pit to dump its load.

As he tottered on his feet, his strength failing his ability to remain upright, the rebbe mumbled, "See, just see, Master of the Universe, what they are doing with Your holy Torah." Then he dropped to the earth.

Two Jews rushed over and began to revive him. The Nazis had no patience for fainting prisoners – the work must go on. When R' Yekusiel Yehuda had come back to his senses, work went on in the former ghetto area as if nothing had happened.

But then came the drenching rain. The work – consisting of carrying heavy boulders and moving mangled beams, and oppressive to begin with – became all the more so in the torrential spring downpour. Many people died of exhaustion and exposure.

One of the exhausted and drenched victims, a man who had lost so much and witnessed even more, walked over to the Klausenberger Rebbe and with a mixture of pain and fury, exclaimed, "Rabbi, does this make you proud to be a Jew? Are you going to continue to recite prayers with the words, 'Ata bechartanu mikol ha'amim' (You have chosen us from amongst the nations) and rejoice that we Jews are the 'chosen nation'?"

The rebbe looked at the man with pity. But when he answered, his tone was firm and sure. "You know something... until this very day I did not say the words 'You have chosen us' with the proper devotion. Indeed, I was lacking in my belief. But today, I realize that if it weren't for the fact that the Al-mighty G-d has chosen us to be His people, then I would be no different than them – than the accursed Nazis. It is better for me to be in my situation than to be one of them, G-d forbid. So, yes, happy is my lot!"

| SATMAR REBBE |

A Giant Among Men

The article which follows about the Satmar Rebbe was written more than fifty years ago, in 1959, by a Hungarian Jewish writer named Dr. Ferencz Kennedy. It appeared in *Uj Kelet*, a Hungarian Jewish newspaper in Israel, to coincide with the rebbe's visit there. The writer vividly recalls the time he was together with the rebbe in what the Nazis named "Zonder Transport." Close to 1,300 Hungarian Jewish personalities, by virtue of Rudolf Kastner's contacts with Adolf Eichmann and considerable amounts in bribery money paid by wealthy Jews abroad, were taken to an internment camp in Bergen-Belsen. After languishing there for more than five months, they were taken by train to freedom in Switzerland. Dr. Kennedy, born into an estranged Jewish family, was in the same barracks as the rebbe in Bergen-Belsen.

I should start by noting that I am not one of Rabbi Teitelbaum's followers, but perhaps I can contribute to portraying this unusual person's travel to Auschwitz, Poland or to Auschpitz, Austria. This was the most important decision for the transport director to make. Each of us understood the difference between Auschwitz and "Auschpitz."

Someone in our group heard from the conductor that his directive was to travel to Auschwitz. This meant that the transport train was heading to the Auschwitz extermination camp. You can just imagine how desperate we were when we found out about this.

In the meantime, the transport train cars moved over to the sidetracks, and we spent two full days inside those cars in an area of three meters on the sidetracks. Along the side of the tracks we noticed a Jew with a nearly gray beard whose face made an enormous impression upon me. Both of his alabaster-white pointer fingers were inside his white vest while he was pacing back and forth, murmuring his prayers or melodies. I do not know whether he was reciting psalms or was thinking about our awful fate. I just saw that he was very upset, moving a few steps among the others with his head bowed. When I asked one of my friends about this man, he replied with certainty, "He is the Satmar Rebbe, Rabbi Teitelbaum. And whoever is with him most certainly has a lot less worries."

I had never heard of a rabbi like him. The world of the Orthodox religious Jews was foreign to me, and I had never before heard of any Satmar rabbi. Therefore, it was no surprise that as a skeptic, I could not imagine how people could be so sure that because the rabbi was with us, we had every hope of surviving our purgatory.

However, I later realized that our hopes were totally justified. The Hungarian police started approaching the train cars, but the S.S. ordered them away. During those dramatic hours, Dr. Kastner in Budapest intervened. Finally, our train was redirected to "Auschpitz," instead of to the Auschwitz death camp. Auschwitz was supposedly filled, and therefore we were sent to Bergen-Belsen.

I lived with the Satmar Rebbe for five months in Men's Block E in Bergen-Belsen. I do not know how this happened, but it is a fact that the Germans themselves permitted him to keep his beard, which the rebbe concealed with a kerchief around his face, pretending to be suffering from a toothache.

The rebbe did not eat the camp food. He lived on water and cooked potatoes. As far as I know, he fasted two or three days a week. You could hear his voice in the barracks almost all day long. It was not talking which we heard, but his prayers and studying. He had a mournful tune and sobbing gestures that kept many of us awake late into the night. I learned those gestures myself, and for years I could hear the tune in my head as a sad memento of those tragic times. The rebbe's mournful tune made many of those living in the barracks nervous, but not me. I knew that the rebbe was using that tune to pray to G-d for mercy; he fought against the decree and prayed for rescue.

The Satmar Rebbe was crystal clean even in the dirty barracks – dirt and vermin had no power over him. He used to sit on his bed, and his wife and his attendant, a young skinny man, devoted themselves to him, helping him to have something to eat so he could continue with his religious activities.

His majestic and wonderful appearance amazed everyone. I admit that I, too, was affected by his influence and appeal. There, among the barbwire, the shadow of the Angel of Death was greatly weakened, and I began believing in Heavenly forces. I often noticed that whenever Rabbi Teitelbaum recited his prayers, or whenever he simply sang his wordless tune, all of our eyes were filled with bloody tears.

On one summer day, I asked the rebbe's young attendant to obtain an autograph from the rebbe. The answer came quickly: The rabbi did not consider my request to be appropriate for now. The weeks passed, and the Satmar Rebbe patiently and modestly suffered through the difficulties.

I subsequently became very close to the Satmar Rebbe, and this happened as follows: I had the opportunity to win the trust of a few S.S. men through some bribery and got along with them very well. In exchange for the bribes I gave them, I received newspapers, and the S.S. provided Goebbels's newspaper, *Das Deutsche Reich*, as well as the *Volkischer Baobachter*, the Pressburg newspaper *Grenzbote*, and other German newspapers. In addition, the German S.S. men would occasionally bring me bread and medicine. However, the newspapers were the most important item and were our intellectual food. In the camp, newspapers were very significant for us. We frequently derived encouragement from the various news reports, and awaited liberation.

We disseminated the news reports every evening in the barracks among the detainees, and for that purpose the famous Hungarian Jewish playwright, Bela Zholt, provided his commentaries and opinions on the dry news that the camp consumed with great curiosity. This is how we found out about the Allied invasion of Normandy. We heard the news about the capture of Warsaw and Paris, and we also learned about the unsuccessful assassination attempt on Hitler.

One night, the Satmar Rebbe sent his attendant to me to ask for a favor. Since the rebbe's bed was far from mine, he could not hear the news reports that were being read in low tones. In addition, the rebbe did not lie in bed at the same time as the other detainees. He therefore requested me to give him the news before I informed the rest of the barrack. I was more than happy to agree to his request, and each evening, at six thirty, I would go over to the rebbe's bed and report to him the most important news and political events. The rebbe paid close attention and heard the news about the Allied victories with cold indifference and apathy. He commented that "We still need great mercy from Heaven to be able to be liberated from here alive."

The High Holy Days were approaching, and soon it would be Yom Kippur. Several of the barracks held prayer services, and in our barracks the Satmar Rebbe led the *Mussaf* of Yom Kippur. A few meters away, S.S. men were standing outside guarding the camp prisoners in the camp surrounded by barbwire, while inside we could hear the heartbreaking prayerful voice of the Satmar Rebbe, who was expressing age-old laments of the ancient Jewish prayers.

Bela Zholt and Aladar Komlosh (two famous Hungarian Jewish novelists who were also interned in Bergen-Belsen) passed by outside. I approached them and invited them to listen to the prayers of Rabbi Teitelbaum. It was a deeply touching experience to see the rebbe wrapped in his *tallis*, rocking back and forth with all his limbs and pouring out his soul to his Creator. When they left the barracks, the cynical Bela Zholt, who despite being so assimilated had tears welling in his eyes, said to me, "This is quite traditional, but it's very nice!"

Aladar Komlosh replied that if any prayers existed in the world, it was this true prayer service of the Satmar Rebbe. We all felt we were listening to a holy Jewish prayer, and we could not remain indifferent to it.

At the end of November, we heard reports that we would be liberated and would be taken to Switzerland. Our hearts were filled with nervousness, fear, and apprehension. Our minds were filled with doubts as to the veracity of the reports, and the entire camp was in a tense mood.

We got ready to pack our bags and waited for the moment when liberation would arrive. On that very day, filled with physical and emotional stress, the rebbe's attendant approached me and asked whether I still wanted the rebbe's autograph. Some five months had already passed, and we had lived through many difficulties. I had already forgotten about the whole subject. "Of course I would like to have the rebbe's autograph," I replied with a restrained smile.

This is how I obtained the rebbe's autograph in the Bergen-Belsen concentration camp. The rebbe had not forgotten about the subject of my request during all those months, and as soon as it became "appropriate," he fulfilled my request.

Afterwards, on one cold December night when we were actually released and in Switzerland, we marched along St. Galen Street to the barracks that had been prepared for us. On the corners of the street, we were met by fellow Jews who were unable to approach us up close, but tossed apples and sweets our way, which we caught with both hands. However, these Jews who threw us gifts had one question: "Where is the rebbe?"

Bela Zholt strode alongside me, excitedly observing, "You see, Ferencz, I am nothing! No one knows me, even though hundreds of thousands of people have read my novels and poetry. No one is waiting for me; they only know of the rebbe. They are only waiting for him!"

Our group comprised more than 1,300 people, including various famous personalities from the Hungarian Jewish community. The majority of our group was, of course, assimilated and modernized Jews. There were few Orthodox Jews. The transport was comprised of professors, poets, artists, community activists, and leaders of the Hungarian Zionist movement and their families. The Satmar Rebbe, Rabbi Teitelbaum, did not at all fit into our community, whose major leaders were intellectuals and academics who believed that as soon as liberation arrived, they would be greeted with great honor. Yet, suddenly here they were, so bitterly disappointed, since in Switzerland almost no one paid any attention to them. Everyone was interested in the personality known as the Satmar Rebbe, Rabbi Yoel Teitelbaum. Everyone wanted to know where he was in the transport, and how he was feeling.

Everyone asked the same question: Where is the rebbe?

So we all realized that it was not the professionals and academics who were indispensable, but rather the quiet and holy man.

In Switzerland, we all parted ways, but for a long time thereafter, until today, I think a great deal about the fascinating personality of the Satmar Rebbe. I frequently still remember the following little philosophical ideas:

When we consider the significance of faith, and the fact that the Torah and its observance is essentially what has preserved the Jewish people over thousands of years of exile, we must also realize that the Satmar Rebbe is without a doubt one of the holiest individuals produced by the Jewish people, and is the greatest guardian to assure that the Torah of Moshe is not forgotten, G-d forbid. It may be possible that we perceive him as being too fastidious, too stubborn about following every point of the Torah, but without a doubt he is the real and most loyal defender of the Torah, a true leader of the Jewish people!

| R' ELIEZER GERSHON FRIEDENSON |
"*Onus Al Pi Hadibbur*"

On Erev Pesach, April 19, 1943, Nazi S.S. auxiliary forces entered the Warsaw ghetto, planning to complete an *aktion* of deportation and extermination of the remaining Jews in the ghetto. But the Jews were ready for them and began a resistance that lasted for ten days. The ghetto fighters (numbering some four hundred to one thousand) were armed primarily with pistols and revolvers; they had little ammunition and relied on improvised explosive devices and incendiary bottles. German troops suffered losses as they were repeatedly ambushed by Jewish fighters, who threw Molotov cocktails and hand grenades at them from alleyways, sewers and windows.

After initial setbacks, the Germans regrouped and systematically burned or blew up the ghetto buildings, house by house, block by block, rounding up or murdering anybody they could capture. By April 29, 1943, most of the fighters were killed or had escaped the ghetto, and this marked the end of the organized resistance.

The religious Jews in the Warsaw ghetto who were hoping to celebrate the Festival of Freedom were in a real quandary. With great difficulty and under the ever-vigilant watch of the S.S. police and auxiliary troops, they managed to bake a small amount of matzos, and they gathered whatever food they could to prepare for the Seder night. All this was done while mindful that at any moment, the Nazis were coming to liquidate the ghetto.

One of the most respected educators of the Bais Yaakov movement, Rebbetzin Pesya Sharashevsky *a"h*, related that on that fateful day, Erev Pesach 1943, there was a sudden knock at her door. R' Eliezer Gershon Friedenson *Hy"d*, the eminent Agudah activist and leader and educator of Bais Yaakov, was standing there with a nervous look on his face.

When she opened the door, he quickly spoke up. "I've come to inform you," he said quietly, "actually, to warn you and your family. People are saying that tonight the Nazis are planning to liquidate the ghetto..."

Rebbetzin Pesya was so overcome with panic that she immediately blurted out, "The Nazis are planning to liquidate the Jews!" Hysteria was threatening to overtake the women who had been cooking and preparing for the Pesach Seder.

Suddenly, R' Eliezer Gershon rose up to his full height and like a lioness protecting her cubs, his face took on a look of valiant courage. "How can you say such a thing? Liquidate the Jews? Destroy our people? Never! It will never happen! The Jewish people can never be destroyed - there will always be Jews left to carry on the word of Hashem!"

The *rebbetzin* lowered her eyes in shame. She knew she had misspoken and wished she could take back her words. R' Eliezer Gershon felt her shame and realized that she had not meant what she said. Wishing to avoid embarrassing her any further, he quickly spoke up. "If it is alright with you, I would like to join you tonight for the Pesach Seder."

Of course, the honor of having such a prominent person at their Seder was gratifying, and the girls of Bais Yaakov prepared an extra seat of honor in their underground bunker.

The *rebbetzin* recalled that the Seder was as festive as could be imagined under such trying circumstances, but one thing stood out in her memory. During the recital of the Haggadah, R' Eliezer Gershon suddenly cried out in anguish, *"Anus al pi hadibbur* – We Jews are hiding in bunkers, underground; we are *anusim* – forced prisoners!"

He began to weep in a manner that was so heartbreaking to watch and to hear. It was as if his heart could not handle the strain of seeing the Jewish people suffer under such bitter conditions and impending doom.

After a moment, he composed himself and said to her, "You know, I truly envy the Jews in Eretz Yisrael who are able to properly perform the mandate of *Kol dichfin yeisei v'yeichol... kol ditzrich yeisei v'yifsach* – 'Whoever is hungry can come and eat (with us)... whoever is in need can come and join in celebrating the Pesach festival.'" With that, he excused himself and walked out.

Two days later, on the first day of Chol Hamoed, R' Eliezer Gershon's house was razed to the ground. *Hashem yinkom damo.*

| HUSYATINER REBBE |

How the Battle Was Really Won

In the summer of 1942, General Erwin Rommel and his vaunted Afrika Korps had advanced through Northern Africa and were poised on the doorstep of the Holy Land. A huge armada, comprised of elite German and Italian infantry units, was located near El Alamein, eighty kilometers south of Alexandria and 150 kilometers west of Cairo, the Egyptian capital. The entire Jewish population of Palestine was overwhelmed with fear and dread, as Hitler himself had boasted of wiping out the Jewish presence in one day. German bombers had already strafed Tel Aviv, and the *Yishuv* (Jewish community in Israel) knew it was in mortal danger. If Rommel could break through the British defenses in Egypt, there was no stopping them from conquering Palestine. The Jewish Agency in Palestine began destroying sensitive documents and shipping other records out of its headquarters. The Orthodox communities declared days of public prayer and fasting.

On the fourteenth of Tammuz, 5702/1942, Rabbi Yaakov Landau, Chief Rabbi of Bnei Brak, and a close disciple of the Husyatiner Rebbe, R' Yisroel Friedman *zt"l*, visited his mentor at his home in Tel Aviv, as he often did to seek guidance and advice. During the visit, the conversation centered on the great trepidation which had engulfed Eretz Yisrael, with the latest news of the advancing German armies stationed in neighboring Egypt.

The rebbe was in obvious distress regarding the ongoing situation. Rav Landau urged him to do whatever he could to effect Divine mercy on behalf of the Jews of the Holy Land, but the Husyatiner Rebbe kept shaking his head and murmuring to himself, "What can I do? Is there anything I can do?"

His disciple gathered up his courage and replied, "Definitely! Of course! There is no question that the *tzaddik* must intervene."

R' Yisroel looked at his disciple. "Do you really feel that I should become involved?" he asked one last time, and Rav Landau assured him that he must act immediately. After a long pause, the rebbe nodded his head. He accepted his disciple's suggestion and announced that he would visit the tomb of the renowned Ohr Hachaim, Chacham Chaim ben Attar *zt"l*, the following day, on the *yahrtzeit* of the great *tzaddik*.

The Husyatiner Rebbe had formed a deep emotional attachment to the Ohr Hachaim Hakadosh. Every year, on the day of his *yahrtzeit*, the rebbe made a pilgrimage to the gravesite of the Chacham on the Mount of Olives in Jerusalem, overlooking the Temple Mount. Even as he grew older and the journey proved almost beyond his endurance, the rebbe did not relent, demanding that he be taken to the tomb.

That year, as the terrible threat hung over the Jews of the Holy Land, the rebbe, in the company of a large group of Chassidim, ascended to the Ohr Hachaim's gravesite on the fifteenth of Tammuz, the day of the *yahrtzeit*. He was joined there by another great *tzaddik*, R' Shlomka Zhviller *zt"l*. The atmosphere was most somber and spiritual. The rebbe stood at the tomb for a lengthy period of time, engrossed in meditation. Tears streamed down his face as he prayed, even though they remained tightly shut all throughout. Behind him stood one of the rebbe's closest disciples, who felt the need to keep prodding the rebbe to do something by saying, "Rebbe, the *rasha* (Rommel) is already at our doorstep. He is threatening us all..."

Suddenly, the rebbe opened his eyes. He looked around at the expectant faces of the assemblage and his demeanor became more composed. Then, to the utter amazement of all, he said quietly, *"Zurg zich nisht* – Do not worry – he (Rommel) will not make it here!" He later explained that he was able to speak with such certainty about the German defeat because, "While engrossed in deep meditation, with my eyes closed, Hashem's holy Name appeared to me with exceptional brilliance. I immediately realized that the *rasha* would not be successful in his drive to the Holy Land."

The Husyatiner Rebbe then ordered that exactly a *minyan* of highly regarded people gather around the gravesite, along with a *Sefer Torah*. The rebbe personally chose the Torah scroll to be taken. He asked the special delegation to request from the Ohr Hachaim to "act in harmony with him." The small group remained on Har Hazeisim for a few more hours before the oncoming dusk forced them to return home.

After several days the news was announced that Rommel's army had suffered a great defeat at the hands of the British under General Montgomery, and that the Afrika Corps was in full retreat. This Allied victory turned the tide in the North African Campaign and ended the Axis threat to the entire Middle East. It also revived the morale of the Allies, being the first major offensive against the Germans since the start of the war in 1939 in which the western Allies achieved a decisive victory.

Winston Churchill, the prime minister of Great Britain, famously summed up the crucial battle of El Alamein with the words, "Before Alamein we never had a victory; after Alamein we never had a defeat." They also never had an inkling of the mighty power of prayer that the Husyatiner Rebbe brought to bear on a previously hopeless situation.

| VEITZENER RAV |
A Permissible Sukkah

Fulfilling the commandments connected to the holiday of Sukkos in the purgatory known as Auschwitz was unthinkable, for an attempt at religious observance carried the death sentence. There was no *lulav* or *esrog* to be found so that wasn't even a consideration. However, a few Jews were inflamed with the notion of building a sukkah, and thought long and hard about how to make their wish a reality. They were willing to risk their lives for this mitzvah and displayed an extraordinary degree of self-sacrifice.

When a new shipment of wooden barracks arrived in late summer, R' Tzvi Hirsch Meisels *zt"l*, the Veitzener Rav, spirited one bed out of the storage room and used an axe to break it into pieces. Several boards were used as sukkah walls and other sections were broken into splinters, to be used as *s'chach*. Miraculously, no one noticed or heard the muffled sounds of the axe during the day. Of course, under such conditions, there were no decorations in this sukkah.

The location of the sukkah, outside where the walls of two barracks nearly met, was kept a closely guarded secret. To the uninitiated observer, it appeared to be merely a pile of boards. Only a person who knew the secret would be able to traverse the maze that led into the sukkah itself. Once the holiday began, it was decided that each person would make his way inside, quickly eat a *kezayis* (olive-size measurement) of bread, and then just as quickly run out. There was no need to take extra risks and endanger oneself more than necessary.

During the course of the preparations, a unique question arose: Is one permitted to recite the special blessing of *"Leisheiv Basukkah"* (sitting in the sukkah) when dashing in and out of their makeshift structure? The halachah is that if one is in fear of robbers or bandits while sitting in the sukkah, he has not fulfilled his obligation, for a person must "live" in his sukkah the way he would normally "live" in his home. Since in Auschwitz, some argued, we are in mortal danger as we sit in the sukkah, can this really be a true fulfillment of the mitzvah?

The debate raged for a number of days. All the scholars of note chimed in with their opinion, but no consensus could be reached. Finally, all eyes turned to the Veitzener Rav, and it was decided that he would deliver the final ruling. Taking all opinions into consideration, he ultimately ruled that indeed the *brachah* should be said. He based his decision on the words of the Sages: *You shall reside in the sukkah the way you (ordinarily) live.*

Explained R' Tzvi Hirsch: "We ordinarily live under dangerous conditions - living in the barracks in Auschwitz is no less dangerous than sitting in a sukkah in Auschwitz. The Germans could come at any minute and take us to the gas chambers, no matter where we are! Our lives are endangered in exactly the same way - whether we are in the sukkah, or in our 'house' - our barracks. Therefore, this sukkah is quite identical to the way we ordinarily live - and it is kosher!"

| UDVARI RAV |
Being a "*Rabbiner*" Saved His Life

In 1944, soon after the holiday of Shavuos, the Jewish inhabitants of Udvar, Hungary, including their revered rabbi, Rav Shalom Krausz *zt"l*, were herded together and taken by force to the ghetto at the edge of the city of Grosswardein. From there, most of the people were shipped off to Auschwitz and only a small handful lived to tell of the horrors of that ghetto.

After being in the Grosswardein ghetto for three weeks, an S.S. officer approached Rav Shalom on a Shabbos afternoon and asked if he was a *rabbiner*. This was a tricky question since one never knew the sinister intentions of the Nazi S.S. and why they would be inquiring about *rabbiners*. However, since Rav Shalom was dressed in his traditional rabbinical garb, and it was pretty obvious who he was, he answered in the affirmative.

The S.S. man nodded as if he was expecting this answer. Then, he asked if there were any other *rabbanim* in the ghetto. Rav Shalom told him the names of a few other *rabbanim* that he knew of in the ghetto. The officer immediately ordered Rav Shalom and his family to come with him, and led them into a room. Frightened as they were, they had no idea what was going on and spent a restless night in that guarded room.

The next morning, they awoke to the sight of hundreds of Hungarian officers swarming the ghetto with drawn weapons in their hands. A feeling of dread filled them, especially when they saw men, women and children being prodded along roughly by the officers surrounding them. As they observed from the window, the harried and confused people were led to the train station and roughly pushed into cattle cars that were not nearly large enough to hold the large amount of human beings who were forced inside. From there, they were all taken to Auschwitz; only a small minority of them survived while the rest died *al kiddush Hashem, Hy"d*.

The ghetto was quiet after that and in the evening, the S.S. rounded up the Krausz family as well as a few others, and shipped them off to Budapest. In fact, some of the other families belonged to the *rabbanim* that Rav Shalom had mentioned to the S.S. the day before. During the trip, they learned a little more about what was going on – how they alone from the entire ghetto had been saved and how Hashem had disguised the miracle under a facade of nature. They learned that Dr. Rudolph Kastner and his friends had sent a request to the S.S. to save a group of people whose names were written on a special list. Among the people on the list were several Zionist leaders and secular activists. Hashem, who controls the thoughts of human beings, orchestrated events so that when these doctors and professors were asked by the S.S. officers if they had rabbinical ordination, they naturally answered no. The S.S. chief declared that there was surely some sort of mistake as only rabbis were supposed to be sent to Budapest as per Kastner's request. Amazingly enough, the S.S. officers went to seek out more *rabbanim*. When the group arrived in Budapest and the Zionist leaders saw who was being taken on the transport, they were furious. But everything had been predestined already and that was how the Udvari Rav and other *rabbanim* merited to be saved.

From Budapest, the Kastner Transport was taken to Bergen-Belsen. Of the great personages on the train were none other than the Satmar Rebbe and Rav Yonason Steif *zt"l*. When they arrived at Bergen-Belsen, everyone ran to grab a bed so that they could go to sleep and the ensuing melee was loud and boisterous. However, when the lights were finally extinguished, there was still one person walking around. Rav Shalom couldn't make out who this person was and upon getting a closer look, he realized that this was the great *gaon* Harav Yonason Steif, who had no bed to sleep on. The Udvari Rav stood up and offered to share his bed with the *gaon*. Later, when they were free and living in Williamsburg, New York, Rav Yonason once joked that that he still owed Rav Shalom compensation for one night's sleep. (The Udvari Rav also mentioned that the morning after he had shared his bed with Rav Yonason Steif, he found a *kamei'a* inscribed with holy Names. He asked everyone around him if they knew to whom it belonged, but no one had a clue where it came from, not even Rav Yonason. The Udvari Rav closely guarded this *kamei'a* all his life and, as specified in his will, the *kamei'a* was buried together with him.)

On 21 Kislev, 5705 (1944), the Kastner Transport finally merited seeing Hashem's salvation. He delivered them from darkness to light when they finally reached Switzerland. The Satmar Rebbe settled into an apartment after spending a few months in Geneva, while Rav Shalom and Rav Yonason Steif and their families wandered around in various cities, until finally they received visas to America in Iyar of 1949. The Udvari Rav always held a special *seudas hoda'ah* (feast of thanksgiving) on 21 Kislev, the day of his miraculous salvation when he crossed the Swiss border to freedom. He would bring out the special goblet he had in his possession which he had received as a gift from the refugees in the Ku D.P. camp in Switzerland where he served as *rav* right after the war.

| HARDAGA FAMILY |
"Righteous Among the Nations"

In the Land of Israel, there lives a Jewish woman today by the name of Sarah Pecanac. She came to Israel in 1994 together with her mother, and lives in Jerusalem with her beautiful family. She even worked for a while in the museum at Yad Vashem. Her daughter, Esther, was an officer in the Israeli Air Force. What is remarkable about Sarah is that she is a convert to Judaism and that she was once an observant Muslim. The story of how this all came about is truly startling.

In April 1941, the German Wehrmacht invaded the defenseless country of Yugoslavia. Sarajevo, the capital, was bombed into submission from the air. The home of a Jewish family by the name of Kavilio was destroyed and they were forced to flee to the hills. As they were walking to seek refuge at the family factory, they met Mustafa Hardaga, a Muslim friend who was the owner of the factory building. He immediately offered them to stay at his house.

The Hardagas were religious Muslims; yet, they were friendly and kind to their Jewish neighbors and, when they heard the plight of the Kavilio family, they reached out. "You are our brothers. Our home is your home," they said. To demonstrate this point, the women were not even obliged to cover their faces in the presence of Yosef Kavilio - a basic Muslim requirement - since he was now a member of the family.

The Kavilio family stayed with the Hardagas for a short while until Yosef Kavilio was able to move his wife and children into an area under Italian control, where Jews were relatively safe. Yosef himself stayed behind to liquidate his business but before he could make his escape, he was found and imprisoned by the Ustasa, the puppet government that carried out the bidding of the Nazi S.S. He was taken to the local prison house where he was kept under constant surveillance.

Undeterred by the danger, Zejneba Hardaga, Mustafa's wife, began visiting him every day, bringing food and clothing for him and other prisoners. After a few weeks, though, she felt she needed to do more. Taking a huge risk, she went directly to the Gestapo chief in Sarajevo and pleaded for Yosef Kavilio's release. He was obviously very surprised that a Muslim woman would risk so much to save the life of a Jew. It took a generous bribe, but in the end, she obtained Yosef's freedom and he escaped safely to Italy in 1943.

The Kavilios eventually made it back safely to Sarajevo after the war and Zejneba gave them back the jewels they had left with her. They embarked on a ship going to Israel, where they started a new life, but never forgot their Muslim friends and how they helped them during those terrible years of the Holocaust. In 1984, the Kavilios petitioned for Yad Vashem to recognize the Hardaga family as "Righteous

Among the Nations." A year later, Zejneba Hardaga came to Israel to accept the honor, plant a tree in her family's name and be recognized as the first Muslim ever to hold that title.

Obviously, she had no idea that a few years later, the irony of history would indeed come full circle to save her own family's life. In 1992, while Yugoslavia was in the midst of a bloody civil war between Croats and Serb nationalists, Zejneba's family was in mortal danger due to the numerous bombings and attacks in their Sarajevo neighborhood. Yosef Kavilio's children worked tirelessly to save their saviors. They obtained special authorization, directly from Israeli Prime Minister Yitzchak Rabin, to bring the entire Hardaga family to Israel, along with the last few members of the Jewish community of Sarajevo. In February 1994, Zejneba, her daughter, son-in-law and grandchild, arrived in Israel and were welcomed by Israeli government officials, representatives of Yad Vashem and the Kavilios. The Hardagas had sheltered a Jewish family during the darkest period in Jewish history, and it was now time for the Kavilios and the Land of Israel to pay back the debt and help the Hardagas in their time of distress.

Zejneba's daughter, Aida, received a revelation upon entering Jerusalem. "It is only natural that I should want to become Jewish. It is an honor for me to belong to these people," she explained. She then converted to Judaism and was renamed Sarah. She proclaimed that, until her death in October 1994, her mother Zejneba was very supportive of her decision to become Jewish.

R' AHARON DAVIDS

Eating Bread *L'shem Shamayim*

In the spring of 1944, shortly before Pesach, the entire Jewish community of Rotterdam, Netherlands – men, women, and children – was transferred from Westerbork, a deportation camp in Holland, to the Bergen-Belsen concentration camp in Germany. Conditions in Westerbork had been harsh, but continued religious observance had somewhat preserved the Jews' dignity and their will to live. Under the guidance of their spiritual leader, the revered Torah scholar and Chief Rabbi of Rotterdam, R' Aharon Davids *zt"l*, some semblance of communal cohesiveness and optimism had been sustained. Upon arrival at Bergen-Belsen, however, daily existence took a sudden, overwhelmingly drastic turn for the worse, as most of the things that make a human being feel human were taken away from these unfortunate souls. Families were divided, people starved, the absurdly hard labor broke body and soul, and disease was spreading fast.

As for the upcoming Pesach holiday, matzah was, of course, unavailable.

R' Davids, whose wife and three children had been separated from him upon arrival in the camp, yearned to keep the spirit of his flock alive, even as their physical strength ebbed. Yet under such circumstances, refraining from eating *chametz* (leavened bread) would surely bring on illness and death for an untold number of Jews. What should be done during the week of Pesach with their small daily rations of bread?

He conferred with other rabbinical authorities in the camp, and after anguished and lengthy discussions about this complex and most serious dilemma, a course of action was finally agreed upon.

On the eve of the fifteenth of Nissan, the night of the Pesach Seder, R' Davids took his place at the head of a long table in the male barracks, conducting the Seder ceremony, not from a Haggadah – there was none, of course – but from memory. When he reached the blessing, "Who has sanctified us by His commandments and commanded us to eat matzah..." he lifted up his voice and clearly recited the following prayer, as later translated into English by Professor Harold Fisch:

"*Avinu Shebashamayim*, Heavenly Father, it is manifest and known to You that we desire to carry out Your will in regard to the commandment of eating matzah, and strictly refraining from *chametz* on the festival of Pesach. But we are sick at heart at being prevented from this by reason of the oppression and mortal danger in which we find ourselves. We stand ready to perform Your commandments, of which it is said, *You shall do them and live by them* (*Vayikra* 18:5); that is to say, you shall live by them and not die by them. And accordingly, we heed Your warning, as it is written, *Take heed to thyself and keep thy soul alive* (*Devarim* 4:9). Therefore, we beseech You that You will keep us in life and establish us and redeem us speedily from our servitude so that we may in time come to perform Your statutes and carry out Your will with a perfect heart. Amen."

He then reached for a piece of bread and took a bite, thereby urging his brethren to do likewise. And they all did. During the Seder, as well as throughout the rest of the holiday of Pesach, the people ate bread with sincerity – *l'shem Shamayim* (for the sake of Heaven) – as if they were eating matzah.

R' Davids, along with his son Eliyahu, died shortly before the liberation of Bergen-Belsen by the Allied forces, while his wife and daughters, along with approximately 2,800 others,

לִפְנֵי אֲכִילַת חָמֵץ יֹאמַר בְּכַוָּנַת הַלֵּב:
אָבִינוּ שֶׁבַּשָּׁמַיִם הִנֵּה גָלוּי וְיָדוּעַ לְפָנֶיךָ שֶׁרְצוֹנֵנוּ לַעֲשׂוֹת רְצוֹנְךָ וְלַחֹג אֶת חַג הַפֶּסַח בַּאֲכִילַת מַצָּה וּבִשְׁמִירַת אִסּוּר חָמֵץ. אַךְ עַל זֹאת דַּאֲבָה לִבֵּנוּ שֶׁהַשִּׁעְבּוּד מְעַכֵּב אוֹתָנוּ וַאֲנַחְנוּ נִמְצָאִים בְּסַכָּנַת נְפָשׁוֹת. הִנְנוּ מוּכָנִים וּמְזֻמָּנִים לְקַיֵּם מִצְוָתְךָ וְחַי בָּהֶם וְלֹא שֶׁיָּמוּת בָּהֶם, וְלִזָּהֵר מֵעֲשֵׂה הִשָּׁמֶר לְךָ וּשְׁמוֹר נַפְשְׁךָ מְאֹד. עַל כֵּן תְּפִלָּתֵנוּ לְךָ שֶׁתְּחַיֵּינוּ וּתְקַיְּמֵנוּ וְתִגְאָלֵנוּ בִּמְהֵרָה לִשְׁמוֹר חֻקֶּיךָ וְלַעֲשׂוֹת רְצוֹנְךָ וּלְעָבְדְךָ בְּלֵבָב שָׁלֵם. אָמֵן.

The tefillah R' Aharon Davids composed in the camp

were forcibly evacuated by train from the camp. During the two-week journey to nowhere, 570 people died and were buried in a mass grave somewhere along the way. Those who survived the trip were abandoned by the Nazis near the East German village of Troebits and were eventually liberated by the Russians.

In 1947, R' David's wife and daughters immigrated to the Land of Israel, taking with them a copy of the prayer that their husband and father had composed. His wife Erika died in a Hertzliya nursing home in 1997.

Each year, the family and his descendants read the prayer aloud on the Seder night, to hear again how R' Davids asked for Divine assistance, beseeching a shattered people to do the unthinkable – to "live by them" – not die by them.

| R' YITZCHAK AVIGDOR |

Two Rocks Out of One

This is one episode that lasted only a few minutes, with a miracle that required a split second. It happened in the month of Av, 1944, the day after nearly ten thousand Jews were transported from the Plaszow concentration camp in Poland to Mauthausen. The unfortunate Jews traveled six long days in sealed cattle cars, and were given a daily ration of water and a piece of bread.

Mauthausen was located high in the Tyrolean mountains of Austria. There, the Germans had built huge factories for the manufacture of Messerschmidt aircraft and other war material. In order to make the factories as safe as possible against Allied bombing, they were built in long tunnels deep inside the high mountains.

On the day of the episode, a group of Jews was assigned to dig a new tunnel. It was an extremely hot day and they were exhausted from the six-day journey in the sealed cattle cars. Under a heavy guard of S.S. men, nearly five hundred of them were led off to the site of the new tunnel. They were called the Quarry Detail, the Steinbruch Kommando.

The work got underway and proceeded with the famous German order and discipline. First the German experts would install the dynamite and blast a deep hole. Then the prisoners were driven into the crater and ordered to clear out the rubble. The sand was carried out on wheelbarrows or dumped on an electrically operated rubber conveyor belt. Rocks were removed by a different method. The orders were that each prisoner had to lift one big rock or two small ones, and carry them out to a spot where they were to be rolled down the mountain into a deep valley. First the rock-carrying prisoner had to report to a German overseer who made sure that the rock was big enough. If the German was not satisfied with the Jew or with the rock he was carrying, he would send him back into the tunnel, sometimes with the crack of a whip across the shoulders, to get a second rock to carry. Usually, the big rocks were on top of the pile of rubble after each explosion.

Veterans of the Quarry Detail, who knew the system, would leap into the tunnel before the dust of the explosion had settled, grab hold of a rock and quickly line up and be ready for the German overseer's order to march out to the dumping site. The Germans carefully inspected every Jew to make sure that no one was trying to put something over on them by taking a rock that was too small.

Yitzchak Avigdor, the son of R' Yaakov Avigdor, Chief Rabbi of Drohobycz, was not yet experienced in Quarry Detail, and by the time he got into the crater to pick up a rock, there were only huge boulders left, which could hardly be budged by a strong and healthy individual; the others had beaten him to the medium-sized rocks. A few long minutes passed, and he still hadn't found a rock he could lift. He was the only member of the detail who hadn't yet lifted a rock and all the others were already lined up and waiting for the order to march off and be escorted by the armed Germans.

It was inevitable. "Get moving, you lazy Jew; they're all waiting for you," an S.S. man rasped at Yitzchak. It sounded like the devil himself speaking, the way his words reverberated inside the tunnel and through the high mountains. Frightened, Yitzchak seized a rock, lifted it with great difficulty, and finally crawled out of the tunnel and got into line. First he carried the rock with both hands. Then he put it on his right shoulder, then on his left shoulder, and so on, back and forth until he saw the blood start trickling down his shoulders where the rock was eating into his flesh. The blood and sweat ran down his body, and the German who was keeping an eye on him relished the sight. Thus, Yitzchak had no choice but to keep on walking at the tail end of the formation, feeling the strength draining from his already weakened body. At that precise moment, he knew he would never make it to the dumping site.

Usually, those who lagged behind were either shot or shoved down the mountainside, with a report being given that they had slipped and fallen through their own clumsiness. In this horrific manner, thousands of Jews perished on the Quarry Detail, assignment to which meant a 90 percent chance of early death.

The minutes seemed like years. Yitzchak felt himself losing the will and the hope to carry the rock to the destination. He was about to collapse, but at this point he really didn't care anymore: "Let them shoot me, or throw me off the mountain," he thought helplessly. "All I want to do is let the rock drop to the ground."

And then - the miracle happened. The huge boulder slipped from his grasp, hit the ground, and split in two. Quickly, unnoticed by anyone - prisoner or overseer alike - he picked up one of the pieces and, with new resolve, resumed marching. Half the weight allowed him to have double the strength! There may have been a natural crack in the rock that caused it to split the moment it received a blow. Nonetheless, a threefold miracle happened to Yitzchak Avigdor on that day: the rock split in two pieces, he had enough presence of mind to realize and take advantage of the opportunity, and most amazing of all - no one noticed.

At that moment, Yitzchak would later relate, he recalled the story of the Patriarch Yaakov and how, when he was wandering alone in exile, twelve individual stones grouped themselves together into one stone - just for him. In this case, Hashem caused one rock to split into two. Apparently, Providence had decided that he was to go on living.

R' Yisroel Meir Lau and Chazzan Yossel Mandelbaum

After being brutally torn away from his mother on the train platform in Piotrokow, young Yisroel Meir Lau and his older brother Naphtali were transferred by cattle car to Czestochowa, where they arrived on Friday, November 26, 1944. They had arrived at a factory which had been converted into a labor camp, a diabolical place known as Hassag. The Nazis sent them to one of the miserable camp barracks. They were just two brothers, alone in the world - the world around them had come crashing down in sheets of overwhelming grief. Naphtali, the older brother, had sworn a vow to their mother to protect Lulek (Yisroel Meir), taking upon himself a mission that was to prove incredibly difficult in that horrifying place. As they lay down in what was to be their new residence, Naphtali spread a wool blanket on the ground and lay his younger brother on it. Lulek cried bitter tears, missing his mother dearly.

That first night in Czestochowa was a Friday night, the eve of Shabbos. As Naphtali lay down beside Lulek, a familiar tune from far-off days reached their ears from the end of the barracks. Cantor Yosef Mandelbaum was singing the words "*Mikdash Melech*" from *Lecha Dodi*, the traditional song for welcoming the Shabbos on Friday evenings. The tune, a distant reminder of home, allowed Lulek to forget the events of the last few days and lulled him to sleep.

Naphtali, however, could not sleep. Upon hearing the melody, he recalled this song from Krakow, the city of his birth. The memory of his childhood permeated the atmosphere, filling him with emotion, a vestige of vastly distant times. As a child, Naphtali had gone many times to visit his mother's cousin, the revered Admor of Bobov, R' Benzion Halberstam *Hy"d*, a descendant of the Sanz dynasty, who died during the Holocaust. Yossel Mandelbaum, a Bobover Chassid, was the *chazzan* of Krakow and a world-renowned cantor.

Naphtali crawled over the ground toward the singing voice. Yes, it was really Yossel Mandelbaum, encircled by Chassidim. He saw not a trace of Mandelbaum's impressive beard, nor his imposing *shtreimel* and *gartel*, two of the symbols of Chassidic prayer. Except for the hint of a mustache, Mandelbaum and all those surrounding him were clean-shaven. Only the cantor's marvelous voice remained, unmistakable and unique.

Naphtali sat down among the Chassidim and introduced himself as the son of Rabbi Lau of Piotrokow. They all knew his father and his family, as well as his mother and her family. Indeed, they knew the entire Lau family genealogy better than Naphtali did. They smothered him with warmth and love that night, offering a ray of light within the darkness they inhabited.

Yossel Mandelbaum also remembered the Jewish holidays in Hassag. One December eve, he lit the first of the Chanukah candles, fashioning an oil lamp from an empty bullet casing. He led a rousing version of *Ma'oz Tzur* ("Rock of Ages") inside the barracks, and all those in attendance shared baked potatoes. For the first time, the hungry and hardened Jewish prisoners tucked away in a cold and heartless labor camp actually felt as if they belonged somewhere, a part of something. They were among close friends, like the friends they had known and cherished in better times.

But Yossel reserved a special place in his heart for Lulek and Tulek (Naphtali) Lau. As Naphtali would later tell his younger brother, Yossel Mandelbaum saw in the two Lau boys a reflection of his own sons, who were killed along with their mother. Yossel took them under his wing, speaking to them and comforting them in their suffering during those first days of orphanhood. They loved and trusted Yossel and knew he would take care of them as best as he could. However, in January 1945, the Nazis sent Yossel Mandelbaum and a number of his fellow Chassidim who had come with him from Krakow, to a camp in Germany, and the Lau brothers lost contact with him.

(Before they left, Naphtali gave Yossel Mandelbaum a souvenir: a *Chumash* that had belonged to their uncle, Rabbi Mordechai Vogelman. Later, when Naphtali and Yisroel Meir were transferred to Buchenwald, they arrived in the camp and were ordered to throw all of their meager possessions into a pile for burning. Naphtali looked at the pile and saw his uncle's *Chumash* – the same one he had given to Yossel Mandelbaum – poking out from among the heap. They knew right then and there that Yossel had arrived before them, but they never actually saw him in the concentration camp and they assumed that, like most of those who arrived there, he was immediately sent to his death.)

Forty years later, Naphtali Lau served as Israel's consul general in New York. For a family event, he went to Brooklyn, to the grand *beis medrash* (study hall) of the Admor of Bobov, R' Shloime Halberstam *zt"l*, son of R' Benzion, who had likewise survived the war. The Bobover Rebbe treated Naphtali with the utmost respect, seating him to his right, to the great surprise of the crowd of Chassidim. Naphtali didn't look like a Chassid, and most of them were unaware of the family relationship between the *admor* and Naphtali. They attributed R' Shloime's warm hospitality to his respect for the official representative of the State of Israel.

During the evening, the rebbe and Naphtali conversed off and on, and Naphtali told him about Yossel Mandelbaum, who had sung those fateful words from *Lecha Dodi* - "Too long have you dwelled in the valley of weeping, He will shower compassion upon you" - on that first Shabbos night in Czestochowa, thus unwittingly making a valuable contribution to his and his brother Lulek's spiritual lives.

"Chazzan Mandelbaum brought us back to the bosom of family despite the threatening conditions at the camp," intoned Naphtali with the glint of a warm memory etched in his eyes. "What a pity that we lost track of him in Buchenwald," Naphtali lamented.

R' Shloime nodded compassionately and then quietly whispered something in the ear of one of his *gabba'im* (attendants). A few minutes later, the *gabbai* reappeared, holding the arm of a tiny, stooped-over Chassid with an impressive white beard. The old man walked up and stood respectfully next to the Bobover Rebbe. R' Shloime waited expectantly, but Naphtali had no idea who this man was.

Suddenly, R' Shloime called out, "Here is Yossel Mandelbaum!" Naphtali was overwhelmed and stunned into silence. The rebbe then asked the elderly Chassid, who was more than eighty years old, to sing that same tune for *"Mikdash Melech"* from *Lecha Dodi*. Naphtali listened, astounded. Despite the forty years that had passed and his diminished height, Yossel Mandelbaum's voice had not changed, and remained as clear and strong as it was then.

As Yossel sang the phrase "Arise and depart from amid the upheaval," Naphtali no longer saw the Chassidim of the Bobover Rebbe in Brooklyn, but the miserable wretches who sat on the cold, damp ground of the barracks in Czestochowa that Shabbos eve in late November 1944.

| A TASTE OF FREEDOM |
Sinking One's Teeth into It

The Nazi occupation of Salonika, Greece began in 1941, and with it the persecution of Jews, as it had in other parts of Europe. In 1943, the Jews of Thessaloniki were forced into a ghetto near the rail lines, and soon after, the Nazis began deporting them to concentration and labor camps, where most of the sixty thousand deported men, women and children died. This resulted in the near-extermination of the entire community.

Yakob Masito was among the tens of thousands of deportees to Auschwitz. In the spring of 1943, he found himself herded into a cattle car together with his entire family and shipped away to a distant location. Fortunately, he was part of the small percentage of Greek Jews who were spared immediate death.

The prisoners who greeted them upon their arrival in Auschwitz seemed dispirited and despondent. As far as they were concerned, all hope was lost. They had seen too much death and destruction in the camps to believe that there was any hope for the future. The new arrivals from Greece, however, had an unusual advantage over the others which kept them in good stead; due to their unfamiliarity with Yiddish, Jews from Greece kept to themselves. As a result, the pervasive feeling of death and despondency that overtook the prisoners from Europe who had already experienced the worst that humankind had to offer, was not in place. For the newly arriving Jews of Greece, the taste of freedom was still tantalizingly fresh. For Yakob Masito and his friends who were sent to the right – to life in the camp – their sense of hopefulness was prevalent, and they refused to give in.

Upon arrival, every inmate received two utensils – a bowl and a spoon. These two utensils were vital for survival. No utensils, no food. As it was, it was nearly impossible to complete the inhumane tasks their captors demanded of them on their meager daily ration. If a prisoner had no utensils to eat with, he was finished.

So, Yakob Masito accepted the bowl and spoon he was given and guarded them well. But in truth, Yakob was less worried about what he would eat that very day or the next and the next after that. What he was most worried about was the upcoming holiday, and specifically, how and where he and his friends would obtain matzos for Pesach.

Although the other Greek Jews may not have been as concerned, Yakob was obsessed with this problem. He schemed and pondered, but a solution eluded him. Until an incident occurred and the problem was solved.

Yakob and several of his friends were assigned to work on the railroad line. It was arduous, backbreaking labor. Occasionally, Yakob and his friends were able to make contact with the local populace. It was during one of these rare times that he got lucky. After describing to the Polish farmer what he needed, the Pole understood and agreed to procure two matzos for him – but for a price.

"Yakob, where are we going to get the money?" one of his friends moaned.

Yakob was silent for a long time as the group of men returned to their work. His mind continued to mull over the possibilities. They were so close to having matzos; surely there was a way.

And then, as if touched by a Divine light of inspiration, he had a brainstorm. "I have it!" he shouted.

As the group watched, curious to see what plan he would come up with, Yakob extracted his spoon from his pouch and held it up for everyone to see.

"A spoon?" the others laughed. "The Pole is not going to trade matzah for a little spoon!"

"No, no," said Yakob, smiling, "just watch."

The men stared as Yakob placed his precious spoon, his life's support, on the railroad tracks next to him. Then, he waited. It wasn't long before a train roared by, flattening the spoon into a long pointy tool.

"And now," Yakob announced with a wide grin, "we use this to pry out our gold teeth!" Yakob held the elongated utensil as it glinted in the sun.

Slowly, painfully, Yakob pried and prodded until he had extracted all of his gold teeth. His friends quickly followed suit. When they put together a considerable amount of gold, they offered this unusual currency to the Pole, and he happily accepted their payment for the two round matzos. That year, on the night of Pesach, Yakob and his friends made Kiddush and fulfilled the mitzvah that they came to with such determination.

Many years later, at Yakob Masito's eighty-first birthday party, he told over this story. All the guests sat in openmouthed wonder at the devotion and sacrifice of Yakob and his friends. "We didn't have enough matzah for everyone to have the correct amount," Yakob said, harking back to that dark period of time, "but at least we all had a little taste of freedom."

There are those who "break their teeth" on a minimal amount of matzah each year, complaining about the difficulty in eating the bread of freedom. Yet Yakob Masito literally "broke his teeth" just to eat a small piece of matzah on Pesach.

| R' YEHOSHUA MOSHE ARONSON |
To Eat or Not to Eat

The deportation of Hungarian Jewry began on April 29, 1944. The first transports to Auschwitz began in early May and continued incessantly even as Soviet troops approached from the east. By July 9, 1944, an astonishing 437,402 Jews had been deported and most had been sent directly to their deaths.

In Auschwitz III (Buna-Auschwitz), R' Yehoshua Moshe Aronson *zt"l* was one of the old-timers, having been deported from Poland years earlier and forced to experience numerous slave labor camps. When the shipments of Hungarian Jews began arriving in mid-1944, he was surprised to learn that the derogatory term "Magyars" that the Polish prisoners used to describe the Hungarians was a total distortion of the truth. These Jews of Hungary - pious and G-d-fearing Jews (among them quite a few prolific Torah sages) - were his flesh and blood. They were Jews like him who trembled for the word of G-d and valued Torah and *mitzvos* above all else. The most exceptional thing about the Hungarian Jews, however, was their simplistic naivete. R' Yehoshua Moshe was a hardened concentration camp prisoner and he knew what it meant to live and survive under the Nazi boot. But these Hungarian Jews, they knew nothing; they believed what the Germans told them and they followed orders. Indeed, their simplistic naivete was strange to behold.

Upon the arrival of one prisoner at Auschwitz, all could see that he was a great sage. His name was R' Yisroel Ephraim Fishel Roth, the *rav* and *dayan* of Vajdasca, and he had been sent to Auschwitz together with his two young sons. R' Yehoshua Moshe befriended him and the two would speak for hours in matters of Torah and halachah (Jewish law), in which the newcomer was very well-versed. However, no matter how much they spoke, the Hungarian *rav* could not be convinced that he was in a death camp; that Jews were brought to Auschwitz to be gassed and cremated. The simple rabbi of Vajdasca believed, like many of the Hungarian Jews, that he was in some kind of "health" camp, a place of rehabilitation, as the Germans had informed them earlier. No matter of persuasion on R' Yehoshua Moshe's part could convince him that these were falsehoods, elaborate German schemes, and nothing more. He refused to believe the truth and did not put credence into the veteran rabbi's words.

One night, the Vajdasca Rav came into the barracks, swollen, his entire body beaten and sore. He could barely walk and he whispered to R' Yehoshua Moshe that his strength was waning and that he would not survive much longer. Just then, the *kapo* of the engineering squad entered the barracks. He was a young, former Chassid and yeshivah student and he had a good heart. The engineering squad was one of Auschwitz's "good" assignments. Eighteen men worked there, doing specialized work for the S.S. Only intelligent men, knowledgeable in engineering, could work there. Additionally, the members of this squad received extra food rations.

R' Yehoshua Moshe told the *kapo* of the terrible plight of Rabbi Roth, the Hungarian scholar, who was working in one of the hardest squads, breaking stones, and that at this rate, he wouldn't survive long – a couple of days at best. "Isn't it possible," asked R' Yehoshua Moshe earnestly, taking a page out of the Purim megillah story and the words of the sage Mordechai, "that you only merited to be appointed to this position in order to help this Jew? And it is not just one Jew you will save, but three, since you will be saving his two sons."

The Jewish *kapo* hesitated. A long moment passed before he said, "Okay, I can take the risk. Tomorrow, the rabbi will join my engineering squad."

Within a few days, the rabbi of Vajdasca began to recover. He became healthier with each passing day. Additionally, his sons, sustained by the extra rations, recuperated as well.

But then, one evening, after a day of grueling labor, R' Yehoshua Moshe was told that the *kapo* wanted to see him. What was so urgent? He wanted Rabbi Aronson to preside over a *din Torah* (rabbinic court case) that he was bringing against Rabbi Roth!

"For what purpose," asked the *kapo* in great anger, "did I assume on myself an enormous risk to move Rabbi Roth from the rock squad to my commando? Why did I put myself in such great danger? So that in the World to Come I could come and say, 'I saved a soul in Israel! I saved a rabbi and a Torah giant!' And what did our rabbi do? From the time he joined the engineering squad, he avoided eating the S.S. soup because it was not kosher. He subsists only on dry bread. He does not want to eat *treif* food. Yet if he does not eat this food, he will soon die. So why did I take this great risk? I took a simple prisoner and masqueraded him as an engineer! I didn't do this so that he might die of starvation! If the rabbi does not meet me at a *din Torah*, tomorrow morning I will return him to the stone quarry."

R' Yehoshua Moshe tried to convince the *kapo* to let the issue ride. A *din Torah* in the death factory of Auschwitz seemed absurd. But the *kapo* would not back down: either there would be a *din Torah* or the quarry squad.

So, early the next morning, a *din Torah* was conducted in the barracks at Buna-Auschwitz. The *kapo* presented his case: he risked his life to save a Torah giant, a living Jew, one with the ability to stay alive and disseminate Torah in Israel. And what does the rabbi do? He refuses to eat the food he is given; he would rather starve himself to death.

Now it was the turn of the rabbi of Vajdasca to respond to the charges. He spoke succinctly, short and to the point. He greatly appreciated the sacrifice that the *kapo* had done for him; however, now that he was not doing backbreaking labor and undergoing beatings on a daily basis, he felt as if he was no longer in danger and his health had improved quite considerably. The little kosher food he could find would suffice for him. He had a little bread (half a kilo a day) and so he had no need to eat the nonkosher food that the engineers received. He hoped that the *kapo* and the other rabbis would understand how important it was that he kept to his strict kosher diet.

The debate raged, as neither side wished to relent to the other. It took quite a bit of haggling until R' Yehoshua Moshe succeeded in convincing them to accept a compromise: the rabbi would eat the nonkosher soup at the first sign that his health was once again failing. The *kapo* would keep him in the engineering squad but would closely monitor his health. The *kapo* wasn't particularly happy with the decision, but he finally acquiesced.

With G-d's help, Rabbi Roth never did eat the nonkosher fare. He survived Auschwitz, but he collapsed and died on the second day of the death march. His two sons survived.

| BADISCHLE RAV |

A Father's Prophecy

One of the great *rabbanim* of prewar Hungarian Jewry was the Kapashnover Rav, R' Yochanan Hirsch *Hy"d*. He was a massive Torah scholar as well as a *dayan*, a halachic arbiter, and he served his community of Kapashnov devotedly. But he was most renowned for his humility. It was said about him (by none other than R' Yosef Tzvi Dushinsky *zt"l*, head of the Eidah Chareidis in Jerusalem) that were it not for R' Yochanan's intense humility, he would surely have been recognized the world over as one of the leading halachic authorities. His son, R' Yisroel Chaim *zt"l*, followed in his father's footsteps and became known at a very young age as the Badischle Rav.

In the spring of 1944, as the majority of Hungarian Jewry was being rounded up and deported to Auschwitz, both father and son – the Kapashnover Rav and Badischle Rav – and their families were stuffed into cattle cars and sent to Auschwitz-Birkenau. When the trains stopped, they were told to leave all their belongings on board and were forced to disembark from the train and gather upon the railway platform, known as "the ramp."

The ramp is where history's saddest, most unmerciful, and bloodiest tribunals would take place. Millions were given the death penalty there and not one sentence was ever commuted. The horrific judge, that slender Nazi officer with a slight smile, who waited with remarkable patience until everybody dragged his body off the train, was already preparing the judgment, death by a slight hand movement. He waved to the left and to the right. Whomever he sent to the left died within the hour; the rest he sentenced to death by starvation, slave labor and exacerbated cruelties. Nobody in this world ever rampaged with such a quiet, polite, almost pleasant demeanor as this officer.

It was there, on that fateful platform, that R' Yisroel Chaim was torn away from his father, his mother and the rest of his family. It was there, amidst the din and tumult of the rampaging S.S. guards and their barking menacing dogs, that R' Yisroel Chaim heard his father speak for the last time. As men and women were being forcibly separated and families brutally torn apart, his mother began yelling in a hysterical voice, "How can this be? No, no, no... It cannot be. I worked so hard - I put so much effort into this child of mine! How can he be lost in Auschwitz?"

R' Yochanan attempted to calm her down; her hysterical cries were attracting unwarranted attention from the Nazi guards and their truncheon-wielding cohorts. "Mama," he said, "this is a decree from Heaven and we must accept it."

But she refused to calm down and continued screaming over and over again, "What will be with my son? How can he be lost to this hideous place?"

R' Yisroel Chaim writes in his memoirs (the *hakdamah* of *Ohr V'Chaim L'Yisroel*) that the next words out of his father's mouth were truly prophetic. "Mama," he told her in a calming, soothing tone, "stop crying. All will be well with Yisroel Chaim. I see him now, standing there with three young children surrounding him. What more do you want?"

He never saw his parents again. They were taken directly to the gas chambers where their holy and pure lives came to an end. R' Yisroel Chaim, however, survived. He underwent the horrors of Auschwitz - the starvation, the torture, the cruelty; he was once beaten into unconsciousness and lost his hearing as a result of the terrible blows. But he survived. In particular, he was highly vigilant with respect to anything that passed his lips, notwithstanding the starvation prevalent in the camp.

R' Yisroel Chaim lost his entire family in the war, but, like many of his heroic generation, he remarried and rebuilt his life, raising a family with three wonderful sons. Later, tragedy struck him as his oldest son, Yochanan, died before his time – at the young age of thirteen, However, in true fulfillment of his father's vision, within a few short months his wife gave birth to another son. Indeed, R' Yisroel Chaim could practically hear his father's final words, "All will be well with Yisroel Chaim. I see him now, standing there with three young children at his side. What more do you want?"

| VEITZENER RAV |
Tzitzis Are "G-d's Clothing"

To hide one's personal possessions in the Auschwitz death camp was nearly impossible. As soon as an inmate was brought into the camp, he was stripped of everything he owned. Those who were sent off to the barracks of the slave labor camps were given a flimsy prison uniform, a pair of wooden clogs, a piece of bread – and nothing else.

The *tallis* of the holy Sigheter Rebbe, the Yetev Lev, was the prized possession of R' Tzvi Hirsch Meisels *zt"l*, an *einekel* (grandson) of the rebbe, later to be known as the Veitzener Rav. When the Nazis forcibly removed him and his family from their home, his first thought was to take this *tallis* and keep it with him at all times. This would be his *shemirah* – his protective amulet – that would allow him to make it through the hardships of the Second World War.

Alas, it was not to be. The moment he entered the confines of Auschwitz, he was stripped of his family, his clothing, and his very identity. His prized *tallis* was taken as well, which added insult to injury and caused him an untold amount of extra grief. It was not until later, when R' Tzvi Hirsch was taken to the slave labor division, that he learned the location of the barracks where the Nazis kept all the stolen artifacts, and after a great deal of searching, he found his grandfather's *tallis*.

R' Tzvi Hirsch was ecstatic. The first thing he did was remove the silver *atarah* – the strip of silver sewn into the top of the *tallis*. Then he shortened the long garment down to the size of a small *tallis katan*, which he slipped over his head, carefully hiding it under his prison uniform. His heart soared with hope and he truly believed that he, together with his son Zalman Leib, would survive the war in the protective merit of the holy *tallis* of his ancestor.

Indeed, on more than one occasion, he was accosted by various S.S. guards and *kapos*, and he was even beaten once on account of his unique *tallis katan*. But he held onto it – literally for dear life – and when he was asked by German and Jew alike why it meant so much to him, he replied, "I am wearing 'G-t's *kleid*' (the clothing of G-d)." Miraculously, he kept this exceptional garment on his body throughout the war and no German *kapo* forced him to remove it.

It was not until ten days before the end of the war that R' Tzvi Hirsch's luck in keeping the *tallis* on his person ran out. There was one *kapo*, an especially malevolent villain named Willy, who took great pleasure in torturing those under his "care." As the war was drawing to a close and the bombs dropped by Allied warplanes could already be heard inside the camp, the Nazis herded all their prisoners onto cattle cars in order to transport them away from the advancing armies. The war might have been all but lost, but these villains would stop at nothing to finish the job of imprisoning, torturing and ultimately eradicating every Jew from their midst.

The Jews were ordered out of the barracks and onto the train tracks. But before they could run outside, every *kapo* was ordered to inspect his prisoners to see if they were actually worth transporting. During this hurried inspection, Willy, for the first time, detected a bulge under the prison garb of R' Tzvi Hirsch, and he pulled the material out from under his shirt. It took a moment to register, but when he realized that this prisoner had been wearing a Jewish religious article right under his nose, his rage boiled over. Amidst blows to R' Tzvi Hirsch's person, Willy began shouting like the madman that he was. Then he tore the *tallis* into bits and shreds with his bare hands and tossed the ragged material into a nearby burning fire.

R' Tzvi Hirsch stood in his place, unbelieving of what had just transpired and inconsolable over the loss of his precious keepsake. If not for his son Zalman Leib pulling him by the arm onto the train, R' Tzvi Hirsch would not have been able to move. His distress knew no bounds and he was so heartbroken that he believed he didn't have the strength to go on.

That night, as the prisoners huddled in the narrow cattle car, sleep was hard to come by. Tens of emaciated inmates were forced to stand or sit in place leaning against one another, while the evil Willy prepared himself a cozy makeshift bed in the middle of the car, and lay himself down to sleep. R' Tzvi Hirsch had stood mournfully in one place all afternoon, the loss of his most precious possession continually on his mind, his devastation near totally complete. By night, he had no more strength to stand up straight and he began resting his head on the shoulder of his son, while Zalman Leib stood in place.

At some point in the night, R' Tzvi Hirsch was nudged awake when Zalman Leib whispered loudly, "Please, Tatte, take your head off of me. I simply can't hold it up any longer!" Zalman Leib bent his body forward and his father – a bit surprised and slightly annoyed – was forced to pull his head back and off the shoulder of his son, thereby creating a bit of space between father and son.

Suddenly, the droning of Allied aircraft could be heard and the strafing began. The prisoners could do nothing but stand in place as chaos and mayhem surrounded them from the skies on all sides. At that very moment, a burst of artillery fire broke through the walls of the car and shot directly in the space where father and son had been huddling – head to shoulder – seconds earlier. And then, with an audible thud, two bullets pierced the two hands of the evil *kapo* Willy, the same two hands that had torn the precious *tallis katan* to shreds earlier that day.

He screamed in agonizing pain, but not one prisoner moved to help him. It was clear that Divine retribution came swiftly to the one who took such pleasure in destroying the cherished possessions of others.

| MOTELE'S REVENGE |
A Tale of the Youngest Partisan

By profession, he was an engineer and his real name was Misha Gildenman. But in the forests of Zhitomir, Soviet Ukraine, he was known as Dadia Misha (Uncle

Misha), the legendary commander of a detachment of Jewish partisans numbering in the hundreds. These Jewish partisans were fearless in their attacks on German army positions, and after the war, they were commended many times over for their bravery. One incident in particular stood out for the scope of its effectiveness and the little hero who made it all happen.

His name was Motele, a twelve-year-old boy who was not at home the day Germans and Ukrainians swept down on the village of Zhitomir and massacred his parents and little sister, Basha. Young Motele had no place to go, so he headed out to the woods, where exhaustion caught up to him and he fell asleep. He was found by Dadia Misha's partisans, and he soon became an active member of the group. Being a child, though, he did not partake in major activities against the enemy, but rather the clever, daring and alert boy was utilized for intelligence and espionage work.

One day in late summer, a Ukrainian contact brought news that a Greek Orthodox holiday, "Sfas," would be celebrated on August 20 and on that day one would be allowed to enter and leave the town of Ovrutch without the special permission usually required by German and Ukrainian police. This was important because Ovrutch was where the Soldiers' Home was located. The Soldiers' Home was a large restaurant and inn which the Germans had set up for their military forces, where they received the best food and the finest French wine. Since Ovrutch was a transit stop through which soldiers were often shipped to the front, it was a busy and usually packed building, where soldiers would eat, sleep and be entertained during their stay. All this was to raise the spirits of the soldiers on the way to the terrible eastern front, from which few returned alive and unwounded.

Dadia Misha decided to take advantage of this situation and that day sent out several partisans to familiarize themselves with the town, find out which institutions were functioning, which military units were stationed there and, generally, to assess the mood of the town. Together with the band of partisans, he sent along Motele. The least suspicious looking of the group, the boy was to observe the partisans from a distance, and inform Misha if anything happened to any of them.

Motele took along his violin in its wooden violin case and posed as a beggar playing in front of the church, collecting alms. A whole gallery of beggars and cripples, some standing, others squatting, tried to evoke sympathy from the holiday crowd in a variety of voices and gestures. Motele was the last in the row. He sat down, took out his violin, and placed between his legs a clay saucer he had bought in the market.

Motele had learned many Ukrainian songs from his violin teacher. Now he tuned up his violin and began to play a popular Ukrainian folk song, singing along in his pleasant voice. His young voice and violin playing set him apart from the rest of the beggars' chorus. A crowd began to gather around him and when he finished the song, peasants threw lead coins into his clay saucer and applauded.

Suddenly a commotion arose and people began to push back and make way for a German officer who had appeared in the crowd. The officer walked up to where Motele sat and stood there, listening to his singing and playing. Motele did not notice him at first. When the German touched Motele's shoulder with his riding crop the boy raised his head and, seeing the officer, rose to his feet and bowed.

"Come with me," the German commanded. Frightened, Motele put his violin back in the case, gathered up the coins in the saucer, and followed the officer. After passing several blocks, they came to a one-story building in front of which were parked many limousines and motorcycles. A German guard stood at the entrance. They went up one flight to a large bright hall where officers sat around tables eating, drinking, and talking loudly. In one corner of the hall stood a brown piano at which sat an elderly gray-haired man, wearing a black dress coat. The officer led Motele over to the man and said something to him.

The pianist selected a sheet of music and placed it before Motele, who tuned up his violin and began to play, with the man accompanying him at the piano. When they finished, there was a burst of applause. On the spot, Motele was offered the job of playing in the Soldiers' Home for two hours at lunchtime and from seven to eleven in the evening. For this he would receive two marks per day, plus lunch and dinner.

Of course, the German "offer" was more like a command, and with little choice, Motele had to agree to this proposal and remain in the Soldiers' Home. But Motele was smart and he realized the potential of his situation. He was literally "in the lion's den," where he could scout and keep an eye on the Germans and their movements in the region. Dadia Misha was cautiously pleased with the turn of events.

Motele played at the restaurant and memorized the numbers of units and the types of uniforms the Germans wore on the way to the front. He eavesdropped on conversations of those who had returned from the front. Between lunch and dinner he wandered around town, read the signs on government institutions, and noted the streets he was on, later relaying all this information to Dadia Misha through a discreet contact. The director of the Soldiers' Home was satisfied with the talented and modest young musician and even had a miniature German uniform and cap sewn especially for their little "Ukrainian" musician. A few days later Motele came into the Soldiers' Home dressed as a little soldier. The commandant and the other employees seemed highly pleased.

Motele ate lunch and dinner in the kitchen, which was located in the basement. On the way down from the first floor one had to pass through a dimly lit corridor. On its right were the kitchen and laundry, on its left some storage rooms. One afternoon when Motele came out of the kitchen, he noticed that the door to one of the storage rooms was open. Out of curiosity, he peered in and by the dim light from a small grated window, he saw a large cellar filled with empty wine cases, herring barrels, and other useless things scattered about in disorder. He noticed that the wall opposite the entrance was cracked, apparently by a bomb explosion nearby during a bombardment. It was a crooked crack, veering leftward.

Remembering the stories he had heard the partisans tell about their various sabotage acts, an idea flashed through his mind: If a bomb could be stuck in the crack of the wall, the explosion would destroy the Soldiers' Home together with the hated German officers. The idea gave him no rest, and every time he passed the corridor he peered into the basement and thought of such a sabotage act. He wasted no time and passed on his plan to Dadia Misha, who liked the idea and arranged for a precise amount of explosives – eighteen kilograms according to his calculations – to be smuggled into the town.

Motele secretly met with another partisan who taught him how to assemble the little blocks of that explosive and how to make a mine, how to insert the capsule detonator, and other necessary details. All this was not entirely unfamiliar to Motele, as he used to watch the partisans do it when he lived in the forest. The really difficult task was transporting the explosive material to the cellar of the Soldiers' Home, but

Motele found a way. In the evening, after dinner, when he said goodbye to the cook, he took his violin with him. He passed through the cellar door and hurried inside. Then he took the violin out of its case and put it inside an empty barrel and left the Soldiers' Home with the empty violin case.

On the second day, when he came to the Home at lunchtime to play, he hid three kilograms of the explosive in his violin case. Before he went up to the hall to play he first went, as always, to the kitchen for his lunch. He entered the cellar, took the explosives out of the violin case and put the violin back in. In several days he had thus transported all the eighteen kilograms of the explosive into the cellar.

Later, he used every opportunity to go down to the basement and remove some stones from the wall to enlarge the opening in which to place the bomb. He inserted the capsule with the long wick and camouflaged it. All that was left to do was to ignite the end of the wick and realize the act of revenge which was his dream. Everything was ready. Motele was merely awaiting the proper moment.

There was much excitement in the Soldiers' Home. High-ranking guests were expected. A division of the S.S. was on its way to the eastern front to rescue the situation and to encourage the disorganized German armies after the severe blows they had received in the area of Kursk.

One day, at about three o'clock in the afternoon, automobiles and motorcycles began to arrive in front of the Soldiers' Home. The rooms were filled with elegantly uniformed S.S. officers. They ate and drank. Above the din of clanking dishes, clinking glasses, and loud laughter, Motele's violin was heard to the piano's accompaniment. The officers amused themselves and sang. With few interruptions, Motele played throughout the afternoon and evening.

At eleven o'clock, Motele took a break and went down to the kitchen to have his dinner. He was too exhausted to eat and explained to the cook that because he had played for eight hours without a stop, he had no appetite. Soon afterward he said good night to the cook and left the kitchen. The corridor was dark. His hand groped for the cellar door and found it. He went inside and closed the door behind him. In the dark he found the end of the bomb wick and ignited it. Then he slipped out of the cellar and ran through the corridor.

Motele left the Soldiers' Home and quickly disappeared into the darkness. After running about two hundred yards, he heard a powerful explosion. The earth trembled and windowpanes shattered. Moments later he heard police whistles and sirens. Red rockets lit up the sky over the town. Both frightened and elated, Motele hugged the walls of buildings as he ran toward the lake. He entered the cold water which in some places reached his neck and held his violin above his head with both hands. He glanced back at the city and saw a big fire shooting up into the sky.

On the other side of the shore, at the foot of a small hill, a wagon waited for Motele. On it were five well-armed partisans. Ten hands reached out to hoist the boy into the wagon. With lightning speed the horses galloped away and disappeared into the nearest woods.

For the first few minutes Motele was speechless. Gradually, he calmed down and, raising his clenched fists to the red sky, said in a trembling voice, "This is for my parents and little Bashale."

| MINCHAS YITZCHAK |

Rescue and Salvation

As German troops occupied Hungary on March 19, 1944, the lives of Hungarian Jewry changed abruptly. Anti-Jewish laws, which had long been in place in German-occupied regions, were now being applied to Hungary's Jews. They were disenfranchised and herded together in ghettos. In the spring of 1944, two ghettos were established in the city of Grosswardein, not far from the city's center. About thirty thousand Jewish citizens, and some from nearby areas, were forced into the ghettos. Most endured the inhuman conditions; many were tortured; some committed suicide; and very few escaped.

The ghettos in Grosswardein were evacuated at the end of May 1944. The evacuation was organized and scheduled by sectors, and 2,500 to 3,000 people left the ghettos each day. Within weeks, the ghettos were emptied and all were forced aboard freight trains in the area of Balcescu Park, two or three thousand people a day, in a total of seven shipments. They were delivered to Auschwitz-Birkenau, where the vast majority met the fate of the six million European Jews lost in the war.

R' Yaakov Yitzchak Weiss *zt"l*, the *Av Beis Din* of Grosswardein before the war, was determined to avoid the deportations, and continuously moved himself and his family from bunker to bunker. Each time he thought he was safe, something or someone managed to sabotage his plans and usually, under cover of night, he would steal away to another hiding place.

As the last of the evacuations were taking place, the remnant of Jews hiding out was dwindling, as fewer and fewer hiding places were left undetected. On the day before Shavuos of 1944, a lady by the name of Mrs. Rothbart came to the *rav* with a halachic query. She happened to mention that her husband had a hiding spot that was virtually undetectable to the Germans, and she offered to bring the *rav* and his family to the site. Mr. Elchanan Rothbart was a wealthy businessman who owned a soap factory on Kapistran Street in Grosswardein, and, through a great deal of ingenuity, he had cleared out an area in the attic of one of his factory buildings. To the naked eye – and even to the prying eye – one could not tell that there was room enough for habitation, and it was to this spot that the Rothbarts brought their family. With the addition of R' Yaakov Yitzchak, his wife and their young son, a total of twenty-eight souls squeezed into the loft, and managed to remain undetected for close to seven weeks.

Rothbart's gentile partner, Mr. Offem Kolman, was at first startled to learn that his partner and a sizable group of family and friends were hiding out on the factory premises, and although he agreed to provide a limited supply of food and water to the fugitives, he never really embraced the idea of concealing them. He was too afraid of the consequences. This led to a constant strain and uneasiness on the part of R' Yaakov Yitzchak, who recognized that this loft was not a long-term solution.

In a stroke of good news, R' Yaakov Yitzchak learned that his brother-in-law, R' Aharon Zimmetboim, had escaped one of the transports and was currently holed up in Peliks, one of the towns that was situated on the border of Hungary and Romania. With the help of a Hungarian gentile by the name of Miklos, he was involved in helping Jews escape across the Romanian border to comparative safety. After making contact with Miklos, the Weiss family decided that their best option was to get to Peliks and eventually over the border to Romania.

Plans were set and Miklos arrived at the factory gates on the evening of July 13, 1944. He brought a car with him and when those in the loft spotted him standing at the side of the gate, Rebbetzin Weiss crawled out of the space and walked cautiously out to the gate to meet him. A minute later, R' Yaakov Yitzchak and his son walked quickly to the front gate and out onto the street. They looked both ways but to their chagrin, Miklos was not there. They stood there for a minute, looking to the right and to the left, but they couldn't find him. To compound matters, at that exact moment, a man walked by and began asking R' Yaakov Yitzchak for directions. He refused to speak lest he give away his Jewish accent, and his little son told the man they were sorry. But by now, they were totally confused – as well as totally exposed.

Grabbing the child by the hand, R' Yaakov Yitzchak turned to the right and began walking hurriedly, but as Providence would have it, they turned in the wrong direction and never did find Miklos's car. Not willing to stop even for a moment, father and son walked for over an hour, nearing total desperation, when R' Yaakov Yitzchak recognized the area and remembered that the well-known Goldring family lived nearby. Although the Goldring family was probably gone, taken away with the rest of Grosswardein's Jews in the Nazi "evacuation," the large and noble house did have a sizable cellar where they could hide just until alternative plans could be made.

They hurried to the house and were surprised to find that Mrs. Goldring was still living in her stately home. When they asked to be admitted to the cellar, she took them down the stairs where they were shocked to find a worried Rebbetzin Weiss, sitting by herself. Their joy was indescribable at the unlikely reunion, but when Miklos walked into the cellar a few hours later, he was furious, because the mishap had set them back quite some time. He had gone out to look for them and came back to report that he was unsuccessful. Somehow, the family had found each other, but now, at ten o'clock at night, Miklos refused to accompany them to Peliks and he insisted that they take a taxi by themselves. Thankfully, the taxi ride to Peliks went without a hitch, and they met up with a very worried Aharon Zimmetboim that very night.

| BOBOVER REBBE |

Survival of the Five Minzer Brothers (2)

On a rainy and dark August night in 1944, eighty-five Jewish prisoners of the Stalowa Wola *arbeitslager* escaped into the forests of southern Galicia, near the city of Rozwadov. Michael Minzer, one of five brothers present that fateful night, took the sledgehammer provided to him by a kindly Polish overseer and gave a mighty pound on a vulnerable section of the camp's wall. Amazingly, the thick wall made up of numerous wooden boards fell away and a large hole was created through which the eighty-five inmates burst forth and escaped. The German guards who had been sleeping in their guard towers began shooting at the fleeing prisoners but they missed in the dark. (One Minzer uncle, an older man over fifty years old, was too afraid to escape that night and he remained in the camp. The next day, the Germans liquidated anyone who was still there and sent them to Auschwitz.)

The group stayed together and ran through the night. Apparently, due to the disarray in the camp, the Germans did not chase after them, but they were not taking any chances. With superhuman strength, all eighty-five Jews ran until their strength gave out. Then, they dropped to the ground and hid among the forest trees and underbrush. They remained there for the next ten days, drinking water from a nearby stream and eating any vegetation that was deemed edible. They were lucky. Blackberries, pine firs and wild mushrooms were plentiful and the group did not starve. But the danger was ever present and they knew they could not continue on in this way indefinitely.

From time to time, it was necessary to cross over from one tree cropping into another. This required traversing a paved road, and the task was not as simple as it seemed. The constant hum of army vehicles heightened the danger. One did not know if they were German troops retreating or Russian troops advancing. Either way, it was in the Jews' best interest to stay clear of both armies and they would only cross the road at night and under the most guarded conditions.

The sound of gunfire and mortar shelling was constant. Obviously, the war front was getting closer to their position and although they understood that this signaled the Red Army's continuous push further and further into Poland, with the obvious repercussion of German defeat, they could not celebrate yet, or even let down their guard for a minute. Nearby explosions and bullets whizzing by nonstop precluded them from rest and only served to heighten the danger.

The oldest of the five Minzer brothers, Hertzka, decided that he needed to take matters into his own hands. The group needed information and they wanted some bread, so Hertzka set off on his own to the nearest town to try to obtain both. When he arrived, it was clear that this town was occupied. Russian soldiers, tanks and armored vehicles were everywhere and the local tavern was packed with Russian-speaking patrons.

Hertzka stood out. He didn't look like a local and he certainly wasn't a Russian soldier or civilian. Immediately, he was spotted and taken for what he was: a Jew. Suffice it to say, the crowd wasn't pleased to see him, and he was hauled into the tavern by a rowdy crew. Hertzka was frightened. This definitely did not bode well for his survival and he tried to protest – but nobody was listening. The Poles derided him and the Russians harassed him.

Before the situation could spiral any further out of control, a Russian commander at the bar stood up and faced the mob. While the others looked on in amazement, the fearless Russian spoke to Hertzka in Yiddish.

"What are you doing here?" he asked. "Don't you know how dangerous it is?"

Hertzka could barely get the words out. He explained how he and eighty-four other inmates had escaped from Stalowa Wola and were hiding in the forest. They were subsisting, for the time being, on berries and vegetation, but they couldn't go on much longer this way. They needed real food and security.

The Russian nodded his head. This was no typical Russian soldier; this was obviously a man with a Jewish heart. How he came to be a commander in the Red Army is anyone's guess, but the fact that he was in this place at this time to help his fellow Jew was no coincidence. Immediately, he escorted Herzka out of the rancorous tavern and spoke to him with heartfelt, yet intense words. "Yid, you must hold out just a little longer! The Red Army is about to liberate you. Don't leave the forest and don't show yourself to anyone. Someone will come for you and then you will be safe!"

He ordered a local villager to give Hertzka some bread and then he turned and disappeared back into the pub. Hertzka didn't even have time to thank the man. Who was he? An angel? Eliyahu Hanavi? A repentant Jew? Who knew? Not wasting another moment, he hurried back into the darkness of the forest. Finding his compatriots, he told them what had happened and what the Yiddish-speaking Russian had told him. Grateful for the bread, they sat tight, ate and waited.

Early the next morning, the sound of horses and hoof beats rang out against the silence of the forest underbrush. The Jews heard the sounds and froze in terror and fear. Who had found them? Who was coming for them?

Two riders on horseback came into the clearing. The Jews looked on with a combination of curiosity and wonderment. They had never seen such odd-looking men before. Short and stocky, they were dressed as warriors in ritual battle clothing, with wooden shields and metal pointed helmets. Both carried a battle axe, a curved sword, a lance, and a quiver full of bows and arrows. Their horses were small but they moved with agility and speed. They were, as was later learned, Mongolian scouts who served the Russian army.

The two riders approached the Jews and began to speak in a language that nobody recognized. The Jews did not move. The scouts kept on speaking until even they realized the futility of their words. Finally, one spoke up and said in a clear voice, *"Privetstvuyem Tovarishchey"* ("Welcome, Comrades"). They gestured for the group to follow them. After a moment's hesitation, all eighty-five Jews began to walk in the direction they were being led. Nobody knew where they were going or to what end they were headed. But they followed nonetheless, until they reached a road they were unfamiliar with.

The two Mongols pointed ahead and indicated that they were to go in that direction. The group continued to walk and it soon became apparent that they had passed far beyond the war front. The Red Army was long past this place and there was no trace of the Germans or their retreating soldiers. They now knew that they had been led to safety. Indeed, the war was over for them and it was time for them to begin their lives anew as free men.

Hertzka always believed that these two Mongol scouts were sent by the Jewish Russian commander to find them in the forest and lead them to safety.

The amazing story of the survival of the five Minzer brothers from Poland, who remained together all throughout the war, was a topic of wonderment and incredulity for years to come, especially in the close-knit Bobover community to which the Minzers belonged. Thirty-two years later, when Hertzka, the oldest of the five, passed away during Chanukah of 1976, the four remaining Minzer brothers sat *shivah* all together in the deceased's small apartment in Boro Park. Of course, the story of their escape and survival was the main topic of discussion, dominating all other areas of conversation, and nary a single visitor to the house failed to comment on their miraculous salvation, let alone the unprecedented occurrence of five brothers outliving the Nazi camps. Indeed, it was quite a sensation, literally the talk of town.

Exactly sixty days later, Yossel (Joe) Minzer had a heart attack and died. When the Bobover Rebbe, R' Shloime Halberstam *zt"l*, heard the sad tidings about the second Minzer brother, he immediately proclaimed that the remaining three brothers should sit *shivah* separately, not all together in one home as is customary.

"Obviously, a terrible *ayin hara* (evil eye) was cast upon the Minzer brothers after so many people visited the first *shivah* house and commented on their miracle. They do not need another one to wreak more havoc on the family!"

R' SHIMON SCHWAB
A *Sefer Torah* for Sale

It was sometime in 1944 when R' Avraham Kalmanowitz *zt"l* brought the desperate cables sent by Rabbi Weissmandl of the Slovak Jewish underground to Baltimore, in an attempt to arouse the help of the Jewish community. An opportunity existed to bring refugees from Poland across the border into relatively safe Slovakia at $1,000 a head – an enormous sum at the time.

R' Kalmanowitz went to see the Jewish leadership of Baltimore, the established Associated Jewish Charities, and all the rabbinical organizations. In emotional terms, as befitting the horrible crisis, the Mirrer Rosh Yeshivah sought to arouse the local leadership into creating a special emergency campaign, in order to rescue as many Jews as possible.

After delivering his impassioned plea, as only R' Kalmanowitz could, the rabbis and organized Jewish leadership had an opportunity to assess the situation. Most would neither believe R' Kalmanowitz nor heed his call. Some dubbed him "hysterical" and a prevaricator, while others said, "Let's not make waves; we can't do anything about it anyway." And so they voted to ignore his pleas.

A few of the more Orthodox rabbis, unwilling to stand idly by as untold millions were being persecuted in Europe, decided to make their own emergency appeals. R' Shimon Schwab *zt"l*, leader of Congregation She'arith Israel, himself a refugee from Germany, made such an appeal on the Shabbos of *Parshas Bo*.

Standing up at the podium, R' Schwab began his speech by declaring to the surprised congregation, "Today, I will be delivering the most important speech of my life."

Paraphrasing Rashi's comment on the words of Moshe Rabbeinu to Pharaoh, he thundered: "Why are we acting like poverty-stricken and lowly people in the face of this enormous need that has arisen?" He went on to read the demands of Rabbi Weissmandl, that unless the American communities responded immediately and with more than they could afford, they would be held accountable by Heaven for the Torah's injunction of "*Lo Sa'amod*" – not to stand on the blood of their Jewish brothers and sisters.

Fortunately, the people did respond to the call of their prestigious rabbi. Straining their resources, many, especially the women, gave selflessly, even donating their personal jewelry to the cause.

R' Schwab himself gave abundantly and even pledged a very personal heirloom. Standing at the pulpit, he told the congregation the following:

"As a refugee, I have no resources of my own. However, I do have a small Torah scroll which I cherish dearly. It was entrusted to me by the *parnassim* (benefactors) of the small town of Kleinurdlingen, where I served as a rabbi, but which by 1936 no longer had a *minyan*. The Talmud notes that one may not sell a *Sefer Torah* except for three important reasons: to enable one to study Torah, to get married, and for questions involving *pikuach nefesh* – life and death. Today, it is clearly a question of *pikuach nefesh*, a matter of life and death, and I hereby offer this treasure of mine for sale as my contribution to the appeal."

One of the congregation's trustees, a wealthy man with a big heart, bought the precious Torah scroll for $1,000 and placed it back in the ark, where it remains to this day. Despite the small size of the congregation, the appeal raised over $10,000, an immense sum, yet so pitifully small compared to the need.

| KALIVER REBBE |

The Power of Faith – The Power of "*Shema Yisrael*"

The "final solution" of the Jewish question in Hungary got underway with a speed and efficiency that surprised even the Germans: between mid-April and late May 1944, practically the entire Jewish population of the Hungarian countryside was ghettoized and, in the largest deportation operation in the history of the Holocaust, between May 15 and July 9, over 437,000 people had been transported to Auschwitz-Birkenau. The speed with which the Hungarian authorities cast out Jews from society, then robbed, segregated and deported them, was unprecedented in the entire history of the Holocaust.

Menachem Mendel Taub (the current Kaliver Rebbe living in Bnei Brak) was only twenty-one years of age when he found himself on a transport to Auschwitz. He arrived there, starving and thirsty, on May 25, three days before the festival of Shavuos was to begin. The sight that greeted him was an enduring one; he never fails to mention it when he speaks publicly about his ordeal in the camps. "I will never forget the sight that met my eyes when we came to Auschwitz, three days before Shavuos. I saw, revealed before me, the eternal core of Am Yisrael, unquenchable, even though all of the forces in the universe strive against it."

The rebbe relates that as they exited the trains, disoriented and bewildered, each group of one thousand Jews was surrounded and enclosed by electrified barbed-wire fences. One touch would kill a man on the spot. Indeed, they saw prone bodies lying at the base of the fence and it was quite obvious that these people had chosen to end their wretched existence and meet their Maker by touching the electrified fence.

Suddenly, they noticed a commotion. A number of men were struggling to reach a certain object which was just beyond the fence. With as much caution as they could muster, they were reaching through the wire to try to grab a piece of paper. R' Menachem Mendel did not understand what was happening and asked what they were doing. Someone told him that beyond the electric fence, they had spotted a page of a *machzor* with the poem of *Akdamus* (a liturgical poem read on Shavuos) printed on it, and the men were trying to reach through the fence and get hold of it.

The sight made an incredible impression on the future Kaliver Rebbe. He lifted up his eyes to heaven and said: "Master of the Universe, who is like Your people, Yisrael? They are a unique nation on earth!" Jews in such a terrible situation, with death staring them in the face; yet at that very moment their faith moved them to risk their lives to get a single page of praise to Hashem.

R' Menachem Mendel did not stay in Auschwitz for very long. He was transferred to what was once the Warsaw ghetto, where the Nazis required strong, healthy prisoners to clear away the ruins of the decimated ghetto (the Klausenberger Rebbe was also among this group). There were no gas chambers or crematorium there, but frequently, for the amusement of the Nazis, men were thrown alive into bonfires, particularly anyone who was worn down and could no longer work.

Once, a group of four men, R' Menachem Mendel among them, was selected to be tossed into the flames. Facing death, he once again looked upward and declared, "What will my last *'Shema Yisrael'* on this world add to You? Master of the World, give me life and save me, and I will bring Your *'Shema Yisrael'* to so many." He had no doubts about Hashem's justice, no complaints to lay before His throne. Rather, he knew, with the strong faith that his father and grandfathers had imbued in him, that he was simply giving back his soul to the One Who had put it within him.

But lo and behold, a miracle occurred just then. The gate opened, and a group of S.S. officers entered, searching for a few more men to do some extra work. In the momentary confusion that ensued, R' Menachem Mendel said to the other three men, "Let's run for it!"

They argued, "They will shoot us if we run," but R' Menachem Mendel insisted, "And if we stay, will it be any better for us?" So they ran for shelter, and somehow managed to stay alive.

From Warsaw, he was subsequently transferred, first to Breslau and then to the Bergen-Belsen concentration camp. His faith in the Al-mighty never diminished. He relates that when he was in one of the forced labor camps, the Nazis ordered him, as a form of abuse, to take a horse-drawn wagon loaded with garbage and drive it in the middle of the night to a neighboring camp several kilometers away. It was a black and moonless night, and there was no defined road leading to the other camp. How would he be able to stay on the road without veering off and getting lost? The German officer looked at him menacingly, as if to say: that is not my problem; that is your problem! He was ordered to drop off the foul-smelling load and return immediately. "And if you are not back by daybreak..." The sentence wasn't completed but the implication was understood loud and clear.

With no choice, R' Menachem Mendel took the wagon and began the impossible journey. Not being adept at wagon-driving and barely able to see the road in front of him, the inevitable came to pass: after going only a short way, the wagon overturned on the bumpy terrain. He was thrown to the ground, and the wagon tilted on its side.

He wasn't hurt - but he was scared. Sitting on the ground, he took stock of his situation. He was far from his family, far from his home, far from his friends. But right then and there, he reminded himself that Hashem, the Master of the Universe, was still there, right with him. There is no place that is without Him.

Musical person that he was, he remembered a Yom Tov melody that his father, the previous Kaliver Rebbe, used to sing in his house, and the tears began to flow. He sat on the ground and sang and wept. Later, the Kaliver Rebbe would recount, "I can honestly say that I wish people would cry like that on Yom Kippur."

With the tune on his lips, the Kaliver Rebbe stood up and sprang into action. To this day, he maintains that he does not know how he had the strength to do it - he has no idea even how it happened; beyond any shadow of a doubt, it was the all-powerful hand of Hashem that did it. Within minutes, the heavy wagon was up on its wheels, the garbage was loaded back on top of it, and he was in the driver's seat, moving toward his destination. It was as if the wagon was driving itself! Indeed, he accomplished his mission and arrived back at daybreak - it was daybreak, he would always say, for both his body and soul - and the villains could not believe their eyes.

Only with faith and stubbornly clinging to Hashem, only taking the example of the righteous men who walked in His way no matter what happened - that is what saved the Jews in those days. R' Menachem Mendel would say: "It seems to me that such incidents (and thousands of such events occurred during the Holocaust) should be capable of destroying the power of the Heavenly adversary and of awakening mercy in Heaven for all of Klal Yisrael. I do not think that even the angels in heaven believed that after all the calumnies against Am Yisrael during the war, and after all the bloodshed and the agonizing death of millions - that after all this the Jewish people would still stand forth as the torchbearers of faith in G-d, declaring, 'Despite it all, we have not forgotten Your Name!' With perfect faith we still shout from the depths of our hearts, '*Shema Yisrael!*'"

| R' AVRAHAM JUNGREIS |
Administering to His Flock

The city of Szeged was the second largest city in Hungary at the beginning of the war. With the 1941 invasion of Yugoslavia, the Germans acquired large copper mines in the area of Bor. As the majority of Yugoslav Jews were already annihilated by 1942 and all Serbs were seen as potential partisans, the Germans turned to Hungary for a slave labor force. The Hungarian government agreed to provide the requested contingent and the first companies left for Bor in the summer of 1943. By the summer of 1944, approximately six thousand Hungarian servicemen were sent to the copper mines. Most of these laborers were Jewish boys who were conscripted into slave labor battalions, which quite often meant death. As Szeged was near the border with Yugoslavia, it became a major staging point from which servicemen and slave laborers alike were sent to the mines.

R' Avraham Jungreis *zt"l* served as the chief Orthodox rabbi in Szeged and he was determined to save as many Jewish men as possible. It took some ingenuity, but he finally came up with a plan. The only thing that would deter the Hungarians from shipping out these young men was the fear of an infectious disease that might contaminate their own soldiers. Taking this into account, R' Avraham discreetly consulted some physicians, who suggested that an injection of raw milk into a person's bloodstream would induce a mysterious fever, and a paste made from soybeans, smeared on the said person's eyelids, would simulate trachoma. It was definitely worth a shot but, as R' Avraham quickly realized, the problem was not giving them the shot; the problem was how to get these concoctions to the conscripts.

Rabbi and Rebbetzin Jungreis found a way. As the rabbi of the community, he was entitled to visiting rights with the labor battalions; however, he was always thoroughly searched before being allowed to enter the barracks. Rebbetzin Jungreis thought of a solution; she sewed pockets into the linings of the coats of her eight-year-old daughter Esther (founder of the renowned Hineni organization) and her younger brother, Binyamin. Then, she secreted the potions into the inner pockets of the coats, together with some sweets and messages from home. And so, every time the rabbi's two children accompanied their father on his visits, they were able to pass the medicine to the men and boys when no one was looking. Indeed, they managed to rescue many Jewish boys who would otherwise have perished in the mines.

On the freezing night that the Nazis entered Szeged, the lives of all of its Jews became tenuous, as a ghetto was hastily erected and, soon after, the deportations to the death camps began. The Jungreis family worked hard to save countless individuals and they were remarkably effective. Among the many people who arrived at the ghetto in Szeged was a well-known rabbinic family from Hungary. As was their wont, the Germans singled out the Jewish leaders and respected rabbis immediately, and this rabbi and his sons were from the first to be deported. His wife, however, who was in her last months of pregnancy, was permitted to remain.

R' Avraham, fearing for the life of this woman and her unborn child, converted the *mikvah* (ritualarium) of his synagogue into a makeshift hospital, which immediately had the effect of making it off-limits to the Germans, who were afraid to contract any of the "Jewish diseases." When the woman, attended by her mother, went into labor, it was on the floor of that *mikvah* that she delivered her baby son. Of course, the baby needed a layette and other sundries. At the risk of his life, Yankie Jungreis, the eldest Jungreis son, took off his yellow star and jumped over the wall of the ghetto to purchase supplies. When that was accomplished, his father prepared for the baby's *bris* (circumcision) and arranged for the rabbi of Zenta to act as *sandek*, obtaining for him a temporary release from detention.

That baby and his mother miraculously survived the horrors of the camps and today he is the esteemed rebbe of a great Chassidic community in Williamsburg, Brooklyn.

| NOAM ELIMELECH |

Holy Earth

Late in the war, the tide had turned against the Germans. Towards the end of 1944, as the armies of Great Britain and the United States approached Nazi concentration camps from the west, forces from the Soviet Union were advancing from the east. The Red Army was heading straight for Poland and the Nazis needed to hide their crimes, moving or destroying evidence of the various atrocities they had committed there. Mass graves were dug up and evidence was burned. Numerous slave and labor camps were evacuated. Documents were destroyed.

The Jewish prisoners that were taken from the camps were sent on the terrible "death marches." Although the prisoners were already weak or ill from enduring the routine violence, backbreaking labor and starvation of concentration camp life, they were now marched for dozens and dozens of miles in the snow and bitter temperatures to railway stations, and then transported for days at a time without food, water or shelter, in freight carriages originally designed for cattle. On arrival at their destination, they were forced to march again to a new camp. Any prisoner who refused to walk, or was unable to keep up and fell to the ground, was shot on the spot.

As a group of exhausted, desperate Jews trudged along on one of these death marches, one of the men recognized his surroundings and realized that the trudging column of skeletons was passing the city of Lizhensk. This city, although small in size, is world-renowned by virtue of the holy rebbe, R' Elimelech (Noam Elimelech) of Lizhensk *zt"l*, who had lived there and was buried there.

What an opportunity! As exhausted and distressed as he was, he could almost feel a charge of spiritual energy by just being in the environs of the righteous man's burial site. He knew he had to do something to act on this impulse. Feeling that he really had very little to lose, he managed to slip away from the walking column and ran off in a sprint to the cemetery and *kever* (burial site) of the Noam Elimelech. He knew he didn't have much time as patrols were everywhere and in his prison garb and emaciated condition, there was no way he could conceal himself.

Arriving at the grave of the rebbe, he silently began to pray. His mind raced wildly, trying to recall even a small prayer, something from Tehillim. When he finished his short but meaningful prayer, he bent down and scooped up a piece of earth from the gravesite. "This," he thought, "will protect me over the coming days. It will be as if the rebbe, R' Elimelech himself, will be with me all throughout these difficult times."

He slipped the clump of earth into the pocket of his prison uniform and slowly withdrew from the *kever*. He was gone for barely a few short minutes and could just make out the end of the column of prisoners trudging down the road. He decided that rather than risk getting caught by a German or turned in by a Polish informer, which he knew meant instant death, he would cling to his newfound source of hope. He quickly ran back to walk alongside his fellow Jewish inmates. With the rebbe's protection, he smiled inwardly, he knew he would survive.

Wherever he went, he took with him the piece of earth from Lizhensk, and amazingly, he survived one crisis after another, witnessing miracle after wondrous miracle, until the war finally came to an end. He and his fellow prisoners were liberated near the Hungarian border, and he was absolutely certain that he had survived only due to the merit of protection of the great *tzaddik* from Lizhensk.

Very soon after his liberation, the man had a dream. In his dream, he saw a short man with a glowing red beard appear to him. He had never seen this man before. The short man spoke in a soft voice and said, "Now that the war is over and you no longer need this protection, please put back the missing clump of earth." It was a strange dream, indeed.

When he awoke, he dismissed the dream as meaningless, but when it recurred for several nights, he realized that the man in his dream was none other than R' Elimelech himself, who wanted him to travel back to Lizhensk and return the earth to his gravesite. It was dangerous to return to Poland after the war, but mindful of his obligation, the man persevered. As soon as he replaced the earth, the dreams ceased.

A Soldier's Commitment

On December 7, 1941, two very important events occurred. One was renowned and forever "will live on in infamy"; the other was less known. One changed the course of world events; the other changed the course of a young man's world.

On that fateful morning, the Japanese Imperial Navy launched a surprise air attack on the U.S. naval base at Pearl Harbor, in Hawaii. After just two hours of bombing, more than 2,400 Americans were dead, twenty-one ships had either been sunk or damaged, and more than 188 U.S. aircraft destroyed. The attack at Pearl Harbor so outraged Americans that the U.S. abandoned its policy of isolationism and declared war on Japan the following day. This officially brought the United States into World War II. On that very same morning, a young Jewish man by the name of Armand (Avraham Aber) Prince was attending college at the University of Buffalo. Like so many Americans after the attack, his world collapsed as the ships in Pearl Harbor sunk to the bottom of the ocean and the Japanese retreated in victory, leaving behind carnage and a once proud nation in shock. As the planes of the enemy flew back across the Pacific, the lives of American youth changed forever. Armand's was no exception.

He met with some of his friends the day after the attack and all of them agreed it would be better to enlist in the armed forces rather than wait for the inevitable draft notice. At least this way they might have their choice as to which of the military services they would enter. Armand had his heart set on the Army Air Corps. And so, this bunch of Jewish kids from Buffalo, New York, went down to the local army recruitment station and enlisted.

The young men joined the army, and like many in the armed services at the time, they felt scared and alone, wondering what the future held.

As was the case with many Jewish kids of the day, Armand had grown up with traditional Jewish values in his home. War, however, is a frightful thing and it was anyone's guess as to how the young men who went off to war would reenter the world of their youth if they were lucky enough to survive. Undoubtedly, in the chaos and tumult of training camp, deployment, battle and transport, most of those Jewish boys from Buffalo didn't have time to think about Jewish traditions; Shabbos, holidays or kashrus. They only knew of the meal packs provided by the military and ate whatever they were served.

Armand finished training camp and was shipped off to the South Pacific. He served for a stint in the Philippines and saw battle at Guadalcanal, a small island off the coast of Australia. It was some time after that that Armand found himself on a military transport ship when a Japanese submarine lurking in nearby waters found its target and torpedoed his vessel out of the water. Many of the soldiers on board were killed, including a number of Armand's close friends. Those who escaped the direct hit managed to jump onto rafts or cling to fragments of the vessel that could be used as a flotation device. Our young Jewish soldier was able to latch onto one such piece to keep himself afloat in the warm waters of the South Pacific.

He drifted for quite some time – no one ever found out how long it was – and spent his time doing something he hadn't done much before in his life: beseeching the Al-mighty G-d he was raised to believe in. If only he were lucky enough to survive, he told G-d, as his weary body held on for dear life. If only he were lucky enough to be rescued. If only he were lucky enough to survive and be rescued by the Allied troops and not the Japanese! At that moment, somewhere in the middle of the vast ocean, with the sun beating down on him mercilessly, hanging by a thread to a flimsy flotation device that was keeping him alive, this brave soldier turned to the only One he knew could help him; he turned to Hashem. He vowed that he would never, ever, eat nonkosher food again. He vowed to work at being a better Jew, keeping more *mitzvos* and helping his fellow man. He vowed to put on *tefillin* every day. He vowed to Hashem and waited for a reply. It was not long in coming.

Lo and behold, his prayers were answered! Somehow, an American troop ship found him floating in the water and rescued him. He was taken to the nearest hospital in

Australia where one of the attending physicians happened to be his brother-in-law. (His sister's husband, Joe Roufa, was a physician with the United States army stationed in Australia. The army had sent him to Australia from his hometown of St. Louis.) Thankfully, Armand recuperated and was eventually discharged. Everyone thought that the coincidence was too striking, but Armand knew better. He knew this was no coincidence; he knew this was Divine providence. G-d kept His word and saved him; now he would emulate G-d and keep his word as well.

That was the first and last time he would ever utter a word about his horrific experience to anyone. Like many of that great generation, he refused to discuss what happened in the war. Word of his time at sea only survives from the bits and pieces his brother-in-law passed to his sister, who later told Armand's wife after they were married. At some point, she mentioned it to her children, under the condition that they never bring it up with their father.

The soldier healed, and the war ended. He returned to his native Buffalo, got married some four years later, and he and his wife were blessed with four children. His home, like that of his parents, was traditionally Jewish, but his renewed commitment to kosher was fierce, much greater than theirs ever was.

Because of his pledge, his strict adherence to eating only kosher food, two of his children wanted to learn more, to attain greater knowledge about their Jewish roots. They eventually decided to expand their commitment and become completely observant Jews. He ended up with twelve religious grandchildren, and if that was not enough, at the end of his long and fulfilling life, he lived out his remaining years as a Torah-abiding Jew. For the last fourteen years before he passed away during Sukkos of 1994, the connection that was forged in the vast Pacific years earlier was solidified when Armand – Avraham Aber – chose to follow a fully committed religious Jewish lifestyle. He had finally made it all the way home.

Avraham Aber's daughter, Judith Bron, and her sister, Faigy Pollack, fondly recall that even before he was fully committed to religious life, he was a man who never stood still in his Judaism. He was always adding to his knowledge. If you went downstairs in his house on any given Shabbos morning, he was reading the *parshah* in the Soncino *Chumash* he got from his synagogue, Beth David Ner Israel, where he later served on the board and was president of the men's club. They would tell their children and grandchildren the story of their dad and always stress the point that if he hadn't survived the initial blow to his ship, if he hadn't spent his time in the water pleading with his Father in Heaven, and if he hadn't survived to go back to Buffalo, marry and raise four children, they would not be here today. Though he did not speak of his story in actual words, he passed down a connection, a feeling, a heritage, for generations to come.

| R' CHAIM STEIN |
The *Goral HaGra*

On the occasion of the first *aufruf* of a grandchild in 1999, R' Meir Zelig Mann *zt"l*, executive director of the Telzer Yeshivah in Cleveland, Ohio, gazed around and surveyed his entire family in the throes of celebration. It was a deeply satisfying feeling for him, and although he was an extremely private person – the last person one would expect to get up and make a public speech – the joy of the moment moved him to the point where he felt the need to make an announcement.

"My dear children," he began in his clear and melodious baritone. "Being that this is my first *aufruf* of a grandchild, and it is *Shabbos Parshas Mattos*, and I received *Shlishi* (the third *aliyah* when called to the Torah) today, I would like to tell the family an important secret that I've kept with me for almost sixty years." Of course, no one could resist such an opening line and the entire extended family crowded around to hear the words of their patriarch.

"What I am about to tell you took place around 5701 (1941), during the second year of the war. The *rosh yeshivah*, R' Chaim Stein *shlit"a*, and I had run away from our beloved Telzer Yeshivah ahead of the Nazi onslaught and, *baruch Hashem*, we managed to stay one step ahead of the wicked ones almost the entire time. At one point, we arrived at a small town and found twenty-eight other *bachurim* from various *yeshivos* who were escaping like us. We joined up with them and remained in that town for a short time. When the Germans were getting too close for comfort, we all recognized that it was time to go. But to where? Where was a safe haven that all thirty of us could escape to? Nobody knew."

R' Meir Zelig paused for a moment, recalling how he and R' Chaim excelled in understanding maps and making calculations that were – more often than not – right on target. "As our group made our way out of the town, we arrived at a fork in the road. R' Chaim suggested to me that if we turn to the right, there was a lake that he remembered from one of the maps, where we could hide and eventually make an easier escape from the Nazis. However, most of the *bachurim* in our group knew nothing of this way and insisted that the only correct way to go was to the left, in the opposite direction. Of course, we attempted to convince them that we knew what we were talking about, but it was no use. They felt that they knew what was best and were prepared to move on, with or without us.

"My children, you must understand that the *rosh yeshivah* and I went through so much during that difficult period, and we became quite skilled in employing a technique known as the *goral haGra* to make these most important life and death decisions. (This is a practice based on tradition, whereby a righteous and qualified petitioner is able to "capture" Heavenly advice for what he should do in a certain situation. A *Chumash* or Tanach may be utilized and a technique of seemingly random page-turning is done after proper prayer and spiritual preparation. The *pasuk* that comes up after using this system gives an answer to the person's question.) Here too, we felt that it was absolutely necessary to use the *goral* to decide on the best course of action, both for ourselves, as well as for the entire group of *bachurim*."

R' Meir Zelig smiled wistfully. "We did the *goral haGra* and the *pasuk* that we arrived at was in this week's *parshah*: *Bilti Calev ben Yefuneh Haknizi v'Yehoshua bin Nun ki mil'u acharei Hashem* – 'Only Calev ben Yefuneh the Knizi and Yehoshua bin Nun [survived] for they followed Hashem fully' (*Bamidbar* 32:12). R' Chaim and I looked at each other and it seemed clear what the *pasuk* was telling us." R' Meir Zelig flushed as his voice rose to a crescendo. "But we could not just leave the remaining twenty-eight *bachurim* and only save ourselves! There had to be something for us to do to help them. I suggested that perhaps we do the *goral* again and maybe the positive outcome would include them as well.

"So we did it again! We turned the pages of the *Chumash* back and forth, and this time, the *pasuk* that came out was from *Parshas Shelach*: *V'Yehoshua bin Nun v'Calev ben Yefuneh chayu min ha'anashim hahem* – 'And Yehoshua bin Nun and

Calev ben Yefuneh lived from among those men' (*Bamidbar* 14:38). At this point it was quite obvious and R' Chaim and I turned to the right, while the others went left."

With a tremendous sigh, R' Meir Zelig fought back tears. "What can I say, children?" he asked. "We lived – and they died, just as the *pasuk* had indicated!"

The room was quiet as everyone absorbed the amazing story, until one person had the temerity to ask how they were so sure that Yehoshua bin Nun and Calev ben Yefuneh was an obvious reference to him and the *rosh yeshivah*.

"That is a good question," R' Meir Zelig said, "and here's the answer. My name, 'Zelig,' is the Yiddish form of the Biblical name Yitzchak. Thus, my real full name is Meir Yitzchak Zelig." The family members gasped in surprise. They had never known that their father and grandfather's name included Yitzchak. In shocked silence they listened as R' Meir Zelig continued.

"R' Chaim, too, recalled that as a child, some of his relatives referred to him as 'Yankele,' even though as far as he knew, his only given name was Chaim. Based on this information, I made the calculations. The *gematria* of Meir Yitzchak Mann (549) is identical to the *gematria* of Yehoshua bin Nun, while the numerical value of Chaim Yaakov is equal to Calev ben Yefuneh with the *kolel* (250). It was an obvious sign from Heaven!"

R' AHARON KOTLER

The Heart of a Jew

As the war inexorably turned against them, the Nazis entertained a number of Jewish ransom plans, none as bold or broad in scope as the Va'ad Hatzalah's Musy Negotiations. Named for Jean-Marie Musy, the pro-Nazi former president of Switzerland who served as the Va'ad's intermediary with S.S. Chief Heinrich Himmler, the Musy Negotiations highlighted Orthodox Jewry in its finest and most painful hour. No rescue action was of greater scope; none had a more heartbreaking conclusion. Towards the end of 1944 and into the beginning of 1945, it was a nearly successful attempt to ransom the six hundred thousand Jews remaining under Nazi control.

What was needed was one million dollars. Surely it was ambitious, it was unheard of, and in the minds of just about every figure in the U.S. during the Second World War – political and otherwise – it was impossible! But to the leaders of the Va'ad Hatzalah in New York, led by R' Aharon Kotler *zt"l*, it was the only way to save thousands of European Jews from their Nazi captors.

Irving Bunim, the renowned American activist and lay leader, served in large part as a spokesman for the Va'ad Hatzalah, and in particular, he carried the message of his *rebbi*, R' Aharon Kotler, to the numerous politicians and government officials who needed to hear the great rabbi's words. With regard to implementing the terms of the Musy Negotiations, the main opposition came from American Jewish organizations, who were afraid to make waves in the halls of the U.S. government. It took a great deal of cajoling and perseverance by Bunim on behalf of the Va'ad before these wealthy organizations would agree to lend their support to the plan. And even when they finally did give their consent, there were strings attached. One major condition was that the United States government grant the Va'ad Hatzalah a license to transfer the funds overseas to Switzerland and then, through their agents, to Himmler. It was a condition which these organizations felt the Va'ad could never meet.

For their part, the Va'ad quickly accepted the terms. "But suppose you cannot get the license," one of the naysayers said. "After all, what you are really asking for is permission to trade with the enemy. The government will ask what you intend to do with the money. You will tell them and your request will not be granted because this ransom is tantamount to sending money to Germany!"

Bunim told the man in no uncertain terms, "We will get the license. If we have to, we will storm Washington. Rabbi Kotler and all of us will go, and we will use every contact we have. But we will get it."

There was no time to waste. They had accomplished the impossible in Washington before, and they would simply have to do it again. This was the Va'ad's single greatest rescue opportunity. Hundreds of thousands of Jewish lives were at stake. They had nothing but a begrudging promise of American Jewish support, the persuasiveness of the *gedolim* and their strong contacts. The license stood between them and rescue.

The gravity of the situation weighed heavily on Bunim. Every word and every personality was critical. The Va'ad discussed strategy and used their best Washington contacts. They decided to go right to the top, to President Roosevelt himself. In February 1945, with great trepidation, Bunim called the Oval Office for an appointment. He was referred to Henry Morgenthau, the secretary of the treasury. Bunim fought a feeling of despair. Hundreds of thousands of lives depended on government approval to transfer $937,000 ($63,000 had already been transferred to the Sternbuchs) to American agents in Switzerland. Henry Morgenthau was their last and only chance.

Once in Morgenthau's office, Bunim explained the Musy Negotiations. Crisply and articulately, he told the treasury secretary what was needed.

Morgenthau's reaction was predictable.

"What?" he asked, bewildered. "Ransom!" The secretary's hands sketched large arcs. "Surely you know that the motto of the United States is 'Millions for defense but not one cent for tribute.'" Morgenthau shook his head. "We can't do it."

Bunim usually translated for Rabbi Kotler and Rabbi Kalmanowitz, but this time the secretary's tone and facial gestures were self-explanatory. Bunim hid his disappointment while he framed a response, but R' Aharon could not hold back his emotions. As he stood shaking, his blue eyes blazed, and then he pointed a finger at Morgenthau. "Bunim," he snapped in his rapid-fire Yiddish, his words coming in agitated bursts, "you tell him that if he cannot help to rescue his fellow Jews at this time, then he is worth nothing, and his position is worth nothing, because one Jewish life is worth more than all the positions in Washington!"

Although Morgenthau did not understand the words, there was no mistaking the intensity of R' Aharon's fury. After an awkward moment of silence, he asked Bunim to translate.

Sensitive to the protocol involved in speaking to top-level officials, Bunim decided to take the edge off a difficult situation. He cleared his throat and told Morgenthau that Rabbi Kotler had said, "Perhaps because of your high office in government you cannot force the issue. But please understand that in this case there are mitigating circumstances. Perhaps something might be worked out."

When Morgenthau looked relieved, R' Aharon realized that his powerful message had not been conveyed accurately. "No, no!" he shouted in Yiddish. "Bunim, tell him exactly what I said!"

Morgenthau looked quizzically from R' Aharon to Bunim.

Bunim paused and exhaled slowly. He knew that their chance to save countless Jewish lives had all come down to this moment. It all depended on what he said. He spoke slowly, deliberately, never taking his eyes from Morgenthau's face. "Rabbi Kotler thinks that you may be unwilling to help us because you are afraid of losing your position in the government. He wants you to know that one Jewish life is worth more than any office."

Morgenthau looked at R' Aharon's fiery stare, R' Avraham Kalmanowitz's anguish and Bunim's quiet determination. He put his head down on his desk. Minutes went by in the silent room until finally Morgenthau stood up and sighed. Standing directly in front of R' Aharon, he asked Bunim to translate. "Tell the rabbi that I am a Jew. Tell him that I'm willing to give up my life – not just my position – for my people!"

Bunim breathed a sigh of relief. It seemed as if the license would be forthcoming. It looked as if thousands of Jews would be spared. Still, Bunim knew that Morgenthau had a difficult task before him. Through the War Refugee Board's bureaucracy, he would have to create a feasible policy permitting large fund transfers from one Va'ad office to another, from New York to Switzerland. The fact that the funds would be used for ransom made matters all the more difficult.

Indeed, in the end, the negotiations fell apart and the plan – and the salvation of thousands of our brethren – never came to fruition.

| YISMACH MOSHE |

Save from the Grave

As a soldier in the Czechoslovakian army during World War II, Shlomo Zalman Markowitz had to endure the dangers and deprivations that came with army life, along with the continuous challenge of remaining a faithful Jew. Despite the torments to which he was subjected, Shlomo Zalman remained firm in his resolve.

One day, his unit was passing through the town of Ujhel, Hungary, home of the Yismach Moshe, R' Moshe Teitelbaum *zt"l*. Shlomo Zalman could recall visiting Ujhel as a child, when his father had taken him to pray at the *tzaddik's* grave. He had been young then, and unable to appreciate the importance of this holy place. Now, however, Shlomo Zalman wished he had the chance to make up for that lost opportunity. He watched longingly as the column of soldiers marched right past the Jewish cemetery and he could even make out the *ohel* (enclosed structure) that contained the Yismach Moshe's grave. How he wished he could step out of line for a few minutes to say the fervent prayers that were in his heart!

Just then, Shlomo Zalman felt a tap on his shoulder. Having gotten his attention, the soldier behind him pointed at Shlomo Zalman's leg. Shlomo Zalman looked down and discovered, to his astonishment, that the bottom of his trousers was ripped and his foot was covered in blood. He hadn't felt a thing!

Looking up in bewilderment, Shlomo Zalman caught sight of a wild dog running away from the column of soldiers. The dog must have attacked him. He had been so involved in his thoughts that he hadn't even noticed.

Shlomo Zalman quickly decided to take advantage of the situation. He broke away from the column and sat down on a nearby stoop. Holding his foot, he began moaning in pain and calling for help.

Moments later, the commanding officer spotted him and came striding over.

"Soldier, get back to your squad!"

"I can't," Shlomo Zalman protested. "I was just bitten by a dog."

The commander peered at his injury, and then signaled to several nearby soldiers. "Take this man to the hospital at once."

Shlomo Zalman enjoyed a few days of calm in the hospital, where his wound was treated and healed. On the third day, the commanding officer walked in just as the doctor was checking up on his progress.

"Doctor, what is the prognosis on this soldier?"

"He was bitten by a wild dog. We think he'll be okay."

With a sinking heart, Shlomo Zalman waited for his commander to order him back to duty. Instead, to his astonishment, he heard the officer say, "We don't want any soldier who was bitten by a wild dog! He doesn't belong in my army."

Shlomo Zalman was elated. He was finally free of army duty! As soon as he was dismissed from the hospital, he went into hiding and lived through the war. Today, he has a wonderful family who are all committed to Torah and *Yiddishkeit*.

Shlomo Zalman did not return to the site of his miraculous release until the late 1990s, when his son Dovid convinced him to visit Ujhel. He located the stoop he had rested on over forty years earlier, when a seeming misfortune had turned out to be a blessing in disguise. Finally, Shlomo Zalman was able to properly offer his heartfelt prayers and thanks to Hashem at the grave of the Yismach Moshe.

The Shabbos Trial

The inmates of Bergen-Belsen were suffering collective punishment. On Friday, the eighth of Av, 1944 (5704), someone lit a mattress on fire and burned it to a crisp. The Nazis were incensed and, in retribution, decreed that no one would receive any food that entire day.

There was one woman in the camp who was well-known for her kindness and dignity. This was no ordinary woman; she retained her modesty when others didn't bother. She kept her head covered the entire time she was in the camp even though she could have wrapped herself with the extra cloth to keep out a bit of the winter chill.

Even when she became ill and could barely walk due to her exhausted and starved state, she could always be found tending to the sick in the hospital ward. One day, she heard a woman weeping. She walked toward the sound and found a Rebbetzin Dessberg lying there in critical condition. When the woman asked her what was causing her tears, she answered feebly that she had finally gotten a bit of milk to drink, but it was so cold that she was unable to drink it. (When one is dying of starvation and typhus, the frustration and despair this situation would cause is unimaginable.)

The woman took the cup of milk and, without a word, went outside with it. A few minutes later she came back in, her face smudged with soot and her eyes red; but in her hand was a cup of warm milk for Rebbetzin Dessberg. She had warmed it over a fire she lit from scraps of paper and bits of wood she had gathered, one by one. She did this despite the absolute prohibition the Germans had placed on lighting fires. She would not pass up the opportunity to aid the sick.

On that fateful day, when the Germans refused to provide any nourishment to the inmates, the woman was only looking out for the children. Somehow, she managed to obtain some oats which she cooked into porridge to feed some children, including her four-year-old daughter. Sadly, though, just as the porridge was cooked and ready to be served, she was caught by two of the *kapos*, who threatened to report her to the Nazis. She would have to appear before a tribunal that very night – Friday night – to answer for her "crime."

The judges were Jews themselves but served the Nazis slavishly. They made short work of the trial and the woman was "sentenced" to two days without her bread ration, which she would have to hand over to the *kapos*. Throughout the entire "trial" the woman refused to utter a word. She did not even bother to deny several of the trumped-up charges, which were totally untrue.

When she was released, she walked back to her barracks, where her family was waiting for her. Upon her arrival, she told them what had happened. Her children asked her why she had not defended herself against the false charges, but she gave no answer, and instead became quite upset and agitated.

A while later, one of her sons, R' Yonah Emanuel, was bold enough to ask her again why she had refused to say anything in her defense. Why hadn't she at least argued that on that day there was no food and she couldn't let her young daughter and other children starve? These extenuating circumstances might have led them to give her a lighter sentence. This time she responded, "The judges, the prosecutor, the defending attorney, and the court recorder were all Jews. They actually pretended to conduct a real trial and they used an actual person to capture each word. The recorder was writing down everything – each and every word that I would have spoken was causing a Jew to write on Shabbos! I had to keep silent. It is better to be hungry a while longer than to cause a Jew to desecrate the Shabbos."

| ARUGAS HABOSEM |
A Grandfather's Promise

Duvid'l was a young Hungarian Jew who shared the fate of his brethren. He, too, was deported to the kingdom of death camps. In the winter of 1945 he was slaving for the German war industry in Gusen, Austria. An epidemic of typhus broke out there and Duvid'l was one of its victims. For some time, his friends were able to shield him from the searching eyes of the *kapo* and the S.S. men and save him from the certain doom awaiting the sick and dying. Every morning they dragged him out from the barracks to the *appell* and propped him up against a board, its base anchored into the ground and its top concealed under Duvid'l's striped jacket, thus creating the impression that Duvid'l was well and standing on his own two feet. At work his friends placed him near his machine and worked alternately on their own machines and on Duvid'l's, thereby completing his daily quota in addition to theirs. When the German overseer passed by, Duvid'l moved his hands to give the impression that he was working at full speed.

But Duvid'l's body could not take the strain; his fingers became numb and his feet could not move. One morning, as his friends were about to drag him to work, they discovered that his body was cold. He did not respond to any of their attempts to revive him. They begged forgiveness for being unable to save his life, though they had tried to the best of their abilities. They walked out to the *zeilappell* without Duvid'l, and from there they marched to their daily jobs at the ammunition factory.

At night, when they returned to their barracks, Duvid'l's body was gone. It had been taken away with all the other corpses and placed in the death shack where the bodies were collected for disposal.

That night, Duvid'l's closest friend, who had shared the top of the three-tiered bunk bed with him and others, had a dream. In his dream, he saw a man with a long beard. The man told him, "You are Duvid'l's friend. Go to the death chamber and wish him a full and speedy recovery."

The friend woke up. Although the dream made a strong impression upon him, he did not consider it anything more than a dream and he fell asleep again. Once more, he dreamed the identical dream. He woke immediately, as before, but this time he was very frightened.

The dream was in fact a command to go to the death shack, which was located at the other side of the camp. To go there at this hour meant risking his own life, for to leave the barracks at night was a violation that carried the death penalty. The fear for his life was stronger than the dream and Duvid'l's friend decided not to leave for fear of being shot by the German guards. Once more he fell asleep.

He dreamed again. This time the old man with the flowing beard said, "I am the Arugas Habosem, Duvid'l's grandfather. Go and tell Duvid'l that I say that he will have a speedy and complete recovery. To you no evil will happen and your merit will be very great."

This time, Duvid'l's friend jumped out of his bunk in great fear and without thinking, ran in the direction of the death shack. Miraculously, there were no German guards around and no one noticed him.

The death shack was filled with corpses stacked together like logs of dry wood. It took many minutes before he was able to locate his friend Duvid'l's corpse. Once he was sure he had found his friend, he placed the stiff and cold body on the floor, stood next to it, and announced as he had been commanded in his dream: "Your grandfather, the Arugas Habosem, wants you know that you, Duvid'l, will have a complete and speedy recovery."

The shack was quiet; not a sound or movement was heard. Suddenly, Duvid'l lifted his hand, grabbed the hand of his friend, and said, "Repeat what you just said."

Terror and panic filled the man but he still managed to force the words out of his mouth. "Your grandfather, the Arugas Habosem, lets you know that you will have a speedy and complete recovery!" The friend wanted to run away from the death shack, but Duvid'l would not let him. His frozen fingers were intertwined with his friend's and his grip was like that of an iron vise.

"Tell me once more!" Duvid'l commanded his frightened and nearly hysterical friend. The friend repeated the same sentence about twenty times. Finally, Duvid'l eased his grip and released his friend's hand. Frightened to death, the friend ran back to his barracks with as much strength and speed as he could muster.

In the morning, the German in charge of the death shack arrived to find an unusual sight. Duvid'l, shivering with cold, was sitting up amidst the corpses. A spark of humanity flickered in the Nazi's heart. He took Duvid'l to the camp's hospital where he was treated and nursed back to health. Duvid'l recovered fully and was liberated by the American army in the spring of 1945. He remained a pious Chassidic Jew and moved to Williamsburg, Brooklyn, where he raised a family and ended up living just a few doors away from his friend who had literally brought him back to life.

| REB CHAIM YOSEF RUSSAK |
Chain of Miracles

The final insult to the inmates of Stempeda and Rotelbraude, two concentration camps deep in the German hinterland, was the death march of April 1945. The war was all but lost but the Nazi guards still felt compelled to torture their prisoners in every possible way.

Early one morning, the Germans woke the weary inmates and forced them to begin a strenuous march. Many prisoners felt weak and could hardly walk. Chaim Yosef Russak was one of these tortured souls and it wasn't long before he began to fall behind the long column of marching men. After a few hours, he was almost at the back of the line and he knew his life was in danger because the S.S. officers did not hesitate to shoot those who could not walk. He looked around to see if there was any place that he could hide but they were passing open plains and it was impossible to even think of escaping.

Chaim Yosef raised his eyes to Hashem and prayed, using the words of Shimshon: "*Chazkeini na hapa'am* – Hashem, strengthen me just one more time. Enable me to survive this day and I will attempt to hide when night falls. I don't want to lie down at the side of the road and be shot by the Germans without attempting an escape and I want very much to live and carry on my family chain."

When he finished his prayer, he felt a new flow of energy. He was able to drag himself through the rest of the day. At night, the entire column came to a village called Drakenstat where they were led into a huge silo. A massive threshing machine stood in the center of the room, surrounded by bundles of straw stacked high as a house. Chaim Yosef decided to dig a hiding place in the straw. In order to cover the full length of his body and leave himself a safe distance from the opening, he estimated that he needed to dig a tunnel through three bales of straw.

He lay down near the back wheel of the threshing machine and began to pull straw from the first bale. He tried to pull out as much straw as his hand could grab but the bale was packed so well and was so tightly pressed that nothing budged. It took some time before the bundle became looser and he was able to draw two straws, then three, and finally, a handful. In two hours, a small tunnel took shape in the first bale of straw. He crept inside and began to pull straw from the second bundle. By this time he was experienced, and the second bale loosened quickly. He worked another hour and burrowed a hole in the second bundle of straw. The tunnel was now deep enough for him to stretch out his hand and still remain concealed.

Now, he started to work on the third bundle and made a hole that was large enough to insert both hands. People started complaining that it was very late at night and he was disturbing their sleep. They needed to refresh their energy to continue the grueling march waiting for them in the morning. Chaim Yosef begged them to let him work another half hour to finish preparing his hideout, but no one would hear of it. They advised him to rest and complete his work in the morning. He had no choice but to stop and decided to wake up early the next morning to close the opening of his tunnel.

Exhausted, he immediately fell asleep. It wasn't too long before he was woken by the shouts of *kapos* yelling at the prisoners to line up outside and prepare to continue the march. Chaim Yosef was very tired as he had worked most of the night and hadn't eaten for almost a day. He knew he couldn't walk and would have to remain hidden. The others rose to leave and they parted from him with warm blessings for success.

As quickly as he was able, Chaim Yosef heaved himself into the tunnel, feet first. He kept his head toward the air source. The hole was tight and narrow and he could barely turn over because the ceiling was so low. And to make matters worse, he couldn't stick his hand out and take straw to cover up the hole, as just then two Jews came and lay down between the wheel and the hole and covered themselves with the straw that he had dug out from the bales. When he asked them to move so he could close his hole, they refused. They felt that they would be safer near the wheel. He argued with them but they warned him to stop because the noise would attract attention and they would all be caught. They promised to leave as soon as the Germans left and Chaim Yosef realized there was nothing more he could do.

Meanwhile, all the prisoners were taken out of the silo. Chaim Yosef was glad to rest his feet and decided to accept his fate. He had done whatever he could and his life was in the hands of Hashem. Feeling weary, he fell asleep.

A short time later, he was awakened by the sounds of German S.S. officers opening the door of the barn, followed by gunshots. He realized that the Germans were pulling people out of their hiding places and killing them. Every few minutes, he heard footsteps of people being led out of the silo, followed by gunfire. Lying in the cramped, narrow hole, he became extremely nervous and felt sick from the apprehension of waiting and not knowing what the next few minutes would bring. Would his six years of suffering end with his life being taken now?

He tried pulling himself close together. He squeezed his body into the tunnel as far as he could from the opening. He experimented putting his body in different positions. He placed his feet this way and that way to see how he could take up the least amount of space. He stuck the edge of his foot into the third bundle of straw.

The hours passed slowly. Chaim Yosef prayed and napped. Suddenly, he heard some Germans begin to search his area. They discovered the Jew near the wheel of the threshing machine and yelled at him to get up. The man pretended to be dead. They shouted repeatedly, *"Aufshteyn!"* Finally, he rose. They took him outside and a shot rang out. The Germans returned and found the second man who lay near the tunnel entrance. He, too, was removed and shot.

As soon as the second man stood up, light entered the hole. The man's back had been covering the entrance. Now it became light and Chaim Yosef felt a cold wind and assumed that the barn doors were open. To his horror, he saw that he did not have nearly enough straw at the opening. With little effort, anyone could see through the skimpy pile.

He yanked desperately at the bundle to the side of his hand, but it did not fall. He realized that only the mercy of Hashem could save him now. He laid his hands near his head and began to pray fervently: "*Ribono shel Olam*, the midrash states that Hashem helped Moshe Rabbeinu escape from his Egyptian executioners by making them blind and deaf-mute. In the merit of *Toras Moshe*, may the same miracle happen here. Please confuse the Germans; blind them so they don't see me. If I am saved, I will relate the story of Hashem's miraculous help."

One of the Germans began to search the area. Chaim Yosef heard him walk past the hole and was relieved that he did not notice the opening. However, he soon returned with a pitchfork, poked it into the hole, and began to sweep away the straw he had carefully laid at the entrance. He kept pushing the tool deeper and deeper into the hole.

Chaim Yosef watched in horror as the steel teeth came closer and closer. He squeezed himself together as tightly as he could but the German pressed the pitchfork against his hand. As soon as he touched it, he realized that he had made a discovery. Now, he turned over the fork and began to bash it into the hole with great cruelty. He banged so hard that the straw began to fly.

Miraculously, instead of directing the pitchfork downward towards where Chaim Yosef was laying, the German kept the fork pointed upward. He banged the pointy steel teeth several inches above his body.

The German banged the pitchfork three times to his right, to his center, and to his left. He repeated this pattern several times. Had he pointed the fork an inch lower, Chaim Yosef's body would have been riddled with holes.

Eventually, he tired and dropped the pitchfork in the hole. A shiver went through Chaim Yosef's bones as he felt it resting on his back. When the German moved the fork, he felt the heavy tool sliding off his body.

Now the German became angry and began to shout, "*Raus, Raus!*" Chaim Yosef was so frightened; he was not able to move a limb. As soon as the German had started to bang at the straw, he became terrified; his mouth sealed shut and he could barely breathe. His heart stopped as if he was a dead person.

The German summoned his friends. He made a loud commotion as if there was a fire. Apparently, it was a major catastrophe that whoever was hiding inside did not want to exit. Chaim Yosef lay lifeless for several minutes and finally, he felt his heart start pumping again. "*Ribono shel Olam*," he whispered a prayer, "he didn't touch me! Please help me further!"

The Germans began to remove some bales of straw that lay on top of Chaim Yosef. Instead of removing all the bales and uncovering his position, however, they left four large bundles over his hiding place.

A German climbed up on the straw and began to stab downwards with a long pointy iron. Chaim Yosef was laying with his face down and his feet stuck in the hole of the third bundle of straw. Suddenly, he felt a bang on the back of his shoes and he quickly moved his foot. Before he was fearful of the front; now he began to guard his rear.

When he shifted his foot, the German recognized that he was on to something because a hard spot had become soft. This gave him fresh energy and he intensified his blows. More miracles occurred. Each thrust of the pointy iron missed Chaim Yosef by millimeters. The German stabbed the straw next to his knees, then near his elbow, but somehow he kept missing his body.

Since Chaim Yosef had loosened the third bundle of straw, the Germans thought he was hidden there and aimed in that direction. They did not realize how close to the opening he was. Chaim Yosef silently thanked Hashem that the people had prevented him from digging deeper into the third bundle because they wanted to sleep. He kept praying: "*Ribono shel Olam*, please confuse them! Let them search in the wrong location!"

Suddenly, he heard a German call, "To the machine!" They were so intent on catching him that they decided to move away the threshing machine to have a better view of the straw.

Chaim Yosef lay very quietly. He was too frightened to breathe. He heard them call, "One, two, three, push!" Hard as they tried, the machine did not move.

They summoned another person who began to bang on the machine. They tried again to move the machine but it remained glued to its spot. Seeing that it was a difficult case, they decided to hunt for other prisoners and return later.

About noontime, Chaim Yosef heard the Germans leave. He heard the silo doors lock and it became very quiet. He assumed they were eating lunch and thought that it would be a good time to slip out and hide in a different spot. He was torn with indecision. On one hand, it was risky to remain because the Germans were aware of his hiding place and could discover him at any moment. On the other hand, it was dangerous to leave because the Germans might have left a guard to observe the area. His life was hanging in the balance. Should he stay or go?

What should he do? He decided to remain in his hiding place because Hashem had performed so many miracles in that spot.

Several minutes passed and suddenly a German voice called out, "You - near the machine - come out immediately or you will be shot!" Chaim Yosef realized that a guard had been posted to watch his place and he thanked Hashem for the good sense to remain hidden.

When lunch was over, the silo doors slid open and the Germans returned to their murderous work. One group came over to the threshing machine and again attempted to push it out of the way. With renewed vigor after their meal, they shouted, "All together, push!"

Suddenly, the earth began to shake and sounds of loud crashes filled the air. The Allies were bombing the city of Magdinburg, only eighteen kilometers away, where a large German force was gathered. It was a massive attack with the participation of thousands of Allied planes. That bombing, on Tuesday afternoon, April 10, 1945, saved Chaim Yosef Russak's life.

When the earth started to quake from the bombs, the Germans ran out of the silo. Chaim Yosef did not have the strength to move from his hiding place. The afternoon passed and night fell and it finally registered in his mind that a miracle had really occurred; the Germans had left, and he was no longer in danger.

The night passed quietly. The next morning, farm workers entered the barn and Chaim Yosef remained in his hiding place. He was very frightened because he did not know what they would do if they found a Jew on the property. Eventually, evening fell and the workers left the barn.

He began to formulate his plan. He would leave the barn and walk back in the direction he had come from. He assumed that the Allies must be near because the Germans were running away. He felt very weak but was determined to leave this place.

Late at night, the barn was dark and it seemed safe to leave his hideout. He slowly crept out of the hole and slid under the threshing machine. When he tried to stand up, his knees buckled and he fell. He was surprised at his weakness and thought, "What do I do now? I can't walk!" Crawling on his hands and knees, he managed to find some wheat kernels on the floor of the barn and gratefully, sat down to his "meal" – his first nutrition of any sort in over two days. After eating his fill, he cleaned additional kernels and stored them in his pocket.

The wheat gave him a bit of strength to continue. He began to crawl again and finally located the two silo doors, which, to his dismay, were locked! Each door was secured on the outside with two wooden posts, but the wood was rotten and gave way quickly. He pushed the door at the side and crawled out. He cautiously checked if there were any guards watching the silo. He circled the building and examined all the sides but no one was there.

Now, as he began to search for food, he spotted a farm across from the silo. Painstakingly, he climbed over the fence and entered the yard. He picked and ate an onion, but it made him feel unwell. He entered another yard and found a large pot, used to feed the chickens, and inside there was one hard potato. Apparently, it was too tough so the chickens had left it; to Chaim Yosef the potato tasted delicious and satisfied his hunger.

He spotted an old-fashioned water pump in another yard and crawled under a fence to reach it. There was an empty can laying nearby and he filled it with water which he quickly consumed. He refilled the can five times, drinking more than a gallon of water. Then, he washed his hands and face and finally felt refreshed.

Looking up at the sky, he saw that dawn was beginning to break. The village clock chimed four times, indicating the hour. He wanted to hide before morning so he returned to the silo, cleaned out the tunnel entrance, ate more wheat, and settled himself back inside, thanking Hashem for the unbelievable miracles and hoping for continued protection.

It wasn't but a few minutes before he heard two men crawling out of the straw. One climbed up a large ladder and peered out. He began to shout in Russian, "American tanks are here!" The second man also climbed up to look. He hoped they were judging the situation correctly. Chaim Yosef decided to remain hidden a little while longer. Since he had waited six years for this moment, he wanted to be absolutely certain that it was safe to leave his hiding place.

After about fifteen minutes, however, he could lay no more and crawled out. The lice were biting and he was impatient from excitement. Incredibly, of the seventy-four people who had attempted to hide in the silo, only the two Russians and Chaim Yosef Russak were not discovered.

With heartfelt praises and thanks to Hashem, Chaim Yosef looked around at the silo that saved his life. The men heard workers approaching the barn and they quickly hid. The workers, however, opened the barn doors and announced in several languages that the Americans had arrived and anybody hiding in the barn was free to leave. It was Thursday, April 12, 1945.

{ POSTWAR: }

Liberation and Beyond

Why Me?
by Raize Guttman

Why was I left alive?
Why? G-d, please explain,
Not a single relative survived
Yet — I remain.

I wasn't the type to fight
Or outsmart my plight,
Yet six million Jews were marched to the left
And me — to the right.

My beautiful, big sister Bruncha
In smoke went up to the skies,
Her true identity mocked
By her blonde hair and blue eyes.

My baby brother Dudu,
The child I adore.
Pure, with wide-eyed wonder
Is no more.

Why me? Why was I left
To carry so much pain...
Haunted by my memories,
Was my suffering in vain?

Oh, G-d! Oh, please take notice
What has sprung from all my guilt.
The family I tenderly nurtured,
The generations I have built.

Take pride in my existence,
My tears do not condemn.
My loved ones died for your honor,
But I lived al kiddush Hashem.

| R' YITZCHAK ISAAC HERZOG |
Returning the Lost Children of Israel

On a number of occasions during the war, Rabbi Yitzchak Isaac Halevi Herzog zt"l traveled back and forth to the United States at great risk, in an effort to attract support for the cause of saving European Jewry from the clutches of Nazi Germany. Rabbi Herzog, in his position as Chief Rabbi of Palestine, even managed to secure a meeting with President Franklin D. Roosevelt. At the meeting, Roosevelt smiled and did not reply to the rabbi's pleadings for a promise to help the Jews of Europe. His biographer records that several people noticed that the rabbi's hair turned white when he left the meeting, which he perceived as a failure. Following this, Rabbi Herzog immediately returned home to Palestine, narrowly avoiding passage on a ship that was sunk by a German U-boat, and taking what was said to be the last civilian ship to safely cross the Atlantic during the war.

After the war, Rabbi Herzog dedicated himself to saving Jewish children, especially babies, bringing them back from their places of hiding throughout Europe to their families or to Jewish orphanages. Many of these children were hidden in

Christian monasteries or by Christian families who refused to return them. Rabbi Herzog used any and all influence he had, with whatever clergymen he could, to rescue these children. He also traveled to numerous countries, raising money and utilizing any support he could muster for his rescue efforts.

Rabbi Berel Wein relates that in 1946, as a young boy, he remembers how Rabbi Herzog came to visit the city of Chicago. The entire city; all the adult men and women and all the Jewish children, came to greet him at the airport. They then gathered in Chicago's Beis Medrash L'Torah, Hebrew Theological Seminary, where Rabbi Herzog delivered a lecture on a complex Talmudic issue, as the children stood mesmerized by his oratory. At the conclusion of his speech, his face immediately lost its radiance, and he became somber and staid.

The famous *rav* from Jerusalem paused for a few long moments and then declared: "My friends, I come not from Yerushalayim. I come from Rome. I have just met with Pope Pius XII."

A murmur went through the crowd. Some people were duly impressed; others were waiting to hear why they should be impressed.

"During the terrible war," continued Rabbi Herzog, "many children were sheltered in monasteries across Europe. These Christians saved them from the Nazis. Indeed, they were safe in a physical sense; but certainly not in a spiritual sense. I explained to the pope that there were hundreds, perhaps thousands, of Jewish children who were sheltered in Catholic monasteries throughout the war. Their desperate parents did what they had to do in order to save their children's lives. Today, many of those parents are no longer alive, but those who are would like nothing more than to be reunited with their children.

"I pleaded with him that these are our children and the time has come for them to be identified and returned to the remnants of their families, to be once again embraced by the Jewish people. I asked him to release those children back to their heritage, to let them be raised as Jews."

Suddenly, to the shock of the children and the awe of the adults, he began to cry. "The pope did not acquiesce," said Rabbi Herzog. "He said that once a child is baptized, *Rachmana litzlan*, Heaven help us, he can never be returned."

The great *rav* trembled as he continued to sob uncontrollably. He looked at the assembled children. "My dear children," he wailed, "we lost them!" Then his demeanor changed, as a ray of hope sparkled from his eyes.

"We lost them," he repeated, as he locked his gaze on the young faces, who stared directly at his teary eyes, "BUT WE HAVE YOU! WE HAVE YOU!"

| R' YOSEF FRIEDENSON |
A Simple Declaration of Faith

As the American armed forces continued their march through Europe, liberating towns, villages and cities from German occupation, they came upon numerous sites where atrocities took place, with the evidence in plain sight. Lieutenant Meyer Birnbaum *z"l*, a religious Jew and member of the Fifty-Ninth Signal Battalion of the United States army, arrived in a camp named Ohrdruff, where death and destruction was everywhere. Apparently, in an attempt to silence the witnesses of their crimes, the Nazis forced all the inmates into the main *appellplatz*, where they summarily gunned down thousands of people in cold blood, and left the bodies out in plain sight to rot. When the Americans arrived, only a pitiful few remained alive, and the enormity of the massacre was too much to bear, even for many of the brave American soldiers.

Unlike Ohrdruff, though, there were still hundreds of Jews left alive when the army reached nearby Buchenwald, and the good lieutenant asked his superior officer for permission to remain in the camp to supply the survivors with any assistance possible. Since all that remained of the war in Europe was the capture of Berlin, and it looked like the Russians were, in any event, going to get there first, the officer agreed.

It was not long before a gentile chaplain came running up to him in Buchenwald and wanted to know whether he was Jewish. After receiving an affirmative reply, the gentile chaplain asked if he knew how to administer the "last rites" to those on the verge of death. A makeshift hospital had been set up for the survivors, many of whom had little chance of living, and there was a shortage of chaplains. Although Birnbaum was a soldier, not a chaplain, and really had little idea of what to do by the bedside of a dying man, Jew or gentile alike, he assumed that no one else in the vicinity would know any better than he did, so he headed directly for the hospital.

Indeed, it was a sorry sight. Due to a lack of medical provisions, most of the weak and dying patients stood little chance of recuperating. The first bed that Birnbaum approached held what appeared to be an extremely emaciated adolescent. All that remained, it seemed, were two prominent eyes, cheekbones, and a protruding nose. Hesitantly, he approached and asked in Yiddish, "*Du bist a Yid?*" ("Are you a Jew?") The young man nodded. "*Vus iz dayn numen?*" ("What is your name?") Birnbaum asked, and the sick man whispered that it was Yosef. Seeing that the conversation was off to a promising start, Birnbaum explained that he was a Yid as well, a Jewish officer in the American army, and that he had come to help him.

There was a pause, and the lieutenant was at a loss as to how to proceed. The man looked so sick that Birnbaum was sure he would expire in a matter of time, but he still felt uncomfortable just asking him to start reciting *vidui* (the deathbed confession) with him; especially since he himself didn't even know it by heart. "When did you last pray to *Hashem Yisbarach*?" he finally asked.

"I always pray to *Hashem Yisbarach*," was Yosef's simple reply, more eloquent than any profession of faith that Birnbaum had ever heard.

He asked for something to eat, and the lieutenant gave him some bread. Anything else, the soldiers were warned beforehand, could be dangerous for these people in their emaciated state, as their stomachs probably couldn't handle heavier food.

Yosef, lying in the bed, appeared to be not more than seventeen or eighteen years old. Subsequently, Birnbaum learned that he was twenty-three and only looked younger because of the starvation. In fact, he was married – his wedding had taken place in a cellar in the Warsaw ghetto not long before it was liquidated – and he had been interred in seven different concentration camps since then. This was no youngster and the lieutenant had no idea what to do next. Slowly, hesitantly, he began to recite the words of *Shema Yisrael*, the basic proclamation of faith, a standard prayer one says before death.

The soldier was saying the words but in the middle, he paused. Yosef was looking at him curiously. With a smile, he asked why the lieutenant was reciting Shema with him. Obviously, Yosef believed he was far from dying and thought it a bit humorous that this soldier should be treating him in this manner. Embarrassed and having no answer to Yosef's question, Birnbaum quickly switched the discussion to other topics.

He inquired about Yosef's family, and was told that his family name was Friedenson. His father, Eliezer Gershon Friedenson, had been one of the leaders of Agudath Israel in Poland and the editor of the *Bais Yaakov Journal* from its inception in 1923. He was a close associate of Sarah Schenirer, the founder of the Bais Yaakov movement. Bais Yaakov was almost unknown in America at that time and Birnbaum did not fully appreciate what it meant to be a close colleague of Sarah Schenirer. Nevertheless, he did realize that he was talking to the son of someone of considerable stature in the prewar, Eastern European Torah world.

Fortunately, Yosef Friedenson defied the doctor's predictions, and that conversation was only the first of many over the next sixty-seven years. The two men, liberator and survivor, would meet again in the Displaced Persons' camp in Feldafing, in Israel, and quite often in New York, where R' Friedenson eventually became the editor of *Dos Yiddishe Vort* and one of the most prominent writers in the Jewish world.

It took sixty-seven years, but the two would meet up one final, everlasting time: they passed away less than three days apart and in the Heavenly Tribunal, the lives of these two men, so deeply intertwined, were undoubtedly celebrated, together.

| R' MOSHE SOLOVEITCHIK |

The Grip of the Holy Letters

During the first weeks following the liberation of Buchenwald, many of the former prisoners were drunk with freedom. They could go as they pleased and take what they wanted from the nearby town. During the years of minute-to-minute existence under the oppressive Nazis, they could never allow themselves the luxury of thinking about the future, or even about the next minute. But now that they were free, they thought only of experiencing the present to its fullest. At that point, they could have stayed in Germany forever, enjoying the "good life" there.

Working with these young survivors was an American chaplain, Rabbi Hershel Schachter. He understood that the first step in the long process of the spiritual rehabilitation of the survivors was for them to leave Germany. Working through international relief organizations, Rabbi Schachter succeeded in making an arrangement with the Swiss government, which grudgingly allowed the Red Cross to bring the youngsters to Switzerland for rest and recuperation.

One young man by the name of Yoav Kimmelman had no intention of joining the group traveling to Switzerland and told the chaplain he wanted to stay in Germany. Rabbi Schachter knew about this young man; he was born into a pious Chassidic home of Gerrer Chassidim from Sosnowiec. At the age of sixteen, he was deported to the Nazi concentration camp kingdom where he endured four years of misery, only to learn after liberation that he was the sole survivor of his once large family. He, like many other religious Jews, stopped practicing Judaism in the face of Nazi brutality and its aftermath.

Rabbi Schachter knew what he had to do and he arranged with an American soldier to grab the young man and throw him onto a moving train headed for Switzerland. Although the young man resisted, it was to no avail; he was no match for the soldier. And so, quite against his will, Yoav found himself on his way to Switzerland with the other young men. He was none too happy but could do nothing about it.

It took a few days for the train to reach the Swiss border at Rheinfelden near Basel. The engineer was not too keen on taking the refugees into Switzerland, and an American soldier had to be posted with him in the cabin to make sure that he cooperated. Once in Switzerland, the group was welcomed by the Red Cross and it wasn't long before the camp in Rheinfelden became a center for many Jewish organizations, from Agudath Israel on the right to Hashomer Hatza'ir on the left, each trying to influence the youngsters to accept their particular ideology. Yoav was apathetic to the "soul hunt" going on all around him and refused to be taken in by any camp. He remained staunchly and unapologetically detached.

One Shabbos, a prominent visitor came to Rheinfelden. R' Moshe Soloveitchik *zt"l*, a grandson of the famed R' Chaim Soloveitchik (Brisker) *zt"l*, had evaded the Polish army draft in 1937, and with a group of young men from Brisk, escaped to Switzerland. He continued his meteoric rise in Torah study in Yeshivah Etz Chaim in Montreux, Switzerland, and was already renowned as a *gaon* in all facets of Torah and halachah at a young age. With the outbreak of World War II, however, his idyllic life came to an end. He became a war refugee and was incarcerated in the Schonenberg labor camp near Basel, where he was put to work laying roads. Although it may have seemed harsh to him at the time, in truth, this was the standard procedure for all refugees; they were interned until their papers were processed and it was determined that they were law-abiding civilians who could be trusted that they were not secretly working for the enemy. Later, he was taken to a camp in Lucerne where he was able to continue his studies unabated.

As a guest of Agudath Israel in Rheinfelden, R' Moshe spent a Shabbos in the camp where he surveyed the various factions competing against one another for members. Late in the afternoon, a *minyan* for Minchah was organized and a tenth man was needed to complete the *minyan*. Yoav happened to be walking by at that very moment, smoking a cigarette. Someone approached him and asked if he would be willing to be the tenth man for a *minyan*. At first Yoav turned away – he truly had no interest in partaking in a *minyan*. However, upon further reflection, he realized that although he had no interest in praying, he had no reason to deprive others of *davening* with a *minyan*. He wasn't doing anything of importance anyway, and so he went inside.

Within minutes after the prayers began, it became apparent that they could not continue the services because no one knew how to read the Torah with the proper cantillations and accents. Even R' Moshe Soloveitchik, who was standing at the front of the room, refused to read from the Torah, continuously urging someone else to do the job. But there was no one else; no one recalled the proper way to read from the scroll.

An announcement went out: "Is there anyone here who can read the Torah?" There was no response. Requests for someone who could read the Scriptures continued for quite some time. Finally, Yoav stood up and said that although he had not seen a *Sefer Torah* for a long time, he could probably still remember how to read it.

The others looked at this bareheaded young man and wondered. They glanced over at R' Moshe Soloveitchik, only to see him nodding his head in encouragement. Yoav put his cap on. Then, he took his place at the *bimah*, looked over the reading quickly in a *Chumash*, stood in front of the open scroll of the *Sefer Torah*, and began to chant the ancient melody and words. As he stood before the holy scrolls, he felt the letters reaching out to him from the parchment, fixing him in their grasp, riveting him to the spot in front of the Torah. He finished reading and wanted to step down, but the letters would not let him go; their grip on him was firm.

The entire room was mesmerized by his performance and nobody moved a muscle. Yoav continued to stand in front of the scroll, long after he finished reading, and just stared at the words. The message was being transmitted right before his eyes. It was clearly the turning point in his life. He gave up his carefree lifestyle and embarked on the road to complete Torah observance. As he later observed, "The letters have not relinquished their grip on me to this very day."

| THE REICHMANN FAMILY |
A Loan Repaid

As the winds of war rapidly approached, most Jews in countries occupied by or maintaining cordial relations with Nazi Germany, concerned themselves with the real and mortal threat to their safety. A number of wealthy Jews were also preoccupied with the notion of saving their wealth for later retrieval after the war, by converting their soon-to-be worthless bank notes into gold and precious stones or transferring it to Swiss banks.

One man, though, correctly assessed the risks inherent in these actions and looked for a more concrete manner in which to dispose of his considerable assets.

Growing up in Hungary and later living in Vienna, Austria, Shmaya Reichmann had done well for himself in the import-export business of fresh eggs. He realized that as a Jew, he was ill advised to rely on the strict banking codes of privacy offered by the Swiss, which as a neighbor and friend to Germany, could find themselves, and their billions in hoarded wealth, swallowed up by the Nazis. On the other hand, as a Hungarian national in a country not friendly to the Allies, it was possible that his funds might one day not only be frozen by those very same Allied governments, but also confiscated.

The only other option was to wire his money from his secure Swiss bank accounts to a trustworthy individual in a free country, like the United States, and hope to be able to retrieve those funds at a later time. Of course, this could only work with an American-born individual, with no ties to any enemy countries, in order to avoid the problem of having these assets frozen or confiscated due to the politics of wartime.

The only problem was that Reichmann did not know anyone personally in America who was not originally from Europe and who would fit the profile needed for him to entrust his fortune.

It wasn't long before a friend suggested the well-known Bendheim family in New York, who was willing to safeguard quite a number of people's money in the States. Being that the elder Bendheim was an immigrant from Germany, Reichmann was hesitant to use him as his contact. Instead, he decided to wire a check for $75,000 to his son, Charles Bendheim, then a college student in Easton, Pennsylvania, and a true-blooded Yankee Doodle.

When the younger Bendheim received a call from American Express informing him that it was holding a check for $75,000 in his name, he had no idea who it was from and why it was being sent to him. After initial inquiries, the trail turned cold in Switzerland, and his eminent father advised him to make a written record of when he received the check before depositing it into his private account. Charles waited for word on the source of his surprise windfall, but when none came, he forgot about the whole matter in a short time.

The war ended, and Charles Bendheim became a partner in his father's firm. The check he had received all those years earlier was a distant memory. In fact, it remained as such until 1946, when the Reichmanns, Shmaya and his wife Renee, who themselves had escaped from Europe to Tangier, Morocco, and were heavily involved in Hatzalah operations during the war, traveled to the U.S. on a temporary basis, as part of a Va'ad Hatzalah convention, to discuss Agudath Israel's postwar agenda.

One fine morning in New York City, Shmaya Reichmann quietly slipped away and took a train downtown to the Wall Street office of Philipp Brothers, the commodities firm co-founded by the Bendheim family.

When he arrived, he was told that Charles Bendheim was in a meeting. He asked the secretary to inform her boss that he was there to see him, but when she interrupted the meeting to announce that a Mr. Reichmann was there to see him, he replied that he did not know any Reichmann. Not until the visitor stated that Bendheim did know him and he could prove it, did Charles emerge from his meeting, curious as to who this impatient man was.

Charles came out to the waiting area. With characteristic efficiency, Reichmann introduced himself, cited the exact date and amount of the cashier's check that he had wired to a Charles Bendheim back in 1939 before the war began, and politely asked for his money back. Bendheim stared at this short but elegant European for a moment in uncomprehending astonishment. Then, he remembered, and broke out in a broad smile. Without another word, Charles sat down at a desk, pulled out his personal checkbook, and with flair, wrote out a check for the full $75,000. Reichmann studied the check and thanked him. The two men studied each other for an extra moment, shook hands, and Reichmann quickly departed.

The Sages tell us that wealth does not belong to a rich man. Rather, Hashem wishes to distribute this money to all of His children and safeguards these assets in the hands of wealthy individuals until it is time for them to be distributed. At that time, it is the duty and responsibility of a man of means to return and circulate this wealth.

| R' CHAIM SHMULEVITZ/R' SHMUEL BERENBAUM |
Uninterrupted Torah Study

The story of the Mirrer Yeshivah's escape from war-torn Europe to the foreign shores of Shanghai during the height of World War II is legendary. At the start of the war, the yeshivah moved en masse to Vilna, the capital of Lithuania, where they remained for a while before applying and receiving destination visas to Curacao, a Dutch protectorate in the Caribbean, along with travel visas to Japan. The visa-granting actions of the Dutch and Japanese consuls in Vilna enabled the entire yeshivah, which traveled to Vladivostok on the Trans-Siberian Railway, to find safety in Kobe, Japan, before eventually settling in Shanghai, China, for the duration of the war. Miraculously, the yeshivah managed to survive intact with nary even a slight drop in the students' devotion and diligence in their learning.

After the war's end, the entire yeshivah left China for Palestine and the United States, and reestablished itself with two campuses; one in Jerusalem, and one in Brooklyn, New York.

The ship on which R' Chaim Shmulevitz *zt"l*, later to become the renowned head of the Mirrer Yeshivah in Jerusalem, journeyed from Shanghai to the United States was crammed end to end with refugees. There was barely any space for one to sit comfortably but there was little choice for the refugees. R' Chaim, however, took no notice and totally engrossed himself in one of the most complex Talmudic *sefarim* – *Shev Shmaitsa*. For hours on end, R' Chaim could be found crammed into his tiny area, not taking his eyes out of his precious *sefer*.

At one point, a fellow traveler sitting near R' Chaim wondered about the body of land they were passing and asked out loud, "Where are we now?"

R' Chaim, hearing the question in his subconscious, and thinking that the person was addressing him, replied quickly, "In the third *perek*!"

A similar story is told about another *talmid* of the great Mirrer Yeshivah, who later became the *rosh yeshivah* of the Mirrer branch in New York, R' Shmuel Berenbaum *zt"l*. On the very same ship that R' Chaim traveled with the entire body of the Mirrer Yeshivah aboard, R' Shmuel, who was much younger at the time, was also fully engrossed in his studies.

As the ship drew closer to the port of landing in the San Francisco bay, the ship had to pass under the massive structure of the Golden Gate Bridge, one of the engineering landmarks of the world at that time. Practically every person on board the ship crammed the deck and craned their necks to marvel and gawk at the bridge in all its glory.

All but one student – young Shmuel Berenbaum. He was totally engrossed in his studies and had barely looked out at the vast ocean the entire time as the ship sailed across. When the massive bridge came into view, Shmuel did not join the others on the deck. Some of the other students called to him to come and look but he just continued learning.

"You can always learn," they advised him, again urging him to come up on deck, "but this is probably the only opportunity you'll ever have to see this famous sight, which is one of the *nifla'os haBorei* (wonders of creation)."

The future *rosh yeshivah* was indeed very curious to see the bridge, but nevertheless, did not interrupt his learning. In his characteristic wit he called back to them, "Yes, but this will probably be the only opportunity I will ever have to learn at a time when I could be seeing that famous sight!"

| KLAUSENBERGER REBBE |

What Is There to Do Teshuvah For?

The dominant figure in the Feldafing D.P. camp immediately after the conclusion of World War II was the Klausenberger Rebbe, R' Yekusiel Yehuda Halberstam *zt"l*. What he did for the broken survivors was immeasurable. Although he himself had lost a wife and eleven children, he was a constant source of strength and inspiration to his fellow survivors.

On the first Yom Kippur after the war, the rebbe held a *minyan* for the survivors and, after *Kol Nidrei*, he delivered a tremendously powerful speech. When he had finished, more than two hours later, there was not a dry eye in the shul.

The rebbe stood by the *amud*, *tallis* over his head, looking for all the world like an angel. He held a *machzor* in his hand, and flipped through its pages. Periodically, he would look up and ask, "*Vehr hat das geshriben* – Who wrote this? Does this apply to us? Are we guilty of the sins enumerated here?" One by one, he went through each of the sins listed in the *Ashamnu* prayer and then the *Al Cheit* and concluded that those sins had little to do with those who had survived the camps.

"*Ashamnu* (We have become guilty): Does this apply to us? Have we sinned against Hashem or man? How could we? Let's go on.

"*Bagadnu* (We have betrayed): Are we disloyal to Hashem? Have we betrayed our loved ones? No. *Bagadnu* does not apply to us.

"*Gazalnu* (We have stolen): From whom could we have stolen? There was nothing to steal in the camps. I once woke someone up in the middle of night by accident. *Gezel sheinah*. Perhaps I did steal once – but that was it. There was really nothing to steal. This definitely does not apply to us.

"*Dibarnu dofi* (We have spoken slander): We didn't speak any slander. We didn't speak at all. If we had any strength to speak, we saved it for our S.S. guards so that we would have enough strength to answer them.

"*He'evinu, v'hirshanu* (We have caused wickedness), *zadnu* (We have sinned willfully), *chamasnu* (We have extorted), *tafalnu sheker* (We have accused falsely): No, these don't apply to us. *Latznu* (We have scoffed): Who wrote this *machzor*?

Who put it together? We were so serious in the camps. There was no such thing as smiling or making a joke.

"*Maradnu* (We have rebelled): Whom should we have rebelled against? Against Hashem? We weren't able to rebel at all. If we had tried to rebel against the Nazis it would have been the last thing we did."

When the Klausenberger Rebbe had finished the entire *Ashamnu* prayer in this fashion, he continued with *Al Cheit*.

"*Al cheit shechatanu l'fanecha b'ones u'veratzon* (For the sin we have sinned before You under duress and willingly): In the camps, did we have a *ratzon* (will)? We were way beyond the category of *ones* (by compulsion).

"*B'ma'achal u'mishteh* (with food and drink): Food and drink? What food and drink? We starved for years!

"*B'imutz halev* (with hardness of heart): Our hearts were soft. The Nazis saw to that.

"*B'vli da'as* (without knowledge): Our minds were in such a state that we did not have knowledge of anything.

"*B'dibbur peh* (with harsh speech): We spoke only in whispers.

"*B'yetzer hara* (with the evil urge): To sin with the *yetzer hara* you must first have possession of your physical senses; a desire to touch or see or hear or taste something forbidden. We had none of these nor the ability to achieve them.

"We didn't have any sense of touch. We were skin and bones incapable of touching. The only thing we could feel were the corpses that we carried out every morning. Each morning, we looked around to see who was no longer moving and would have to be carried out from the barracks.

"We heard only one thing: the commands of our guards. We had ears for nothing else. Our eyes were only for looking around to see whether our guards were watching when we wanted to take a rest. Otherwise we were as blind men seeing nothing.

"Smell. Yes, we had a sense of smell. The unforgettable stench of death was constantly in our nostrils, making us nauseous. We never got used to that smell. The dead lay everywhere.

"Taste. The only taste we knew was the thin soup they gave us so we would have enough strength for another day's work - the slop that we saw thrown to the pigs. What the S.S. officers would not eat they threw to the pigs. How we envied the pigs, especially for the potato peels that were thrown to them. How we would have loved to eat those potato peels."

One by one, he eliminated every *Al Cheit*. The rebbe then closed his *machzor* and it seemed he had finally finished. But then he asked again, "Who wrote this *machzor*? These sins don't apply to us." He paused. "What I don't see anywhere is the sin that *does* apply to us. What is that sin? The sin of having lost our *emunah* and *bitachon* (faith and trust) in Hashem.

"What is the proof that we sinned in this fashion? How many times did we recite *Krias Shema* on our wood slats at night and think to ourselves: 'Ribono shel Olam, let this be my last *Hamapil*. I can't carry on any longer. I'm so weak. I have no reason to carry on any more. Is there no end to our suffering? *Ribono shel Olam*, please take my *neshamah* so that I do not have to repeat once again in the morning, *Modeh ani l'fanecha* - I'm thankful before You, the living King, who has returned my soul to me. I don't need my soul. I don't want this wretched existence. You can keep it.'

"How many of us went to sleep thinking that we couldn't exist another day, with all our *bitachon* lost? And yet when the dawn broke in the morning, we once again recited *Modeh Ani* and thanked Hashem for having returned our souls.

"Yes, we did survive, but none of us expected to. Every morning, we saw this one didn't move and that one didn't move, and as we carried the dead out, we looked upon them with envy. Is that *emunah* in Hashem? Is that *bitachon* in Hashem?

"*Rabbosai*, we have sinned. We have sinned and now we must *klap 'Al Cheit.*' We must pray to get back the *emunah* and *bitachon* we once had, the *emunah* and *bitachon* that went to sleep these last few years in the camps. Now that we are freed, *Ribono shel Olam*, we beg You to forgive us. Forgive everyone here. Forgive every Jew in the world, *Ribono shel Olam!*"

| R' YAAKOV AVIGDOR |
An Unexpected Find

As countless Jews sought to rebuild their lives after the horrors of the Holocaust, many complex halachic issues surfaced. For example, the vexing question of the *agunah* arose. An *agunah* is a married woman who is not living with her husband, but has not been released from the bonds of matrimony. Though she wishes to put her nuptials behind her, she is chained to an "unwanted" marriage. For many women who wanted to ultimately start new lives, the question was: What is their status? Are they to be considered widows or women whose husbands have disappeared? May they remarry?

Any rabbi who dealt with this complex issue after the war had to first determine the facts. According to halachah, clear evidence was needed that a woman's husband was not alive. Historical information was desperately needed as the basis for discussion whether to permit a woman to remarry.

One of the rabbis who handled many an *agunah* case was R' Yaakov Avigdor *zt"l*, the former Chief Rabbi of Drohobycz-Boryslaw, Ukraine (later to become Chief Rabbi of Mexico City). The *rav* was himself a survivor of Buchenwald and other concentration camps, and underwent the seven levels of gehinnom while under the Nazi yoke. He lost his entire family during the conflagration, and had despaired of finding anyone after the war, since all of his searches had been to no avail. But he never lost his faith and *bitachon* in the Al-mighty. The huge parade-ground in the Plaszow concentration camp was the last time he saw his two sons, Yitzchak and Avraham. The two youngsters, youthful and fit, were sent to the right, while he was sent to the left, with the older people and females. That was the last he heard from them and naturally he feared the worst.

After the war, Bergen-Belsen became one of the main assembly points for survivors, and a special rabbinical bureau had been set up there which devoted itself exclusively to dealing with all matters of family status. Day and night they were besieged by people pleading to Heaven for help and relief.

As it happened, R' Yaakov, who had held the rank of chaplain in the Polish army and was one of the heads of the Jewish Rescue Committee in Bergen-Belsen, was appointed chairman of this Rabbinical Bureau. He wore a military uniform, so that he should be able to move freely in the occupied territories, and as a result very few people recognized him as R' Avigdor, former rabbi of Drohobycz.

On one occasion, in a makeshift courtroom which serviced the Rabbinical Bureau at Bergen-Belsen, R' Yaakov was hearing the case of an *agunah* from his home town, Drohobycz. The woman in this case had married her husband in the Drohobycz ghetto. She did not recognize R' Avigdor, the former rabbi of the town, as his appearance had been altered so dramatically.

It was a complicated case and the rabbis were having difficulty in reaching a decision. The evidence was unclear and not compelling enough to issue a decision in her favor. R' Yaakov asked her if she could provide any further evidence other than her spoken testimony. She thought for a moment and then with a shudder of remembrance, she rummaged through her valise and produced a single sheet of paper. Here, she claimed, was written testimony from a Jew who had seen her husband lying dead in the main assembly square of the Drohobycz ghetto. She produced the letter and held it out to R' Avigdor. It goes without saying that every applicant produced the same sort of unofficial document, and R' Avigdor told her that it would take some time to check. Angrily, she flung the piece of paper down on his desk and shouted that she had a certificate from a rabbi in Italy.

He looked at the writing and then at the signature. Suddenly, his face went white with shock and he quickly looked up at her. "Who gave you this paper?" he asked her in a hoarsely excited voice. She replied that after the war, she had found herself in an Italian port city, where she had met a man who claimed to have been a friend of her husband from Drohobycz. He reported to her that he had seen the deceased body of her husband and offered to give her written testimony to attest to this fact so she could eventually get remarried. At the time, she was not in the frame of mind to be thinking about matrimony and starting a new home, and really had very little interest or need for such a letter. However, the farsighted individual was insistent and virtually forced her to accept his testimony in case she needed it in the future.

R' Yaakov sat motionless for a few long moments while everyone awaited his verdict. He was stunned to discover that the name of the witness who had signed the document was none other than his son Yitzchak. His son was alive!

Through various channels, R' Yaakov was able to contact his son, and it took another three months before he was reunited with not just Yitzchak, but also his younger son Avraham, who had likewise survived with his brother. The joyous reunion between father and sons was marred only by the tale Yitzchak told of their deportation to the Mauthausen death camp, where they suffered tremendous pain and deprivation until their eventual liberation in Gunskirchen, on May 5, 1945, by the Allied forces. They were bloated with hunger and typhus when American soldiers took them to a hospital in the Austrian Tyrol, and a few weeks later to a UNRRA camp, where one night, members of the Jewish Brigade from Eretz Yisrael smuggled them across the border into Italy.

It was in the city of Milan that Yitzchak met up with a girl he recognized from his home town, Drohobycz. She did not recognize him, as the years in the camps had made him look much older than he really was. She had concealed herself at the home of a gentile for two years, and now she was looking for a certain young man whom she had married in the ghetto. Yitzchak told her the sad news that her husband had been a barracks-mate of his in the Gusen camp and had died at work. He had seen him brought back, dead, to the *appellplatz*. He described it all to her, giving her as many details as he could of her husband's death, and tried to comfort her with words. A few days later she came to take leave of him but before they parted, Yitzchak gave her a signed letter attesting that he had seen her husband, dead, and that she was a bona fide widow, eligible to remarry. At first she refused to take the letter, but Yitzchak, knowing what trouble she might have because of her failure to do so, finally persuaded her to take it. When she met another young man in Bergen-Belsen and decided to marry him, it became clear in retrospect that this letter was her savior.

Amazingly, the letter Yitzchak had written for this woman not only allowed her to remarry; it also led to his dramatic reunion with his father who had practically given up hope of ever finding his son alive. They each looked so different from the way they remembered each other and they could only recognize one another by the sound of their voices.

R' Avigdor was reminded of Yaakov Avinu's joyous reunion with his son Yosef, whom he had not seen for twenty-two years. "Only someone who experienced what I did could appreciate Yaakov's feelings upon learning that his son Yosef was still alive!"

Cleansing a *Neshamah* Once and for All

Six million Jews were killed in the atrocities of the Holocaust, but about three-and-a-half million survived. Some were liberated from concentration camps at the end of the war, some were working with partisans in the resistance, and some were hidden by righteous gentiles or escaped the Nazis before the Final Solution was fully underway. After the war these survivors mostly left Eastern

Europe for other countries. Many immigrated to Israel, America, Canada, and Australia.

One woman came to the United States after having lost everything. Her late husband was a partisan in the forests of Poland and was blown up by an informer who infiltrated their band of brothers and was sympathetic to the Nazis. She remarried and lived for over fifty years in the Brighton Beach section of Brooklyn, New York.

In the early 1990s, the now elderly woman decided to write a *Sefer Torah* as a living memorial to her husband and her entire family who perished in the war. She walked into the storefront of a local *sofer stam* (scribe) on Coney Island Avenue, with only her eyes betraying that which she had seen in her life. Her posture erect, she approached the bearded man behind the counter and informed him of her desire to purchase a *Sefer Torah*. He looked at her for a moment and then led her to a shelf where the stuffed and pre-printed Torahs were kept, thinking that she wanted to buy a present, perhaps for a grandchild for Simchas Torah, or the like.

The woman looked at him incredulously and said, "You cannot read from these!"

Realizing his error, the salesman quickly called the *sofer* from the back of the store, who proceeded to show her Torah scrolls in various stages of preparation, ranging from $36,000 and up. She could afford it. She chose one Torah which was more expensive than the others, the dollar amount not being important, reflecting the fact that she understood what a Torah represents. It is the instruction manual for living as a Jew; instructions to be followed so that those who died as Jews – because they were Jews – did not die in vain.

After making her selection, the woman suddenly became anxious. Turning to the *sofer*, the pain in her eyes all the more pronounced, she asked him, "Please, tell me, will I be able to kiss my Torah?"

Not understanding the depth of her seemingly innocent question, the *sofer* replied, "Of course."

The woman shook her head and proceeded to explain to the *sofer*, Rabbi Pincus, how she survived the war years. Fair of complexion, with the ability to pass herself off as a non-Jew, she spent the war years as a chambermaid, masquerading as an Aryan woman, with a cross around her neck. For a stretch, she even worked in the belly of the beast – in the Nazi headquarters. She told Rabbi Pincus that she once was given the "privilege" of making the bed of Hitler himself, *ym"s*. She took this job over the strenuous objections of her father, who told her on numerous occasions before he died that it was "better to die as a Jew than to live like a *goy* (non-Jew)."

But she continued working there, day in and day out, with the cross around her neck. A cross that represented the silent world who watched as the Nazis carried out their nefarious plans. This was the cross that hung around her neck for the duration of the war, filling her with such a repulsive feeling of impure filth that it would take more than fifty years before she allowed herself to kiss a *Sefer Torah*.

But the time was not yet right. Months went by and shortly before the Torah was to be completed, the woman once again visited the Coney Island Avenue storefront to see her Torah. There it was, lying on a table with the velvet mantle embroidered with the names of her martyred family. She approached it, cautiously, hesitantly, slowly reading the names of her family in a hushed voice. Something was stirring within her, a feeling she hadn't felt for so many years.

Suddenly, she threw herself on the Torah and started to scream in an otherworldly voice. In the middle of a store full of people, the woman's tears pierced the heavens – where her father was undoubtedly looking down and crying too: "*Tatte... Tatte! Zolst mir moichel zain! Ribono shel Olam... Zai mir moichel!* Father... Father... Please forgive me! Master of the World... Please forgive me!"

Over and over she screamed and cried. Over and over her tears burst forth, running down her cheeks and onto the velvet mantle. She cried for what seemed like hours, until... there were no more tears. It was at that moment that it hit her like a ton of bricks: she felt she had lived like a *goy*, while her father, of blessed memory, died like a Jew!

Nobody in the store moved. It took many long minutes of silence before she stood up and looked around the shop. She spied a silver pair of candlesticks. With every eye in the store on her, she turned to the man behind the counter and matter-of-factly declared, "You know, they stole my candlesticks as well; I really should replace them."

The man didn't understand. Who had stolen her candlesticks? He asked her if it was someone in Brighton Beach who took them, and if so, why she hadn't reported it to the police.

"They stole my candlesticks," she repeated again, as if not hearing him. "Hitler stole my candlesticks, and ever since, I have been unable to light." To the stunned people listening, she explained that for most of the years in America her husband was the one who lit the Shabbos candles, because after so many years of working with a cross around her neck, a symbol that represented all that was unholy and impure in the world, she believed she had a "*farshmutzedika neshamah*" – a filthy soul.

She had been angry at G-d for allowing the atrocities to take place, but now her tears had cleansed her soul. She realized that it wasn't G-d, but mankind, who bore the sins of inhumanity. A Torah, a manual for living life, was to be dedicated a few short days hence, and she knew that it was time to start living and spreading light in the world once again.

| BINYAMIN WERTZBERGER |
Shamash of the Kosel

It was another dark day during the Second World War. A hungry Jewish boy named Binyamin Wertzberger was hard at work dragging heavy train tracks with his bare thin hands. When it came time to eat, he hurried to secure his gruel with whatever strength he had left, although the food served was minimal and bland. He needed it to get through another day in the slave labor camp.

One day, while standing in the food line, a Nazi officer gave him and his fellow inmates a dirty look. "Do you dream of getting out of here?" he asked with a sneer. "Perhaps going to your Jewish land, to your Jerusalem?"

Nobody spoke. They just wanted their dollop of nourishment. And besides, what was there to say?

The Nazi beast wasn't finished. "I doubt you will ever get there. Maybe your ashes will get there, though, through the chimneys of the crematoria." His taunts and barbs were unceasing.

Binyamin Wertzberger recalls being "beaten, humiliated, starved and forced to work in the most difficult of circumstances." But he never forgot the cruel Nazi's words while waiting on line that day. He vowed that were he to survive, he would make it to Jerusalem.

Towards the end of the war, he was forced into the infamous death march. He and thousands of others trudged for weeks to the Austro-Hungarian border. He recalls: "We walked for days without food or drink. Whoever was tired or drifted off was shot to death. Bodies were piling up as we walked." He shivers from the memory.

After weeks that seemed to drag on forever, the group – now much smaller in size due to attrition – arrived at the Mauthausen concentration camp in the Austrian Alps, a camp with the sinister label of "Grade III" (intended to be the toughest camps for the "Incorrigible Political Enemies of the Reich").

Binyamin Wertzberger was only seventeen at the time. He suffered greatly in that inferno where the expected life span of an inmate was no more than a few weeks. On May 5, 1945, the camp was taken over by soldiers of the Forty-First Recon Squad of the U.S. Eleventh Armored Division, who liberated it after they disarmed the S.S. gendarmes.

The teenager, seasoned well beyond his seventeen years, was thankful to be alive, but quickly learned that he was the only member in his family to have survived. "I had a brother and two sisters and they were all murdered by the Nazis," he says, eyes pinched shut to hold back the tears.

He never forgot the promise he made. After a long journey, he made it to the Land of Israel where he married and raised a family. "*Baruch Hashem*, they all learned in *yeshivos* and lead a life of Torah and *mitzvos*," he says proudly.

When he retired from work, the family hoped he would spend more time at home with them, but Binyamin Wertzberger had one more mission in life.

He walked into the offices of the Western Wall Heritage Foundation, the Jerusalem organization involved in physically maintaining and renovating the area surrounding the Kosel Hama'aravi (Western Wall).

At first, nobody paid him any attention. Finally, he spoke up. "I want to work for you," he told a young man at a desk.

A manager walked over and he reiterated his request. The manager looked at him strangely. "With all due respect, you are an elderly man. We don't have a job to offer you."

But Binyamin was not one to give up. If he was, who knows if he ever would have made it out of the numerous camps he labored in? With a shrill insistence evident in his voice, he said, "Sir, I will do anything you ask. Just let me work here - you won't be disappointed."

Wertzberger was given the task of cleaning the stones of the Kosel, and he wakes up at 5:00 a.m. every day to do so. "I never look at the watch when I am at work," he says. "When I stand near the holy stones, I feel like I'm taking revenge on that Nazi officer. This is my Jewish revenge."

Where Are the Children of the Brisker Rav?

After his miraculous escape from the Nazi inferno, together with his three eldest sons, the Brisker Rav did not rest for a moment in his efforts to get his wife and remaining three children out of Europe. As soon as he arrived in Eretz Yisrael, he visited R' Yitzchak Herzog, the Chief Rabbi of Palestine, a man who had a great deal of influence, and asked him to use his connections to try and save the rest of his family. At the *rav's* request, a letter was sent from the central office of Agudas Yisrael in Jerusalem to Aharon (Harry) Goodman, the head of Agudas Yisrael in England. The letter is dated the fourteenth of Cheshvan, 5703 (1942), and it implores all those who have the capability, to assist the *gaon* of Brisk, one of the *gedolei hador* and a founder of Agudas Yisrael. The correspondence concludes: "This is a matter of life and death and if you have favorable news for him, please notify me by telegram."

It was assumed that the *rebbetzin* perished in the ghetto of Brisk along with her three children: Gittel, Naftali Tzvi Yehuda Leib, and Shmuel Yaakov. However, in the month of Av, 5761 (2001), a group of men, including Rabbi Shimon Yosef Meller, who authored a masterful and comprehensive biography on the Brisker Rav, traveled to Brisk to research the *rav's* life and his impact on world Jewry. In the course of their journey, hitherto unknown facts surfaced.

At a meeting with the director of the official archives of the city, Mrs. Reisa Vladimranva, they requested to see documents stored in the archives that would shed light on the history of the vibrant Jewish community in the city before World War II. Gaining access to the archives, as they soon discovered, involved complicated bureaucratic procedures. Generally, access was granted only several days after the original request, but (for a price, of course) the heads of the archives made an exception in their case and agreed to make "special efforts" to allow them to see the documents within a few hours. (Without the help of Reb Shlomo Weinstein, a resident of the city, they would not have gotten anywhere in the outdated system, typical of the government offices in the former Soviet Union.)

Various permits were required, including a special permit to take copies of documents out of the country. Every page of these permits had to be stamped with a special stamp that included the date and a coded number. In addition, one had to pay for each item at the government bank in the city, and the receipt from the bank had to be presented at the archives. Only then did the archives' directors convene a meeting in order to discuss their request in great detail: first, they had to decide whether to allow them to see the particular document they had asked for, then they had to decide whether the copies of a document could be taken out of the country, etc., etc.

Only at three o'clock in the afternoon did they complete all the bureaucratic details necessary to approve their request. A crowd of otherwise bored clerks appeared from all over the building to be present at this "historic" moment: a foreigner had actually showed interest in the archives' documents.

Among the piles of documents they had requested to see were the original protocols of all the residents of the ghetto whose names began with an "S." Of all the ghettos that existed in Russia, Poland and Lithuania at the time of the Holocaust, the Brisk ghetto is the only one for which there still exists a complete set of the original documents that had been issued for each of the residents of the ghetto. In all the other ghettos the Germans succeeded in destroying almost all the documents that testified to their appalling deeds. Thus, the group was able to view the original identity documents of the residents of the Brisk ghetto, each with an authentic picture of the person and his or her personal details.

Only children above the age of thirteen had their own identity papers; any child younger than that was listed on his father's ID papers, or if the father was gone, on his mother's.

They sifted through the papers of people whose names began with "S" and finally came to that of Rebbetzin Hendl *Hy"d*, and her daughter, Gittel *Hy"d*, who was already fourteen and therefore had her own papers. To their great surprise, the younger boys, Shmuel Yaakov and Leibel, were not listed on the *rebbetzin's* papers, where they should have been.

According to the directors of the archives, experts in their field, this could mean only one thing: the Brisker Rav's little children, Leibel and Shmuel Yaakov, were not in the ghetto of Brisk! There was no such thing as a person living in the ghetto without being registered.

They made one last try, asking to see the document of the grandmother, Mrs. Mintz, who lived with her daughter and was also a resident of the ghetto; they wanted to check if perhaps for some reason the boys had been listed on her papers. But, no, there was no mention of children there, either.

Obviously, this does not prove that these children are still alive, having survived the Holocaust. It is possible that the *rebbetzin* succeeded in handing them over to someone in Brisk or its environs in an attempt to save their lives. It could be that the Germans discovered them and executed them. In any event, the fact remains, and demands explanation: according to the directors of the archives, the children were not in the ghetto.

The whole truth will only be revealed at the End of Time, with the Resurrection of the Dead and the Ingathering of the Exiles.

| BLUZHEVER REBBE |
So Much to Be Thankful For

The year was 1960 and the Bluzhever Rebbe had just recently moved his *beis medrash* from Williamsburg to the Boro Park section of Brooklyn. Local residents were overjoyed that the rebbe had chosen to move to their neighborhood and people of all stripes flocked to pray in his quaint, European-style *shtiebel*.

On the morning of the first day of Pesach, the rebbe honored a young man by the name of Chaim Yossel Kofman to lead the morning prayers, including Hallel, which contains chapters of praise for the Al-mighty from Psalms, written by Dovid Hamelech himself. The young man was known to have a beautiful voice and a tremendous command of the *nusach* – not to mention that he was the son-in-law of one of the prominent members of the synagogue; the *rosh hakahal*, R' Leibish Tisser – and a ripple of excitement washed over the congregants as Chaim Yossel began to sing the Hallel melodies.

For the chapter known as "*Mah Ashiv*," Chaim Yossel chose a haunting tune to accompany the uplifting words. The tune (originally put to the words "*Zechor davar l'avdecha*") was reputed to have been composed by the Skulener Rebbe during the harsh years of World War II. The melody as well as the lyrics bespoke the anguish cast upon Dovid by his enemies (*zeidim helitzuni ad me'od*), and his suffering in the face of great torment. Through it all, though, Dovid Hamelech never wavered from his commitment to the Torah, and many Holocaust survivors, some who had experienced excruciating levels of torment and pain, identified with the song and its message of faith in the Al-mighty shining through the pain.

As Chaim Yossel's melodious voice soared in song and the entire congregation joined in, the Bluzhever Rebbe began to noticeably heave with agonized sobs. Although his face was covered by his *tallis*, one could see tears streaming down his cheeks while a series of shuddering cries racked his slim and frail frame. Not everyone in the congregation heard the rebbe crying and the singing continued in earnest, but it was abundantly clear that something had set off the emotions of the Bluzhever Rebbe and caused him to lose control during the song.

When *davening* had concluded, Chaim Yossel and his father-in-law approached the rebbe and respectfully inquired if everything was alright, and why he had cried so stridently during Hallel. R' Yisroel did not want to discuss it in the *beis medrash* and asked them to come upstairs to his private residence.

When they came up to his living quarters, the Bluzhever Rebbe began to explain. "Young man, your *davening* was brilliant today and I enjoyed it immensely. But as you probably know, the tune you chose for '*Mah Ashiv*' is an old classic from the war years. In fact, it was the first *niggun* I sang after I was liberated. As soon as I heard it, it took me back to another place, to another period of time. I began to relive those terrible years and I literally felt the pain and suffering that I had experienced in the valley of death known as Auschwitz."

The rebbe paused for a moment, and it appeared that he was once again reliving the nightmare of losing his wife, his children and his grandchildren. "What was ironic was that you used this specific song to accompany the words of Dovid Hamelech, where he is praising Hashem and offering his thanks and gratitude for all the good that the Al-mighty bestowed on him."

The rebbe's eyes hardened. "I thought to myself, 'This tune reminds me of all that I lost, while these words exhort me to thank Hashem for all that I've gained! What a contradiction! How can I compare one to the other? The Holocaust robbed me of everything – what can I possibly thank Hashem for?' It was then that I broke down crying and sobbed uncontrollably."

Chaim Yossel Kofman and his father-in-law were utterly stunned and stood there transfixed. What was the rebbe saying? The rebbe was a pillar of faith and *emunah*; so many broken individuals looked to him for all forms of moral and emotional support. And he was always stalwart in his faith! What could he be talking about now?

"But then I concentrated on the words of '*Mah Ashiv*,'" said the rebbe, eyes shining with renewed vigor, "and I realized – I have so much to thank Hashem for! I have my life; I have my health; I have a new wife, children, and *eineklach*. I have my Chassidim; I have this beautiful *beis medrash* – what more can a person want? *L'cha ezbach zevach todah* – 'To You I will offer my thanks!' How can I possibly cry when I have so much to be thankful for?"

The rebbe concluded by telling Chaim Yossel, "I want you to sing this *niggun* every time you *daven* Hallel." In fact, Chaim Yossel Kofman still uses this *niggun* every year when he *davens* in the Bluzhever *beis medrash* – fifty-three years later!

| R' MENASHE KLEIN |

A Duty to Fulfill

A number of weeks after the American army liberated Buchenwald, a transport consisting of Jewish youths left the camp and was taken to a convalescent home in Ecouis, France, for rehabilitation and recovery. A secular Jewish organization known as OSE (*Oeuvre de Secours aux Enfants*, Society for Rescuing Children), a French Jewish charity organization, had rented the property in order to revive the spirits of the Jewish youth, and also in the hopes of convincing these young people to remain in France permanently.

Among the young men in the transport was R' Menashe Klein *zt"l*, who was then twenty-one years old. He had arrived in Buchenwald as a teenager and spent his formative years bouncing from one concentration camp to another. After his liberation, he remained in Buchenwald for a while where he completed a postwar military interview, and testified to the horrors he witnessed under the Nazis. Even in the D.P. camp that was set up there, he constantly strove to strengthen the shattered men and women who came from all over to Buchenwald, and encourage them with words of comfort and Torah.

Subsequently, he was included in the transport with approximately five hundred other Buchenwald boys and teenagers and remained with the religious complement at Ambloy and Taverny. To the older boys in Ecouis, he taught *Chumash* and *Rashi*. To the younger boys, he taught *aleph-beis*. One of these young boys later grew up to become the Chief Rabbi of Israel, Rabbi Yisroel Meir Lau *shlit"a*. Rav Lau remembers his *rebbi*, R' Menashe, vividly and fondly.

Although the camp in Ecouis was run by the OSE, an organization that was decidedly non-religious in nature, some concessions were provided to these children to allow them to retain a connection to their past. Right from the start, a kosher kitchen was set up and R' Menashe Klein was instrumental in ensuring that it adhered to the highest standards of kashrus. It was this kitchen that provided food for the entire camp.

One day, a rumor circulated around the camp that a Chassidic rebbe was visiting in the area. R' Menashe was curious and excited, and when he beheld the visage of the Klausenberger Rebbe, R' Yekusiel Halberstam *zt"l*, he almost cried from happiness. Although he had never before met the Klausenberger Rebbe, he had heard of the man and his righteous deeds on behalf of the survivors of the Holocaust. He was anxious to meet him and receive a blessing.

The rebbe was equally excited when he saw the young man standing before him. Here was a Jew with a beard and long curly *peyos*, the likes of which he hadn't seen since before the war broke out. How unusual it was for anyone – especially here in Ecouis, in a non-religious environment – to maintain such a semblance of his Chassidic past. The rebbe spent hours talking to R' Menashe and was impressed with his scholarly abilities, as well as his tenacious adherence to halachah.

At one point in the conversation, the Klausenberger Rebbe asked R' Menashe to join him for the upcoming Shabbos. The rebbe was to remain in the area and very much wished to have this young Chassidic scholar join him for the Shabbos meals. However, his offer was quickly turned down. The rebbe continued to urge him to come but R' Menashe demurred time after time. Surprised and disappointed, the rebbe asked him with mock indignation, "Why do you not wish to be with me for Shabbos? Do I upset or bother you in any way?"

R' Menashe quickly answered, "No, no, Rebbe. It's nothing like that, *chas v'shalom*. In fact, nothing would give me greater pleasure than to spend Shabbos with you." The young man continued his explanation. "The problem is that I am fully responsible for the quality of kashrus in the camp's kitchen. There is no one else I can trust to oversee that everything is properly looked after here. In fact, the one time that I was away turned out to be a disaster. No one was in charge or cared enough to make sure that the food was kept kosher and when I returned, I found the kitchen in such a state of disarray that I spent weeks just trying to restore it to where it was."

With a sad smile, R' Menashe shook his head. "Rebbe, I wish I could be with you, but I know that if I do, five hundred Jewish boys would very likely end up eating *treif* food, and I could not allow that to happen. I am willing to forgo the pleasure of spending Shabbos with the rebbe to ensure that everyone here eats kosher!"

| RECHA STERNBUCH |
A Life of Giving

The *she'eiris hapleitah* – those Jews who had survived the indescribable horrors of the Nazi ghettos and concentration camps – were alive in body, albeit just barely. Emotionally, physically and spiritually, however, they remained every bit the victim. Their frail bodies may have been liberated from torture, but suffering still pervaded their souls. Most were extremely susceptible to disease and depression, and they kept reliving the nightmares of the camp experience. Thus, ironically, thousands of inmates who had made it through the war years now fell prey to illness or shock, and died.

Even for those who did not succumb, the war's conclusion brought no remedy or solace. They had no homes or families to which to return; their parents, wives and children were dead, and their homes had been confiscated by gentiles. For the time being, most of the survivors were sheltered in Displaced Persons camps (D.P. camps), where conditions were generally poor and spirits were dangerously low. As much as they suffered physically, their spiritual needs were ignored by camp officials and United Nations workers who were unaware of the role religion played in these Jews' lives.

Mrs. Recha Sternbuch *a"h* was not a person content to offer aid from a distance. Together with her husband, R' Yitzchak Sternbuch *z"l*, she created a relief organization known as HIJEFS, which became the Swiss arm of the American Va'ad Hatzalah. Throughout the war, she worked tirelessly to rescue Jews and spirit them out of German-controlled lands into neutral Switzerland and to safety. Now, at the conclusion of the war, she felt the need to establish a direct, personal connection with the survivors, specifically by visiting them and learning of their needs on a face-to-face basis. She wanted so much to help her persecuted people. During the end of 1945, and for much of 1946, she was constantly on the move shuttling from one war-ravaged city to the next, bringing precious exit visas to one group of survivors and organizing emergency relief efforts for another. Danger didn't faze her. After scores of Jews were killed in a pogrom in Kielce, Poland in July 1946, she insisted on visiting the city, despite the obvious threat to her safety.

Her presence in the Displaced Persons camps brought the survivors not only much-needed goods but, even more importantly, an aura of hope and a sense of camaraderie. Those in the drab, gloomy camps greeted her sudden luminous appearance with heartfelt gratitude. She was like a magical benefactress who reminded them that a brighter future lay ahead.

The women inmates at the Zeilsheim D.P. camp in Germany were among the many recipients of Mrs. Sternbuch's generosity. She arrived there unheralded one day, lugging suitcases of precious goods and necessities. After welcoming her, one of the camp members asked at which hotel she would be lodging during her stay in the area.

"Hotel?" Mrs. Sternbuch replied, surprised. "I was planning to stay in the camp with you."

"Stay in the camp? In this place?" The other woman was astounded. "But it's not exactly luxurious here, I'm afraid."

"There are more important things than luxury, my dear. I didn't come to live the life of a queen. I came to be with you."

"Yes," the shocked survivor said, "but we aren't able to leave this place. You can - you have a choice."

"Fine," said Mrs. Sternbuch, "then I choose to stay with you!" This elegant lady then settled in to live amidst the squalor of the camp and made herself at home among her fellow Jews. She mingled easily with them, listening to their woes, comforting them and promising to seek their early release. Even if she couldn't free them immediately, she told them, she could make their existence easier. She asked people what they needed and compiled lists of their requests. Later, she followed up by sending as many of these goods as she could - even *sheitels* for new brides who had requested them. Some wishes were satisfied immediately, for even though she arrived with loaded suitcases, they were always empty when she left. Whatever she had brought along remained behind, to be kept by those she had visited.

Her life was one of giving. She gave to others, she said, "Because they will put it to much better use than I would."

| LIEUTENANT BIRNBAUM |

The Feldafing Feast

Towards the end of the war, the Germans attempted to hide the enormity of their atrocities and started to transport Jewish prisoners from camps like Dachau and

Bergen-Belsen to the Tyrol. The conquering Allied forces overtook a number of these transports and liberated the thankful, starving prisoners. However, having no place to put the liberated Jewish prisoners, they decided to use the nearby German army base for the purpose of housing the survivors. This became the D.P. camp known as Feldafing. Later, three other camps developed – Föhrenwald, Landsberg and Dachau – as each previous one became filled to capacity.

First Lieutenant Meyer Birnbaum, of the Fifty-Ninth Signal Battalion of the United States army, had landed on the coast of Normandy, France, during the D-Day invasion, and fought on the front lines all throughout the liberation of Europe. He had seen and liberated a number of concentration camps, including Ohrdruff and Buchenwald, and since he spoke Yiddish, he was able to communicate and provide a measure of solace to the desolate and despondent survivors. Even after their liberation, many of these individuals, having lost their entire families, were unable to cope or go on with their lives, and Lieutenant Birnbaum eventually moved into the barracks at Feldafing to live amongst, and assist, his Jewish brethren. Accompanied by his staff sergeant, a man by the name of Rojo, for the next five months after liberating the camps in April 1945, Meyer Birnbaum gave up the more comfortable army barracks nearby and slept in Block 5A in Feldafing.

Using his status as an American lieutenant, Birnbaum was able to requisition whatever his fellow Jews required. Whether it was *sefarim* from destroyed synagogues in the surrounding villages, food parcels from Agudah activists in the U.S., or *arba'ah minim* (Four Species used on Sukkos) and *gartelach* (a belt used by Chassidim for prayer), Birnbaum was able to get it. And when it was nearing the time to begin reciting *Selichos* prior to the Yamim Nora'im, he succeeded in obtaining a great number of *Selichos* books.

After that, he went to ask the Klausenberger Rebbe, R' Yekusiel Yehuda Halberstam *zt"l*, a former concentration camp prisoner and current resident in Feldafing, if there was anything else he could do. The rebbe thought for a moment and then told him that he had managed to procure a proper *chalif* (knife for performing *shechitah*) from a Jewish chaplain who had passed through the camp, and there was a qualified *shochet* (ritual slaughterer) among the survivors.

His request, then, was if the good lieutenant could possibly obtain any sheep for the Jews to make a grand feast in honor of the upcoming holidays.

Birnbaum and his sergeant, Rojo, commandeered a two-and-a-half ton truck and requisitioned seven sheep from farmers in the region. There was great rejoicing in the camp when they drove up with the bleating sheep. The people took the animals off the truck and the *shochet* slaughtered them right there on the grass. Of the seven sheep, only four were found to be kosher. That was, however, sufficient to prepare a feast for the coming Shabbos, to which the entire camp was invited. For the survivors it would be the first taste of meat in many years. Lieutenant Birnbaum and Rojo were invited as the guests of honor to the *seudah*.

Everything proceeded smoothly on Shabbos night until it came time for Kiddush. There was no kosher wine. Once again, Meyer Birnbaum came to the rescue. He told the Klausenberger Rebbe not to worry as he had plenty of kosher wine that he had made himself.

Part of their army rations was a small package of raisins, and Birnbaum would save these packets and put them into a canteen with a little water and sugar and allow them to ferment. With this "wine," he made Kiddush and Havdalah every week in his barracks. Now, using the homemade wine from the lieutenant's canteen, the rebbe made Kiddush and sat down to drink. No sooner had he placed the first sip in his mouth, however, than he spit it out, saying, "That's not wine, that's vinegar, and I made the wrong *brachah*. One cannot recite *Borei Pri Hagafen* on vinegar."

The rebbe was not really upset and Meyer Birnbaum and his buddy laughed aloud. Apparently, since they had been drinking this wine/vinegar for so long, they had ceased to notice its sour taste and just assumed that's what wine tasted like.

Shabbos day was the eagerly awaited feast. A huge cholent had been prepared and was placed before the rebbe. The rebbe tasted the cholent and then took another big spoonful and passed it to Birnbaum as the guest of honor. Standing behind the lieutenant was Rojo, his faithful companion and the one who had cooked all of the lieutenant's food for the past year. As the spoon was being passed from the rebbe to the lieutenant, Rojo suddenly reached out and knocked it out of the rebbe's hand, sending the cholent flying through the air. Everyone froze in total shock and horror.

"No one does any cooking for my lieutenant. I'm the only one who cooks for him. Don't you know that he eats kosher and only kosher?" Rojo exclaimed.

"*Vus hat der meshugener gezugt?*" ("What did the crazy man say?") the rebbe wanted to know. Birnbaum tried to explain to him how Rojo did all of the cooking for him, using his army helmet as a pot. He even showed the rebbe his helmet of many colors. The rebbe began to laugh as he understood how protective the sergeant was of his senior officer.

All that was left was to explain to Rojo that the Klausenberger Rebbe was no ordinary person. In fact, he was a very holy man and they could surely rely on the fact that anything he served was kosher.

"I'm not sure," said Birnbaum later, "whether Rojo was completely mollified by my explanation. I think his feelings were hurt at no longer being my exclusive cook!"

| R' YOSEF FRIEDENSON |

There Are None So Wise as the Jewish People

In a small *shtiebel* in Monsey, New York, the Yom Tov of Simchas Torah seems to be frozen in time. The total amount of men, teens and young boys in the shul is no more than thirty to thirty-five, but one would not know this by the looks of it; it feels like much more due to the high-strung level of excitement, the loud and passionate singing, and the zealous, energetic, "*lebedik*" dancing that goes on for hours.

The shul played host, almost every Simchas Torah, to a very distinguished guest. Each year, Reb Yosef Friedenson, the renowned historian, editor of *Dos Yiddishe Vort,* Holocaust survivor and author of numerous books on the topic, came to visit his daughter and son-in-law, the Goldings. They were sure to attend *hakafos* in the small *shtiebel*. Mr. Friedenson was not a young man and he was content to watch, with unbridled joy, as the lively dancers circled the *bimah* time after time, their *simchah* palpable and their singing reaching crescendo after crescendo. He, too, got up to dance for his *hakafah*, and while he held the *Sefer Torah* tightly in his arms, his mind took him back to another time and another place. This was when he prepared himself for what can only be described as the "highlight" of the entire day. Midway between the fourth and fifth *hakafah*, the lively group suddenly quieted down and awaited "the story." Mr. Friedenson stood up by the *bimah* and in his inimitable manner recounted a fascinating and inspiring incident that occurred to him in the Starachowice concentration camp, many years earlier.

Although this custom had been ongoing in the *shtiebel* for close to ten years, this past Simchas Torah (5773) was undoubtedly one of the most memorable ones. Mr. Friedenson was not feeling well and his body appeared to be weaker than it ever was. He walked slowly, hunched over, with someone assisting him by his side. When he walked in, he greeted the shul members quietly and sat down heavily in a corner. When the time came for him to give his annual speech - between the fourth and fifth *hakafah* - no one knew if he had the strength to do it.

But Mr. Yosef Friedenson was not one to give in so easily. He knew that he had a responsibility to four generations; to the older men in the shul, to the women watching and listening from the ladies section, to the children who gazed at him in wide-eyed wonder, to the young fathers who will never forget the story that Mr. Friedenson was about to tell them. Shakily and with great effort, he stood up at the *shtender* that was brought to him. The moment he lay his hand on the wood, his posture straightened, his demeanor became distinguished, and his words became articulate. This was what he was created to do. He cleared his throat and began to speak in his elegant Polish accent.

"I will never forget that year. We were in the smithy shop preparing to work for the day, but for some reason, we had not been assigned any work to do. This was unusual but we were not complaining. Somebody remembered that today was Simchas Torah, and we all began singing the appropriate songs. Then, someone started the *niggun*, '*Ein adir k'Hashem,* v'ein baruch k'ben Amram' (There is none as powerful as Hashem, there is none as blessed as [Moshe] the son of Amram.). This is a traditional *niggun* that is usually sung when we dance with the Torah on Simchas Torah.

"Anyway, we were singing the part of this *niggun* that says, '*Ein zechiyah k'Torah, v'ein chachamehah k'Yisrael*' (There is no merit like the Torah, there are no men of wisdom like those in [Klal] Yisrael.), when suddenly the camp commandant, a somewhat civil German by the name of Bruno Papeh, walked into the room. He looked at us singing and he seemed to become angry. 'What is this? Why are you singing? Do you have it so good here that you can sing?' Everybody stopped quickly. We were frightened. Papeh was relatively civil – but he was still a German.

"'Friedenson,' Papeh called to me, 'tell me, what are you singing?' I stepped forward, obviously chosen to be the spokesperson of the group. I explained that today was our holiday and that we were praying in song, a song pertaining to the holiday.

"'You were praying or you were singing?' asked Papeh. 'Were you praying for the downfall of the Fuhrer? Is that what your song is about? Translate the words for me.' I did as he asked and I explained the meaning of the words to him. When I came to the part that there are no men of wisdom like the scholars of Israel, he derisively exclaimed, 'Are you Jews so wise? *Du glaubst in das?* Do you believe in this?'"

Mr. Friedenson paused for a moment to wipe his brow. The strain was tremendous, but the look on the faces of the men and children as they listened to his words was worth all the effort. Like a lion, he gathered up his strength and continued.

"I remember, there was a boy of seventeen or eighteen, just a Jewish boy, not even from our religious group. He jumped up and said in German, 'Yes, Herr Commandant, I believe! *Ich glaub!*' Papeh then began asking each of us in turn if we also believed in this. He went from person to person, starting with me. You have to understand that we were not afraid to say the truth to him, because we knew he was good to us. Each and every person in the shop said, 'Yes! We believe.'

"Papeh looked at us and excitedly gestured with both arms while exclaiming, 'You Jews are amazing. I don't know how the Fuhrer will ever be able to defeat you!' and he walked away. It was an incredible moment of pride and faith."

Mr. Friedenson finished the story and broke out into a huge smile. "How right he was and how fortunate we are today to be able to learn Torah in reestablished centers of Torah and *Chassidus* throughout the world. We must never be afraid and we must always believe. *Nu*, what can I say... '*Ein zechiyah k'Torah v'ein chachamehah k'Yisrael...*'"

This was the cue and the small *shtiebel* in Monsey broke out in joyous singing and dancing.

| VIZHNITZER REBBE |

The Food of Paradise

In the ghettos throughout Eastern and Western Europe, malnutrition and disease stalked the starving, hapless inhabitants. Rations were deliberately fixed by the Nazi oppressors at a level impossible to sustain life, and were often not even delivered. When they were, they were of the lowest possible quality. Only the black market smuggling of food and other essentials made survival possible. Soup kitchens run by local and sometimes international Jewish agencies proliferated in Nazi-occupied Poland, Czechoslovakia, and later in Hungary. Once Jews were concentrated in ghettos, their food supplies were controlled by the Germans. With food allocations limited to only a fraction of that required to maintain life, most Jews were dependent on supplemental nourishment provided by the soup kitchens. However, in almost every case, these free soup kitchens did not serve kosher food, as all meat products lacked proper kosher certification.

In the chaotic days and weeks after the end of the war, a group of young men who had survived the ghettos and labor camps found themselves in the Hungarian capital of Budapest. Another survivor of the German oppression, the Vizhnitzer Rebbe, R' Chaim Meir Hager *zt"l*, also happened to be in Budapest at the time, providing solace to the grief-stricken Jews who remained alive while most, if not all, of their family and relatives had perished in the Nazi conflagration. A nagging concern persistently bothered these young men and they felt it was important to meet with the Vizhnitzer Rebbe and discuss their problem with him.

The moment the rebbe laid eyes on them, he knew that their concern was different than what he had been hearing until then. The leader of the group began to talk and as the spokesman, he came directly to the point.

"Rebbe, we need to do *teshuvah* (repentance)! For the past few years, we have been eating nonkosher food from wherever we were able to find it, whether it was in the soup kitchens or it was the meager rations we received in the camps. To be sure, they never were large rations and the portions we ate were barely enough to stem the tide of our grumbling stomachs. Nevertheless, we feel as if our souls, our very *neshamos*, have become tainted over time."

The spokesman paused for a moment and looked around at the lowered heads of his companions. "Should we have resisted? Should we have starved ourselves? Perhaps. But the temptation to partake in a steady, hot meal caused us to lower our standards. Rebbe, please tell us what form of penance we must do to remove the vestiges of *treif* food and restore our *neshamos* to their purest form."

The Vizhnitzer Rebbe listened in stunned silence. Immediately, his face began changing colors. First he went white; then his cheeks turned varying shades of crimson and pink from emotion. He jumped out of his seat and began pacing the room - practically running from one end to the other. The young men were not prepared for this reaction and did not know what to make of it. Suddenly, the rebbe stopped and burst into tears.

He took the spokesman's two hands in his own and just cried. Minute after long minute went by and the rebbe could not contain his tears. Finally, he paused long enough to speak.

"What exactly do you want? *Teshuvah* for eating in that gehinnom (purgatory)? For not depriving yourselves even more than you already were?" R' Chaim Meir held onto the man's hands and looked directly into his soul. His eyes burned bright. "Now listen to me good and well, for I am about to tell you something very important. After 120 years, when you go up before the Heavenly Tribunal and they check your card to see if you have merit or guilt, a portion of your card will light up as bright as the sun. The portion relating to nonkosher food - and specifically the portion that relates to the past few years when you were forced to eat from soup kitchens, camp kitchens, no kitchens - this portion of your card will suddenly become illuminated; the words will shine so bright that you will not even be able to gaze at them."

The young men were listening with rapt attention as the Vizhnitzer Rebbe painted for them a vivid portrait of what things will be like in the next world. "My dear souls," said the rebbe, looking around at the group of men. "When life is normal and the world is under control, it is almost impossible for a human being to protect himself entirely from placing forbidden items into his mouth. Even the most careful and cautious individual has a hard time with this and nobody is perfect. Nobody! However, during the days of destruction that we all just went through, not only was it permissible to eat whatever you ate, in fact it was a commandment, a mitzvah of the highest order! It was, without the slightest doubt in my mind, an absolute obligation to eat in order to stay alive. Eating *chazer-treif*, the flesh of a swine, in the ghettos and camps was as holy as eating a *kezayis* of the *Korban Pesach* in Jerusalem – maybe even greater!"

Once again, the rebbe broke down in tears. "How I envy you," he said quietly between sobs, "such holy and righteous men like yourselves. *Halevai, halevai*! If only my share in Paradise will be like yours, just on account of the reward you will receive for eating the food you ate during the war! *Halevai*!"

| BOBOVER REBBE |

"So That Future Generations Should Know..."

Anyone who has ever been to the Bobover sukkah in Boro Park will attest to the glory, splendor and majesty of this huge and brightly lit structure. One is struck with wonder at the size and beauty of the sukkah, and when it is filled with the rebbe and his Chassidim singing and dancing to the joyous holiday *niggunim*, there is simply nothing in the world that can compare to it.

On one occasion during the 1970s, the Bobover Rebbe, R' Shlomo Halberstam *zt"l*, was sitting with his Chassidim in the grand sukkah, infused with the joy and happiness of the holiday. The rebbe was engrossed in a Torah conversation with a scholar who was sitting nearby. The entire assemblage was eating and drinking, taking a pause before the next heartfelt *niggun* was to begin.

Two senior Bobover Chassidim, Reb Moishe Braunfeld and Reb Moishe Shia Zanger, were sitting together on the dais, a few seats away from the rebbe. Moishe Braunfeld turned to his friend, Moishe Shia, gave him a look and pointed to the magnificent sight of thousands of Chassidim in the sukkah. "Reb Moishe Shia," he said, "just look at all this... a far cry from years ago. Do you remember what our sukkah looked like back in the *lager* (concentration camp)...?"

Moishe Shia looked at his friend and quickly cut him off. "Reb Moishe, now is not the time – now is *Zman Simchaseinu* (time of joy). Let's not talk about those bitter times."

Just then, the Bobover Rebbe stopped his conversation. He had overheard his devout Chassid saying something but couldn't hear exactly what it was. "Moishe Shia," he asked, "what was that you just said?"

The sukkah suddenly became quiet as all followed the rebbe's movement and all wished to hear what was going on. Moishe Shia smiled a bit uncomfortably, due to the sudden attention directed at him. He looked at R' Shloime and said, "Rebbe, it's really nothing of importance."

The rebbe looked sternly at him, saying, "Tell me what was just said."

With no other choice, he told the rebbe, "Reb Moishe just asked me if I remember the sukkah we built in the concentration camp where we were able to *chap* a bit to eat."

The rebbe nodded. "*Nu!* What did you tell him?"

Sheepishly, Moishe Shia responded, "I told him it's *Zman Simchaseinu; vus darf mehn reddin yetst* (why must we speak of this now)?"

The Bobover Rebbe's face became aglow as all eyes were fixed upon him. He shook his head in disapproval and exclaimed, "It says in the Torah, *L'ma'an yaidu doroseichem ki basukkos hoshavti*. The generations need to know that *Yidden* in all situations and at all times made every effort to sit in the sukkah. Moishe Shia - *yetst darf mehn reddin* (now is the time to talk)!"

Moishe Shia listened to the call of the Bobover Rebbe and retold the story in front of the thousands of eagerly listening Chassidim. "*Ich gedenk* - I remember, it was Sukkos 1944. Reb Moishe Braunfeld and I were in Buna-Auschwitz, together with a number of other Bobover Chassidim. Reb Moishe was a foreman and his job entailed overseeing our group of workers. He had to make sure that every morning, after the *resha'im* counted the prisoners, his group went in an orderly fashion to the gate of the camp for the day's work assignment. At the gate played the infamous orchestra that the Nazis formed to ridicule the Jews, taunting them with the empty words, '*Arbeit macht frei*' (work makes one free).

"After his group left for the day's work, Reb Moishe would return to his block to oversee the cleanup. I was part of the *stubendienst* (barrack-duty) and I also would return to the barracks. Right at the entrance of the gate were loose boards, big and small pieces of wood lying about. I spoke with Reb Moishe about the possibility of making a sukkah with this wood; there were even thin pieces we could use for *s'chach*. We determined that in the few minutes we had from when our group would reach the gate of the camp until the Nazi overseers would arrive to open the gate and let the prisoners out to work, we could take some of the wood and build our sukkah.

"Erev Sukkos, we put our plan into action. We acted as if we were making order of the wood lying around and we managed to put together a small sukkah. The Jews at the gate watched us but said nothing. The plan worked and the sukkah was ready, but we still had a problem since the entrance was quite a distance from the block house where we all were housed at night.

"Of course, roaming around in Auschwitz at night was strictly off-limits. Yet, with the *mesiras nefesh* of a few hundred *Yidden*, that year we all risked our lives to *chap* a *kezayis* (an olive-size measurement) of bread in the sukkah while the Nazis were not looking. The tiny sukkah was able to hold three or four people at a time. Each person would quickly enter the sukkah, make a *brachah* '*Leisheiv Basukkah*' and eat a *kezayis*. Then they would exit and let other people in. In order for people not to have to shlep water to wash their hands for the bread, we even set up shifts of people who would pass forward and backward the cups of water to wash *netilas yadayim* – just like the *kohanim* in the Beis Hamikdash.

"We used our 'beautiful' sukkah on that first night only – we didn't dare to think of trying it again the second night since the danger was so great. We were thankful to fulfill the Torah obligation of the first night of Yom Tov, eating a *kezayis* in the sukkah." Reb Moishe Shia concluded his story, as thousands of Chassidim gazed at him and his friend Reb Moishe Braunfeld with a combination of awe and admiration.

R' Shloime Halberstam slowly nodded his head and uttered the words, *"L'ma'an yaidu doroseichem...* Indeed, we must talk about it..."

"For the Wish of Mortal Man Is Worms"

The following story is told by Rabbi Chaim Kahan, senior lecturer of the Jewish Learning Exchange in Yeshivas Ohr Somayach.

One summer, R' Chaim attended a Torah Umesorah convention, where he was asked to deliver a lecture on Shabbos afternoon, on Pirkei Avos. It was the fourth Shabbos of the Pirkei Avos cycle, and R' Chaim began his lecture by quoting the words of the mishnah which states, *Be exceedingly humble in spirit, for the end of mortal man is worms* (*Avos* 4:4).

"Why does the Mishnah use the words *Tikvas enosh rimah* – 'The end of man is worms'?" asked the guest lecturer. "The word '*tikvah*' denotes desire, as if to say, a person wishes or desires to be a worm! Which person in the world would wish he was a worm?"

The audience laughed at R' Chaim's off-hand wit and he then proceeded to explain based on the words of the Gemara (*Eruvin* 100b): *Had the Torah not been given, we would have learned modesty from the cat; the impropriety of thievery from the ant; chastity from the dove.* With these words, R' Chaim explained, the Sages teach us to derive moral instruction from everything in the world, including the instincts of animals.

After he finished the lecture and the audience began to disperse, a man approached him. "Rabbi," he said, "I have a different explanation for the mishnah."

"Go ahead," R' Chaim said with a smile. "I'm all ears!"

The man raised his sleeve and silently showed R' Chaim the numbers branded on his arm.

"When the Germans came to take us all away to the camps," he said softly, "they squeezed us into cattle cars like animals – a few hundred people in each car. We were so tightly packed that we were hardly able to move. The situation could have deteriorated terribly, but everyone had tremendous respect for one another, and no shoving, pushing or complaining was heard.

"As the trip progressed, someone noticed a slight crack in the back of the car. We all agreed to move inch by inch and allow everyone to pass the crack and enjoy a few moments of sunlight and fresh air.

"Half a day had gone by before it was my turn to stand in front of the crack. I pressed my face up against it and enjoyed the wind stirring against my cheek. I breathed in the fresh air and looked at the tiny ray of sunshine that penetrated into the darkness of the packed cattle car. As I glanced down, I noticed a worm wriggling through the crack into the free outdoors.

"'*Ribono shel Olam*,' I prayed with all my heart, 'how I wish I could switch places with that worm!'

"Miraculously, I lived through the horrors of the concentration camps. And every year, when I learn Pirkei Avos, I realize anew that our Sages do not arbitrarily choose their words. When they tell us, *Be exceedingly humble, for the wish of man is worms*, there is a very important meaning here. A person must always be humble, for he never knows what life will bring; circumstances can change to the point where one actually wishes that he is a worm!"

| REB SHRAGA FEIVEL WINKLER |
Kosher Generations

This is a story about a grandfather who died protecting the values he stood for his entire life, as well as the integrity and the future values of a grandson, great-grandchildren, and hundreds of Jews he never met. They owe their lives to a righteous man they would never meet, yet come to know and hear so much about.

Joe (Yossi) Walis was born in Israel and moved to the United States while still a child. He grew up in New York and learned the streets, fast. Despite the threat of gang life all around him, he was determined to major in engineering at a prominent American university, and he graduated from City College at the top of his class. He married and returned with his wife to Israel where he excelled in his tour of duty in the Israeli army. Later, he moved back to the U.S. and used his military experience to open an aircraft parts, helicopter and weapons business that became very successful. After Joe became well known and established in the industry, he moved his base of operations back to Israel.

He was known to work long hours and become wholly consumed with his work; he left little time for eating and recreation. His employees, however, appreciated his dedication and loved him for it. One late night, after finishing up the work he had to take care of, Joe left his office in downtown Tel Aviv and decided to pick up a bite to eat. Nearby, there was a restaurant he had heard about called *"Mis'ad Hapil"* (The Elephant's Restaurant), known for its *"basar lavan"* (pork) and pita. It was one of the only such establishments in the city that served such blatant nonkosher fare, but Joe didn't have a problem giving it a shot.

It had been a hot and long day, and Joe was tired. The line was out the door. Joe got on line and was waiting patiently for his turn to order when his mind began wandering, taking him back to a story he had heard a long time ago…

Joe's maternal grandfather, Reb Shraga Feivel Winkler *Hy"d*, was a *melamed*, a teacher of children, and known as the most pious man in the town of Feldesh, Hungary. He was respected by all who knew him. In 1944, Reb Shraga Feivel was taken from his home by the Nazi beasts and interned in a slave labor camp outside of Hungary. He had no contact with his family and had no idea of their whereabouts.

As the war was coming to an end and the concentration camps were soon to be liberated, those Nazi soldiers who hadn't yet fled felt the need to humiliate as many Jews as they could before they were freed. They decided to make an example of Reb Shraga Feivel, the one they sneeringly referred to as the "Camp *Rabbiner.*"

The Nazi soldiers assembled all the Jews in the camp and ordered them to form a wide circle. Then, they called for the *rabbiner*, Reb Shraga Feivel, to step forward. "You can already see the Allied tanks kicking up dust off in the distance, and soon you will all be free," the Nazi officer began. Then he pointed to Reb Shraga Feivel and held out his hand, which contained a piece of cooked meat. "But before you are free, rabbi, you must first pass this test. This is pork. If you want to live and see your family again, you must eat it. If you do not eat it, then you will not be freed with everyone else."

Reb Shraga Feivel had starved himself the entire time he was in the camp, refusing to eat anything that was not kosher. He survived on water, vegetables and little else, and he was not prepared to forgo his principles now. "I will not eat this meat," he announced defiantly, to which the Nazi responded with one thunderous shot from his pistol. Reb Shraga Feivel was killed instantly.

Standing on line in this *treif* restaurant, Joe began to contemplate to himself: "My grandfather was willing to die so as not to eat pork," he thought, "and here I am, of my own volition, standing in line to eat it. Either I am not normal or he was not normal! I cannot believe that my grandfather was not normal. I must find out why he would do something that seems so crazy!" With that thought in mind, Joe walked out of *Mis'ad Hapil* and bought dinner elsewhere.

After dinner, Joe and his wife had a long talk, speaking of the emptiness gnawing at their souls. A few days later they heard about a seminar called Arachim (Gateways), given by two scientists, Dr. Sholom Srebrenik and Mr. Tzvi Inbal, and they decided to attend. For four days, Joe and his wife listened, questioned, absorbed, discussed, evaluated and reflected, and by the end of the seminar they were convinced that their previous lives were over.

Yossi Walis, as he became known, was determined to help others understand what he now understood. Yossi became the general director of Arachim and today, he is responsible for a budget of almost nine million dollars a year!

When Reb Shraga Feivel Winkler decided he would rather die than eat pork, he could not know what impact it would have on his family. In fact, as far as he was concerned, his decision cost him to never see his family again. But in the end, that decision was the cause for his grandson to choose to follow in his holy grandfather's footsteps.

| CHACHAM BARUCH TOLEDANO |

A *Mikvah* Built by the Germans

In a quiet little *moshav*, right outside the city of Be'er Sheva, there existed a small community of Jews. They were not the most observant group but they did respect the old traditions and the rabbis. On one occasion, the great Sephardic rabbi, Chacham Baruch Toledano zt"l, visited the quiet *moshav* and inquired about the level of observance there. He was told that on Shabbat they had exactly a *minyan*, for kosher food they would travel to the big city, and there was minimal Torah study.

The Chacham listened quietly. Then he asked, "What about a *mikvah*? What do the people here do when they need to make use of a *mikvah*?"

He was told that most people did not bother with this commandment, and those who did adhere to the ritual purification process would travel infrequently to Be'er Sheva and its environs. R' Baruch was shocked. "Well, then, you must have a *mikvah* here!" he exclaimed, and no sooner than he made the proclamation, did he get right to it.

Within a few short days, he organized a gathering which would take place in the meeting hall of the *moshav*. All were invited - religious, non-religious, Sephardim, Ashkenazim, men and women - the goal was to educate the masses about the importance of ritual purity and the need for a local *mikvah*, to ensure the sanctity, and ultimately, the continuity of the Jewish people in the Land of Israel.

R' Baruch had high hopes. He was sure that a large crowd would turn out for the event and then he would make an appeal to raise the necessary funds. He plastered signs throughout the *moshav* and spoke to many people individually. In preparation for the event, he made sure that food and beverages would be plentiful and he even asked a renowned speaker, R' Yankel Galinsky *shlit"a*, to come all the way from Bnei Brak to give a stirring lecture on the concept of a *mikvah* to the expected large crowd.

He was sorely disappointed. On the night of the event, R' Baruch arrived early and took his place at the front. R' Yankel Galinsky arrived soon after and sat near him. Then, they waited. It was close to an hour before the door opened and one single couple walked in. The man sat himself down in a row midway to the back and his wife took a seat in the women's section. Nobody else showed up.

R' Yankel was discouraged and wanted to leave. It was a clear embarrassment to the honor of the great Chacham, but R' Baruch did not give up hope. They waited a while longer and when it was clear that no one else was coming, R' Baruch said, "Rabbi Galinsky, at least you have an audience of one! Just as one is required to be *mechallel Shabbos* for an individual Jew, one can give a *mussar drashah* to an individual Jewish couple!" R' Yankel accepted the Chacham's words and stood up at the podium.

For the next thirty minutes, R' Yankel gave a masterful lecture. Although he was talking to only one couple, his delivery and content would lead one to believe that he was speaking before an audience of thousands! His message was clear; without the purity that a *mikvah* provides, a community cannot exist and will wither away. R' Baruch was scheduled to speak next and provide a Sephardic perspective on the importance of the mitzvah, but he changed his mind when he realized that the solitary man sitting in the pews was of Ashkenazic descent. Thus, the "event" was concluded.

The man stood up and headed for the door. There, he met his wife and the two could be heard whispering furiously right outside the room. Their conversation became even more animated and their voices rose in the process. Finally, the two stopped talking, reentered the hall and walked up to the front. Together, they thanked R' Baruch for organizing the event and Rabbi Galinsky for his heartfelt words. After an uncomfortable moment of silence, the man cleared his throat.

"Rabbis, I was just discussing your idea with my wife outside. We feel we can help. You see, we are both Holocaust survivors. We both came from Poland and we both lost our entire families at the hands of the wicked Germans. We suffered in the ghettos and then in the camps. But we survived! We found each other after the war, got married and made *aliyah*. Somehow we ended up here, in this *moshav* in the southern part of Israel, and this is where we settled. My business does well and we are not lacking for anything."

The man spoke Hebrew with a heavy Polish accent. His wife, the effects of the war clearly visible on her face, was wiping away a tear from the corner of her eye. "As part of the German reparation program, we both receive a monthly stipend from the German government which is supposed to make us feel better about the fact that they killed our families and made us suffer for years. But it doesn't. The money gets deposited directly into a joint bank account and it has been accruing for years. There must be thousands in that account but we have never touched it! We feel as if it is 'blood money' – money that tries to make amends for the spilled blood of our families. Others may not feel this way, but this is how we feel."

R' Baruch put his hand on the man's shoulder and tried to put him at ease. The man looked at his wife once again, nodded, and continued. "We have a great idea. We want to give all the money in that account, and all the money that the Germans continue to give us, toward the construction of a *mikvah*. This will not only serve the needs of this community, but also serve as a declaration to the Germans – to the entire world – that the Jewish people are forever! This is our revenge against Hitler and his Nazis! Instead of destroying our people, this *mikvah* will serve our people and allow them to grow and prosper in our land."

Indeed, the amount in the bank accounted for more than two-thirds of the necessary funds and, with a few more donations, a beautiful *mikvah* was built and continues to be used until this day.

RUSSIAN WASTELAND

Alone

by Raize Guttman

Alone
So Alone
Kicked about
Like a stone
Or an old broken bone.
From the barracks
I moan
If only
I wasn't
So very
Alone.

Alone
I have grown
For I feel the great soul
That's been blown
Into me.
My body may groan
But inside
I've been shown
That no,
It's not so –
I am not
Alone.

A loan
Is my soul.
In my heart
Is Your Home.
With my tears
I have sown
For I sit by Your Throne
In the barracks
Unknown.
With You
In my soul
I am never
Alone.

| RABBI YITZCHAK GARELIK |

A "Moscow" Sukkah

After seventy years of Communism, publicly building a sukkah in Russia is like the thawing of the snow at the end of the winter. Even in the farthest reaches of Siberia, it warms the Jewish heart. In the last fifteen to twenty years, Judaism has sprung to life across Russia. Jews are practicing their religion openly, where they were once forbidden and imprisoned for doing so. Celebrating the festival of Sukkos is an especially open miracle, for while Communism was in power and the KGB was on the prowl, this holiday was almost completely forgotten due to the dangers and risks of attempting to put up a sukkah or obtain a *lulav* and *esrog*.

R' Avraham Berkowitz, the director of the International Jewish Community of Moscow, recounts a story that he heard not long ago, while visiting Kazan, Russia, a city in the largely Muslim Tatarstan region.

Moshe Adinov, a sixty-five-year-old local dentist and regular participant in the daily *minyan* in Kazan, told Rabbi

Berkowitz a remarkable Sukkos story that must be passed on for further generations.

"My father was Reb Nachum Eliyahu Adinov. He was a *sofer* (Torah scribe) in Kazan before World War II. He kept the traditions in our home, but a lot of tradition was weakened. Being that there was no Jewish school, I went to public school even on Shabbos. Nevertheless, I remember growing up with as many Jewish traditions and holidays as was possible.

"My father was afraid for my future. He always warned me not to repeat to others what we did at home. 'Be a Jew at home and a Russian in the street,' he would always say. In fact, I probably would have never been accepted at university had I been recognized as a practicing Jew.

"We lived in a small wooden home, not in an apartment building like most people. We had a *besedka*, basically a porch, in the back of our home and every year we'd celebrate the holiday of Sukkos. My father would cover the roof of our *besedka* with leaves and foliage and we'd invite over many Jewish friends. It was a well-kept secret that the only sukkah in town was in our house. My father would make Kiddush on wine, tell stories and gently speak to us. It was a most memorable experience and this memory of Sukkos always stayed with me.

"My father died in 1965, and I inherited the house. I wanted to keep that Sukkos tradition alive, to continue the tradition for my children. I thought that, due to his limited means, all my father was able to do was put up trees and foliage. I wanted to do better than him! I had friends in the steel industry, and every year since 1965, I put up a sturdy aluminum roof on the *besedka*. I was proud that I continued my father's tradition."

Moshe Adinov smiled bashfully at the memory. "In 1998, Rabbi Yitzchak Garelik and his wife Chana moved to Kazan. It was so beautiful to have a young Jewish family celebrating in public what I always did secretly. It was incredible for me and I developed a close personal relationship with the rabbi and his family. That year, Rabbi Garelik said to me, 'Moshe, tomorrow night is Sukkos, and I want you to come to the beautiful sukkah we built.' When I walked into the rabbi's sukkah, I saw Rabbi Garelik in his holiday finest, holding an overflowing glass of wine, candles shining in his face – and wouldn't you know it – foliage, branches and trees above his head!

"I couldn't contain my emotions. I began to cry. I suddenly realized that what my father did all those years was the way it was supposed to be done, and for the last thirty years, by placing an aluminum roof above my sukkah, I was not doing it the right way. I had only meant to make my sukkah more beautiful!

"Rabbi Garelik asked me to tell my story, and when I was finished, he said to me, 'Your father is surely looking down from heaven with all the great Jews of the past and smiling. I have no doubt that the Al-mighty had the utmost pleasure from the beauty of your sukkah with the aluminum roof more than any sukkah in the world with the appropriate foliage, because you did it with such love and sincerity.' Since then, I have continued to learn and understand our traditions. I come every day to *daven* at the local *minyan* and my family and I are involved as part of the community. Today, we celebrate all the holidays with their rich fullness."

Rabbi Berkowitz continues to promote Russian Jewry and is quick to point out that in Russia today, *sukkos* are mostly built at the synagogues, since it is very difficult to build near apartment buildings. Sukkos becomes an incredible community event. Despite the cold, everyone comes out, with so many people singing, spending family time, laughing and talking, and enjoying words of Torah. The sukkah keeps everyone warm. Even in the farthest reaches of Siberia it warms the Jewish heart.

This is a true story of Sukkos in Russia – how, like the spark of Jewishness itself, Communism never was able to truly stamp out the Yom Tov of Sukkos.

| BLUZHEVER REBBE |
A "Cold" to Warm Up the Night

At the outbreak of World War II, R' Yisroel Spira *zt"l*, the Bluzhever Rebbe, moved from Istrik to Lvov. Lvov was then under Soviet rule. According to Soviet practice, each person was supposed to be employed in a productive job; otherwise he was classified as a parasite and was liable to be exiled to Siberia. All Chassidic rabbis had to find productive positions, and were forbidden to use the title "rabbi."

The Rebbe of Bluzhev, R' Yisroel Spira *zt"l*, became an insurance agent. At the end of each month, he had to prove that he had earned at least one thousand rubles. In those days the rabbi still had many followers. To produce a receipt at the end of the month for one thousand rubles, together with a list of insured individuals, was no great task for him. Thus, the rabbi was able to satisfy the Russian demands while continuing to serve his Chassidim.

One evening, the Russian commissar called for a regional meeting of all insurance agents. Attendance was mandatory.

Among the insurance agents was one other Chassidic rebbe, the Boyaner Rebbe, R' Avraham Yaakov Friedman *zt"l*. The night of the regional meeting coincided with the first night of Chanukah.

It was customary for many Chassidim to assemble at their rebbe's house for the festive kindling of the first Chanukah light and for the celebration that followed. The Bluzhever Rebbe searched for any way in which to excuse himself from the forthcoming meeting so that he might celebrate the first night of Chanukah in the company of his Chassidim.

Suddenly, he had an idea. He smiled to himself and left for the commissar's office. On the way there he took his snuff box from his pocket and began to sniff tobacco without stopping. By the time he reached the commissar, his nose was red and he kept sneezing. Between one sneezing attack and another, the rabbi explained to the commissar that he had a very bad cold and would be unable to attend the evening meeting.

The commissar, decorated with many medals, sat behind a huge desk covered with neatly arranged piles of paper. He listened to the rabbi with an obvious expression of disbelief.

"A strange coincidence," he said to the rabbi while looking straight into his eyes. "Only a few minutes ago another insurance agent was here, an agent with a beard and sidelocks, and just like you, his nose was red as a flag and he did not stop sneezing. He, too, claimed that he had caught a cold and asked to be excused from tonight's meeting."

It was probably the Boyaner Rebbe, thought the Bluzhever to himself as he tried to conceal his smile. He composed himself and replied, "It is quite natural for two people to catch a cold at this time of the year."

The commissar did not reply. He got up from his chair and walked out of the room.

After a short while he returned with a broad smile on his face and took his seat beneath the huge portrait of Stalin. "Now I understand the cause of your sickness," he said. "I have just checked my Jewish calendar. Tonight is Chanukah and the kindling of the first light. You should have known better. In Russia, when concocting a story, one should make sure it is a good one."

R' Yisroel paled at the thought of being caught red-handed and what the possible consequences for his "crime" would be. But then, the commissar relaxed his tone and said, "A word of advice, if I may? One can never be sure who is hiding behind the uniform of a Soviet commissar. If another commissar were sitting in my chair, you and your other sneezing friend would be nursing your colds in the Siberian plains. However, I am the son of the *shochet* of Mezhibuzh. Go home and kindle the first light of Chanukah."

| PONEVEZHER RAV |
Undivided Attention

The Jewish community in the Lithuanian city of Ponevezh was over two hundred years old when it almost completely disintegrated amidst the stormy days of the First World War. The beautiful city, nestled on the banks of the Nevizhe River, on mountains and plains, was passed back and forth, from one hand to another – from the Russians to the Germans, and from the Germans back to the Russians – each one competing in their hatred for the Jews and tormenting them to the utmost. By war's end, the Bolshevik revolutionists controlled Ponevezh, and they cruelly aborted any attempt to revive traditional Jewish communal life.

The previous rabbi of Ponevezh, R' Itzele Rabinowitz *zt"l*, passed away on Friday, 21 Adar I, 5679 (1919). Within a few weeks, R' Yosef Shlomo Kahaneman *zt"l* was invited to become the *rav* of the large and bustling Jewish community, at the relatively young age of thirty-three. It was then that he entered into the prime of his life. During this time, twenty-one turbulent years from 5679 (1919) until 5700 (1940), R' Yosef Shlomo reached incredible spiritual heights. His tremendous inner strength and multifaceted talents were revealed in their full glory, whether in the field of *rabbanus* and spreading Torah, building Torah institutions, or in communal efforts both in his own city and for all of Klal Yisrael.

Misfortune, however, struck only a few short days after he took over the reins of Ponevezh, when his father passed away in the distant town of Kuhl on Motza'ei Shabbos, 28 Adar II, 5679 (1919), after a long and debilitating disease.

A little over two weeks later, on the night before Erev Pesach, R' Yosef Shlomo sat in his rented apartment, deeply concentrating on formulating a *mechiras chametz* (sale of *chametz*) contract for his community. Due to his father's death and the subsequent *shivah*, he had not had time to prepare a document in advance. Now, he could not find a single form to copy from, nor did he have any books of halachah to consult, and he was forced to reconstruct every detail in the document from memory. This required every last ounce of intense concentration and R' Yosef Shlomo was deeply involved in his writing.

Suddenly, loud banging was heard at his door. Before he even had a chance to stand up, two armed Bolshevik guards burst into the small room. They asked if this was the address listed on their form and then demanded to know what the rabbi was doing. In truth, it didn't matter to them what he was doing, and after R' Yosef Shlomo tried explaining that he was writing an important document, the two motioned for him to follow them outside. R' Yosef Shlomo saw the hate-filled determination in their eyes and he knew what it meant. In the few short steps between the table and the door, he hurriedly whispered the *vidui*.

The Bolsheviks took him down to the courtyard and ordered him to stand against a wall. One of the guards pointed a loaded pistol at him, ready to kill him as per his superior's orders. He seemed to relish his duty and could not wait for the official order. While his finger was poised on the trigger, the second guard, who was apparently his commander, suddenly grabbed his hand. Furious whispers were exchanged between the two, followed by... nothing. For some reason, the superior officer had his doubts if this was the man they were looking for. He told his underling to look in the other entrance of the building, while he stayed behind to guard the rabbi.

A few moments passed, and suddenly two shots rang out in the courtyard. The younger guard came back grinning to report that he had indeed found the right man and that he could now confidently say: "Mission accomplished." The two guards seemed not to even notice R' Yosef Shlomo trembling against the far wall. With smiles and slaps on each other's backs, the two guards left him in the courtyard and walked away.

It took a few more moments for the Ponevezher Rav to compose himself. Finally, his legs began moving once again. Although he had just barely cheated death, R' Yosef Shlomo hurried up to his room and picked up the paper he was writing. He continued working on his *shtar mechiras chametz* with a clear head, as if nothing had just transpired. Unperturbed, he stayed up until four o'clock in the morning completing his monumental task.

Later, he related that when he looked at an old *mechiras chametz* contract he had received, and compared it to the version he had written that fateful night, he saw that he had written the exact same words from memory and even erased a few words, thereby enhancing it.

| R' BORUCH BER LEIBOWITZ |
"They're Tearing Up Holy *Sefarim*!"

The First World War brought unmitigated tragedy to the Jews of Eastern Europe. A quarter of a million Jews died in battle, and over a million became refugees because the Russian czar accused them of being German collaborators. They were forced to leave their homes and settle deep in the belly of the Russian hinterland. The Jewish social, economical, cultural and religious infrastructure in Poland, Lithuania, Russia and the Ukraine was severely damaged during the war. Many of the *yeshivos* were forced to scatter, and many of the Chassidic courts and dynasties were decimated. The Bolshevik Revolution brought on by the war attempted to destroy the practice of Judaism. The anti-Semitism of the Polish and Lithuanian nationalists became overt and violent.

Yeshivah Knesses Bais Yitzchak, led by its great *rosh yeshivah*, R' Boruch Ber Leibowitz *zt"l*, was forced to relocate from its hometown of Kamenitz to the small Polish town of Kremenchug. However, this move was hardly the end of their problems. The level of civilian suffering was very great there, as legions of soldiers from both sides attacked and pillaged citizens indiscriminately. The Jews of Kremenchug bore the brunt of the violence. Many Jews and yeshivah *bachurim* were robbed, beaten and even murdered, and it was not uncommon to see corpses lying in the streets and alleyways.

On more than one occasion, R' Boruch Ber himself was accosted by these marauders, although in each instance, his awe-inspiring presence caused them to suddenly feel uncomfortable and he was immediately released. He once found himself on the street when he got caught in the crossfire between two warring groups. He fled into a nearby cellar and waited it out for several days, while the bloodthirsty animals prowled above him, searching for prey. Thankfully, they never found him. R' Boruch Ber never ceased his Torah learning, even when the Angel of Death was hovering at his doorstep.

R' Shefatya Segal related an amazing incident that happened during this period, which is a testament to R' Boruch Ber's courage and greatness. One day as he was sitting in his home learning, a group of pillaging gentiles broke the door of his house and burst inside. With guns drawn and pointed menacingly at R' Boruch Ber and his family, they commanded every member of the household to stand against a wall and be still, warning them not to budge.

The intruders began a thorough search of the entire house, going from room to room, tearing up everything, searching for hidden silver, gold or jewelry, looting anything of value. Of course, there was little to find, for the refugees did not have an abundance of these materials.

Standing against the wall, everyone watched in deathly silence. At a certain point, one of the pillagers walked over to the bookshelf and began searching for valuables there. Callously, he took a large *sefer* off the shelf and quickly leafed through it, hoping to find money hidden in the pages. When he found nothing, he threw the *sefer* on the floor and grabbed another. When this *sefer*, too, yielded no results, he once again threw it down on the floor, and the scene repeated itself.

This was too much for R' Boruch Ber. Roaring an awesome roar, he broke away from the line at the wall and charged at the man with the gun. The great *gaon*, who spent his entire life poring over the texts of his beloved Gemara, whose legendary kindness prohibited him from hurting a fly, whose aged and stooped appearance belied a strength that drew on inner reserves he never knew he had, began raining down punches on all sides of the pillager's head, screaming at the top of his lungs, *"Sefarim reissen? Gevalt!"* ("Tearing *sefarim? Gevalt!*") For that moment in time, R' Boruch Ber looked like a seasoned warrior, for his outrage doubled the force of his blows.

The man with the gun did not – could not – defend himself! He literally took a beating and ran for his life in terror. When the other intruders saw what was happening, they began screaming in fright, "Run! Run!" and fled for their lives.

| R' YERUCHAM LEVOVITZ |

Caring for Another's Feelings

With the outbreak of World War I in 1914, the famed Mirrer Yeshivah moved to Poltava, Ukraine for a number of years, and only returned in 1921 to its original building in the Polish town of Mir. The yeshivah blossomed, attracting students not only from Europe, but also from America, South Africa and Australia. By the time World War II broke out there was hardly a *rosh yeshivah* in all of Europe who had not studied in the Mir. Although this was clearly the golden age of the Mirrer Yeshivah, world politics had brought tension to all parts of Europe, and the little hamlet of Mir was not spared its own fair share.

Late one night, a group of students from the Mir were returning from a long day at their studies. The yeshivah had no dormitory facilities, so the students boarded with the local townspeople. Small groups of six to eight students banded together in private homes and hired the *balabusta*, the wife or widow of a house owner, to look after them. As the students were walking together down a quiet alleyway, a number of Polish policemen happened upon them. The streets were always empty at this time of night and the policemen became suspicious of the group of men walking together. Immediately, they shouted for them to halt. But the Jewish students knew better than to entrust their fate to a few drunken Polish officers and they started to run to the nearest place of lodging. Panting heavily, they burst into the house and quickly bolted the door from the inside. They thought they were safe and began to relax after a few moments, until they suddenly heard loud banging on the door. The Polish police had found them and they had no choice but to open the door.

The policemen came barging in and held their guns aloft at the terrified yeshivah students. "Do you know how close we were to firing on you after you ran off?" shouted the officer in charge. He then demanded to see everyone's papers.

Apologetically, the boys produced their identification papers, proving that they were not spies but yeshivah students. All but one *bachur* had his papers. R' Shlomo Shimshon Karelitz *zt"l*, a nephew of the Chazon Ish, who was studying in the Mir at the time, did not lodge at this home, but had run together with his friends when the policemen accosted them. Thus, he did not have his papers on him. When the officer in charge surmised that he could at least take one victim with him into custody, he let the other boys go and grabbed Shlomo Shimshon by the arm, marching him out the door.

The officer held him tightly as he headed in the direction of the local station. Young Shlomo Shimshon, thinking quickly, denied being anything other than a student and offered to produce his papers which were located in another lodging just a few houses away. He begged to be allowed to go there with the officer to retrieve them, and thankfully the policeman relented. Together, they walked to his lodging and he showed the officer that his papers were legitimate and in order. Finally, Shlomo Shimshon was able to breathe a sigh of relief as the officer issued a stern warning and then let him go.

The next morning, the entire Mirrer Yeshivah was abuzz over the previous night's events, and word reached the ears of the *mashgiach*, the saintly R' Yerucham Levovitz *zt"l*. But when he rose and walked to the podium at the front of the *beis medrash* to deliver his daily *mussar* lecture, no one could miss the foreboding look that came across his face.

R' Yerucham stood quietly for a few moments before he spoke. He began in a quiet tone which gradually rose in intensity. "I must tell you the truth," he said, "that after hearing about what happened last night, I made up my mind that we must close down the yeshivah! Yes, close it down! I even spoke it over with other members of the *hanhalah* (faculty)..."

The students were shocked. Close down the yeshivah? Why? What had caused the *mashgiach* to feel so strongly?

His voice thundering now, R' Yerucham intoned, "How can it be that a group of *bachurim* allowed one of their own to be taken into police custody, escorted all by himself by the Polish police? Not one of them thought to go with him? Aside from the great danger that this boy was in, can you imagine the feeling of dread and terror that he was experiencing as he was being led away? He was terrified! How can students who learn Torah allow their friend to feel this way? Where is the *derech eretz* that Torah students are supposed to have...?"

| R' MOSHE FEINSTEIN |
A Moscow Miracle

The years immediately following the First World War and the Russian Revolution spanned a most turbulent and chaotic era in Russia, which adopted the title of USSR, or Soviet Union. The country was in a state of anarchy. This did not bode well for the hundreds of Jewish communities that dotted the vast Russian countryside. Horrific pogroms broke out, constantly placing the Jewish population in tremendous danger. It was during this period of time, in 1920, that R' Moshe Feinstein *zt"l* assumed the rabbinical position in Luban, a city with a large population of Torah scholars. R' Moshe had been in his new post barely one year when he was forced to escape a horrific pogrom in Luban.

The worst was yet to come. In 1930, the Bolsheviks established a branch of the notorious *Yevsektzia*, a Jewish division of the Communist regime that sought to eradicate every vestige of the Jewish faith. Hundreds of religious functionaries of the region, including rabbis, scribes and cantors, were either imprisoned or banished to the gulags of Siberia. In those anguished days, R' Moshe acted as a devoted shepherd to his flock, nursing the wounds of the terrorized Jewish community while at the same time attending to his normal rabbinic responsibilities and responding to voluminous halachic and congregational inquiries from all parts of Russia.

Despite the unremitting harassment of the Communist government, R' Moshe continued to lead his congregation in Luban for close to twenty years. When his personal and familial situation became critical in 1936, R' Moshe realized that he had no choice but to get out of the land of his birthplace. He made various attempts to secure an exit visa from the government, but was consistently turned down. Realizing that an imminent threat to his life was looming and that the virulent anti-Semitic local authorities were bent on blocking his departure, he decided to try his luck in Moscow, where some of his friends had contacts with the appropriate government agencies. The big hurdle, however, was to get to Moscow, which was not a simple task. Even within Russia, an internal passport was required for travel, and that relatively minor document was not forthcoming.

R' Moshe hit upon a novel plan. Disguising himself as a Russian peasant who would not arouse suspicion, he successfully evaded the authorities and arrived in the Russian capital. Checking into a hotel was out of the question, since by law all travelers were required to have their identity cards stamped by the local police, authorizing their stay. However, he had *siyata d'Shmaya* (Divine assistance): Immediately upon his arrival he was able to rent a room from a non-Jew who was ready to forgo all legal formalities, despite the dangers, just to earn a few extra rubles. R' Moshe remained in Moscow for several weeks, subsisting on potatoes and water. Part of the day he was busy procuring the required documents, and the rest of the time he spent in a local *beis medrash*, toiling in Torah.

One day, R' Moshe became so engrossed in a complex Talmudic subject that he lost track of time, not realizing that a considerable portion of the nighttime hours had passed. He decided that, considering the lateness of the hour, it did not pay to retire to his lodgings; walking outside alone so late at night was definitely not a safe and secure proposition. Instead, he decided to spend the rest of the night learning in the shul. In the morning, after Shacharis, he returned to his quarters, apologizing to the owner for not returning for the night.

The landlord was shocked to see him. "Are you aware of the great miracle that happened to both of us last night?" the owner asked with palpable emotion. "In the early evening hours, secret service agents encircled the district in pursuit of undocumented residents. They went from house to house and it was impossible to escape them. Many people were hauled off to headquarters, and I need not tell you what awaits them there. Your absence saved both of us from long prison sentences, or worse."

It is noteworthy that even after leaving Russia when the danger to his and his family's lives became unbearable, R' Moshe seriously doubted whether he was justified in his decision to leave. It was only in 1938, when he met R' Elchanan Wasserman *Hy"d* during the latter's visit to America, that R' Moshe discussed his dilemma, which rested heavily on his conscience. He was finally placated only upon hearing R' Elchanan quote from his illustrious *rebbi*, the Chafetz Chaim *zt"l*, who said that a country such as Russia, where Hashem's Name is banned, is considered like a lavatory, where, according to halachah, one may not engage in Torah study.

"It is impossible for a human being to live his life closeted in a lavatory," R' Elchanan stated categorically. "Thus, your decision was absolutely correct."

| MAKOVA RAV |

A Song for the Ages

The Theresienstadt concentration camp was liberated on May 8, 1945. Many of the survivors remained in the camp for quite some time afterward, as they required time to heal from their wounds, recuperate from rampant diseases that had spread through the camp, and simply figure out where to go and how to pick up the broken pieces of their lives.

The Lemberger family was one of the fortunate ones, as they not only survived, but remained intact until the end of the war. R' Nosson Nota Lemberger *zt"l*, the Makova Rav, and his wife and sons could not leave right away due to a quarantine imposed as a result of the diseases that refugees from other camps brought with them during the death march. As a result of the difficult route and their privation, many were stricken by disease, and many died after the war.

After Shavuos, the Lemberger family finally left Theresienstadt for Prague. This was the first stop on their journey after liberation, and they remained there for some time. They then continued on to Pressburg, where their ancestors had lived for several generations.

They arrived in Pressburg on a Friday, and met several surviving family members. On Shabbos evening, R' Nosson Nota and Rabbi Yitzchak Binyamin Mendelovitch, who was the rabbi of Puspokladany, went together to a synagogue to pray. The Russian occupiers had given each of them certificates of liberation, which stated that the bearers did not belong to the German enemy. They had to carry these identity cards with them at all times. A Jew who was caught without the card could be executed or sent to Siberia after a brief trial.

Despite this rule and the imminent danger that could ensue if he did not carry the certificate, R' Nosson Nota was determined not to desecrate this Shabbos after his liberation from the camps, no matter what. He quoted the Talmudic statement: *If the Israelites had observed the first Shabbos, they would not have been dominated by other nations.* This was their first Shabbos after all the wanderings, and they had a powerful desire to observe it according to halachah, and to refrain from carrying even such important items.

Late that night, on their way home, a Russian police officer appeared out of hiding and demanded to see their identification papers. When he realized that they did not have the necessary cards, he immediately arrested and jailed them, suspecting that they were German generals. Of course they protested that they were Jews and that they were not permitted to carry in the city streets on the Sabbath eve, but to no avail. What really bothered the Russian officer was that the language they spoke between them, Yiddish, was very similar to the German language. They pleaded with him, explaining that they had family in the city, and gave them the address so that they could go investigate, but their pleas fell on deaf ears. All the arguments that they mustered, that they had just come from places of severe deprivation and that their suffering was evident on their bodies, were to no avail. Their accusers were certain that they were Nazi officers in disguise. The officer put them in a basement of the jail, which was under the authority of the Russian NKVD. They asked for an investigation and trial so they could prove their innocence, but all arguments were rejected.

"You obviously know nothing about the way our government works," a Russian officer sneered. "With us, you can rot in jail for many, many years and not stand trial. When you do stand trial, it is already a good beginning, because at least you have a way to negotiate."

That Friday night, the Lemberger and Mendelovitch families were certain that the two rabbis had remained with the local rabbi who had invited them, probably because they did not want to walk in the dead of night. However, once morning broke and they saw that the two had not returned, they began to panic. Relatives began racing from one prison to another in search of the two *rabbanim*. In each jailhouse they checked, they did not obtain any authorization or indication that the two men were imprisoned there. Their fears mounted throughout the morning and early afternoon that R' Nosson Nota and R' Yitzchak Binyamin might have already been shipped off to Siberia, a place of infamy from where nobody returned.

It was mid-morning when the drunken contemptuous jailers and their helpers honored the new inmates with the task of sweeping their offices and the prisoners' courtyard. It was at one point when the two rabbis were sweeping the courtyard, that Rebbetzin Lemberger suddenly caught a glimpse of her husband through a hole in the courtyard wall. With the knowledge of which jailhouse they were in, she ran home to bring their identity cards, and took along a member of the family who had some experience with the courts. Unfortunately, her efforts were in vain. The prisoners would not be released.

One of the Russians in charge watched while they were working, and it was obvious to him that these men were not ordinary people. However, he could not be sure that they weren't German spies. After they completed their task in the courtyard, he summoned them to his office. R' Nosson Nota sensed a spark of humanity in his eyes and began to argue that he was a Jew, liberated from the labor camps, certainly not a German spy.

The officer asked them, "How can you prove that you are Jews?" The two rabbis responded by reciting passages from the Talmud and Rambam, and describing Jewish laws and customs. However, despite everything they said, the officer remained firm in his assertion that this was no proof that they were Jews. He said, "You should know that in the course of training spies, individuals and officers are often sent to study the customs of enemy countries in great detail, so that they can blend in easier with the local population. In this war, the Germans targeted the Jewish people and it is known that they sent German spies to places where Jews lived, to study Talmud and Jewish subjects. As a result, we cannot believe what anyone says about his true identity." The Russian officer continued to gaze at the rabbis, while R' Nosson Nota and R' Yitzchak Binyamin found themselves with no logical argument to counter the Russian's absurd assertions.

Then suddenly, the Russian said, "I want you to know that I am a Jew. I was a prisoner of those vicious Germans. Everything you may bring as proof from the Talmud and other such sources is known by the Germans, and it will not help you. But there is one thing that I do know: the Jews have a wonderful custom when they teach their little ones the Hebrew alphabet. They sing it to a tune with movements, in a very stirring and charming way."

He remembered this from his childhood and he was positive that no spy or German officer would ever think of learning this, because why would they ever need such a ruse? "I'll tell you what. If you know this tune, I will believe that you are Jews."

Of course, the two *rabbanim* remembered the tune and immediately recited the *aleph-beis* in the delightful intonation of Jewish children over many centuries, singing the tune for *kametz aleph, ah; kametz beis, bah...*

The officer broke into a wide smile. "Yes, yes. That is the tune I remember as a child." He was pleased and he stood up quite suddenly. "You are hereby released from this prison, for you are Jews. No non-Jew could sing this song the way you just did."

Rabbi Mendelovitch recounted that one of them also recited the entire text of the prayer *Nishmas Kol Chai*, with the spiritual inspiration of a servant of G-d, especially at such a time. The officer was also moved by this, and again conceded that they were true Jews. They were released at the last minute (It was learned that the Russians had planned to send all prisoners to Siberia after Sunday; that was their arrangement – they did not send them on Saturday, because it was part of their weekend of rest.), and everyone thanked G-d for their redemption.

| R' YECHEZKEL ABRAMSKY |
"Great Is Your Faith"

Many countries have grappled with the problem of what to do with petty criminals and political opponents. In the year 1754, Russian officials hit upon their own solution: exile these undesirable elements of society to a place where they could be put to useful work, such as building railroads and working in the mines. The frozen tundra of Siberia fit the bill perfectly. It was vast, underpopulated, and far away from curious eyes.

In the years preceding the 1917 Bolshevik Revolution, many Russian citizens were exiled to Siberia for supporting the Bolshevik cause. After the revolution, the Siberian labor camps were closed down for a brief period of time. However, when Josef Stalin came to power, he reopened and expanded them. The network of labor camps was named "GULAG" (an acronym in Russian meaning "**G**lavnoe **U**pravlenie **L**agerei," or Main Camp Administration). It is estimated that about 1.2 million prisoners were exiled to Siberia under the czars. Another eighteen to twenty million people were imprisoned in Soviet gulags during the thirty years that the prison system was in existence, and it is estimated that about 1.6 million people perished there.

It is not known exactly how many of these people were Jews, but there were many. The first Jews who were sent to Siberia for "eternal resettlement" were mainly businessmen who had been falsely accused of being in possession of "stolen articles," a general term that could be used for any merchandise that was bought and sold. Sometimes a Jew was accused by a jealous gentile competitor; other times, it was a corrupt government official, angered by a bribe that was too small, who leveled the charges against the unfortunate Jew. Many Jews ended up as prisoners and died from starvation or exposure during the trek on foot to Siberia, a journey that could take up to three years. If they survived this ordeal, they were likely to perish from the harsh conditions in the camps, which were made even worse by the cruel punishments meted out to workers who could not meet their daily work quota.

During the Communist era, openly practicing the Jewish religion became a crime, and a Jew could be arrested for owning *tefillin* or teaching Torah. In 1928, R' Yechezkel Abramsky *zt"l* was surprisingly granted permission by the Soviet authorities to publish a Torah journal entitled "*Yagdil Torah*." However, in 1930, in typical Soviet fashion, the authorities suddenly did an about-face and convicted him of being a "counter-revolutionary" who slandered the Communist government. He was sentenced to five years of hard labor in a Siberian prison camp.

What was the gulag like for R' Yechezkel? The typical winter morning in Siberia saw temperatures reaching 40 degrees centigrade below zero. His compulsory morning exercise routine was brutal: a brisk run, while barefoot, over the frost-covered ground. Like the others, he had no choice but to run across the frozen field. Unlike some of the others, though, he never allowed himself to drop to the earth, too cold, sick, and exhausted to go on. Day after day, he put his head down and just began to run, somehow surviving the ordeal. This is how he started his day in the Soviet labor camp.

The camp commanders did not like the fact that they couldn't "break" him and decided to make an example out of this Jewish rabbi. His daily work assignment was to enter the thick forest and chop tree trunks into smaller logs of wood. The problem was that R' Yechezkel was no lumberjack and he could not work fast enough. The commanders knew what to do with such "lazy" workers. As a punishment, they sent R' Yechezkel to string frozen fish on a metal wire. This work was more delicate. In fact, it was so delicate that one could not wear gloves while handling the metal wire. Yet, how can a human being grasp frozen fish with his bare hands in sub-zero temperatures, for hour after hour after hour? That was the world of the gulag.

Eventually, R' Yechezkel was transferred to another job. Now he was required to slice loaves of bread for all the prisoners. Due to this relatively easier job, his hands were no longer bleeding and frozen. Yet, he faced another danger. Gulag prisoners must be tough in order to survive. If they see that the man slicing the bread gives them a slightly smaller piece of bread than another prisoner, even if it's unintentional, the bread-cutter had better watch out for his life!

Faced with such cruel conditions and companions and unable to perform *mitzvos* of any kind, R' Yechezkel admittedly reached his wits' end. His mind and body threatened to succumb to despair. What is the point of going on, he wondered, as he contemplated the words of *"Modeh Ani"* on yet another bitter morning. Should he thank Hashem for another day of painful work in the freezing cold? Should he be grateful that yet another day will pass where he will be unable to learn Torah or do *mitzvos*? What reason does he have to thank Hashem for returning his *neshamah* to him for one more day?

Then he remembered the final words of the prayer: *rabbah emunasecha* – "great is Your faith." *Emunah*! That was something that the gulag commanders hadn't been able to take away from him. He still had his faith in Hashem.

"As long as I am able to hold on to my *emunah*," he resolutely told himself, "I have something to be thankful for. My *emunah* will sustain me. I will be able to bear all the pain and the suffering. And my life will have meaning, because every moment that I live with *emunah* in Hashem is a moment that is worth living." Strengthened by these thoughts, R' Yechezkel stood up and reported for his morning barefoot run across the frozen field.

Thanks to his *emunah*, and with Hashem's help, he bore the pain and suffering. Eventually he was granted permission to leave the Soviet "paradise" and begin a new life in England.

| SKULENER REBBE |

Recognizing the Greatness of a Jew

In 1976, Senator Henry "Scoop" Jackson was campaigning for the upcoming presidential elections. While Senator Jackson was not Jewish, his dedication and respect for the Jewish people were remarkable. He was very active in assisting Jewish organizations and backed many projects that were set up to benefit Israel. R' Moshe Londinski, who at that time was a rabbi in Seattle, Washington, was a big admirer of Senator Jackson. He helped with fundraising and often spoke publicly to help the senator gain support in his quest for the presidency.

One Sunday afternoon in early June, R' Moshe received a phone call from the *gabbai* of the Skulener Rebbe, R' Eliezer Zisha Portugal *zt"l*, with a special request: Can R' Moshe arrange a private meeting between the Skulener Rebbe and Senator Jackson for the following morning?

R' Moshe was taken aback. The next day? Monday morning? The senator was a busy man and he didn't know if he had the clout to pull off a meeting between the rebbe, who was in New York and the senator, who he soon learned was in Arizona at the time. But the *gabbai* explained that the rebbe felt it was urgent – it could not wait another day. R' Moshe promised to do his best.

It took a number of phone calls to important people before R' Moshe's phone rang. "Scoop here!" came the familiar voice on the other line. "What seems to be the problem? My people said it was urgent."

R' Moshe was momentarily at a loss for words. He hadn't dreamed that he would get such a quick response – and from the senator himself! He quickly pulled himself together. "I just got a call from a saintly Chassidic rabbi from New York. He says that he must see you tomorrow morning. He's willing to go wherever you are. Will you be able to see him?"

Senator Jackson thought for a moment. He was traveling back to Washington that night and he could clear his morning schedule to accommodate the rabbi. "Don't worry," he told a grateful R' Moshe, "I'll make sure the rabbi has enough time to tell me what he needs to say."

R' Moshe thanked the senator and called the *gabbai* back with the good news. The *gabbai* asked R' Moshe to hold on while he relayed the news to the rebbe. There was a short pause, and then the *gabbai* got back on the phone.

"The rebbe has one more request. Since he only speaks Yiddish, he would like you to be there as an interpreter." Now R' Moshe was stunned. He was in Seattle, Washington, three thousand miles away from Washington, D.C. But if it meant that much to the Skulener Rebbe, then he would make the effort to be there.

The next morning found R' Moshe in Senator Jackson's office in Washington, D.C. The senator was already in his office, busily rearranging his schedule so he would have time to speak with the Skulener Rebbe.

The rebbe arrived with his *gabba'im*. They met R' Moshe in the outer office and they entered the inner sanctum together. Senator Jackson's inner office was very impressive, complete with magnificent paneled walls and a rich oak mahogany desk. The senator was, after all, the head of the U.S. Foreign Relations Committee, and a very powerful man.

The senator greeted his guests and sat down behind his desk, ready to begin the meeting. But instead of speaking to the senator, the rebbe whispered something to his *gabbai*, who in turn whispered something to R' Moshe.

R' Moshe turned pale. He looked helplessly at Senator Jackson.

"What is the problem?" the senator asked curiously.

"Well, ah..." R' Moshe took a deep breath. "It seems that the Grand Rabbi has not had a chance to finish his morning prayers. He needs a place where he can concentrate. Would he be able to use your office for a little while?"

R' Moshe held his breath, but Scoop smiled broadly. "Of course, no problem!" The senator immediately stood up and walked with R' Moshe out of the inner office. The two of them stood in the hall, making conversation, waiting for the rebbe to finish.

Twenty minutes went by. By this time, both men were pacing the hall. R' Moshe didn't know what to say to the senator. After all, it was his office! Fortunately, the office door opened just then, and the Skulener Rebbe himself stood there, beckoning R' Moshe and the senator back into his office.

Senator Jackson once again seated himself behind his desk. "Now," he said with a smile, "what can I do for you?"

R' Moshe stood next to the rebbe, ready to interpret every word. The rebbe opened his mouth to speak. But he said just two short words and then burst into tears.

"What's wrong?" the senator asked in concern.

"I don't know," R' Moshe said in bewilderment.

The rebbe was trying to speak through his tears, but R' Moshe couldn't understand a single word. He stood, waiting for the crying to stop, but the tears continued to pour down the rebbe's face.

Senator Jackson beckoned to R' Moshe. "Tell the rabbi that I know what he wants," he said abruptly.

"You do?" R' Moshe said, startled. "How?"

"Just ask the rabbi what he wants me to do about it," the senator told him.

R' Moshe stared at the senator for a moment, but then he obediently turned to the rebbe and relayed the senator's statement. The rebbe stopped crying.

"I want it stopped immediately," he told R' Moshe.

R' Moshe translated the rebbe's statement.

"How does he want me to stop it?" the senator asked.

Again R' Moshe relayed the question to the rebbe.

"The senator knows which buttons to press," the rebbe replied.

The senator reached for the phone, punched in a number and began to speak. As R' Moshe listened, the story slowly became clear to him. It seemed that a few days before, the Romanian government had arrested twenty Jews and falsely accused them of currency speculation. They were imprisoned and due to be executed in a few days. The whole situation was a ploy by the Romanian government to pressure the United States into giving them the Most Favored Nation status. The senator, as the head of the Foreign Relations Committee, was also very involved with Soviet Jewry, and he knew of this action by the Romanian government. He had immediately understood what the rebbe had come for.

The senator was speaking to the Romanian ambassador. "As head of the Foreign Relations Committee, I strongly suggest that you immediately call the prime minister. Tell him that if those twenty prisoners are not released within forty-eight hours, I guarantee that Romania will never see a cent of American aid. Hair will grow on the palm of your hands before you ever receive America's Most Favored Nation status."

The senator put the phone down and looked up at R' Moshe. "Tell the rabbi that it has been taken care of." The rebbe smiled and warmly shook the senator's hand.

Within forty-eight hours, all twenty prisoners had been released and brought to the Land of Israel. Once again, R' Moshe had seen Senator Jackson's concern for the Jewish people. R' Moshe was curious about this, and he once took the opportunity to ask the senator why he cared so much about the Jews.

Senator Jackson smiled. "Three reasons. One; I was a prosecutor during the Nuremberg trials. I saw how much the Jews had suffered in the concentration camps, and I resolved to do whatever I could to help them.

"Two; my mother, a widow, was a housekeeper for a Jewish family in Everett, Washington. They treated her very well. They gave her extra food and money during the Depression years to help her raise her family. In her will, my mother asked that her children should always be good to the Jews.

"And finally, when I was a young boy, there were a few Jews I would always help out on Saturday. They always treated me nicely and gave me tips after their Sabbath was over."

The Jewish people, by practicing their Torah-true values, had instilled a feeling of mutual respect into a man who later rose to a position of power and was able to reciprocate their kindness.

R' CHAIM BERLIN

Of Sheep and Shepherds

One year, the Chief Rabbi of Moscow, R' Chaim Berlin *zt"l*, walked into the Great Synagogue on the morning of Yom Kippur to find it empty of congregants. Not one person showed up to *daven* on this, the holiest day of the year. R' Chaim was at first upset with his constituents, but then he realized that in the "Proletariat Utopia" that was the Soviet Union, missing work was a crime that earned the offender a hefty punishment, and no one was willing to take that chance.

Heartbroken, R' Chaim was forced to *daven* alone all day and he poured his heart out to the Al-mighty to forgive the people for their weaknesses. All afternoon, the large sanctuary remained empty, devoid of anything resembling a religious atmosphere, but as soon as darkness began to fall and the workday was completed, an interesting thing occurred: the people came streaming into the shul in droves. Families hurried to the synagogue; men, women and children packed the pews and in a very short time, there was not an empty seat in the building.

R' Chaim sat in his place up front and watched with fascination. The people came in, took their prayer books and without a word began to pray in earnest.

R' Chaim stood up, quickly walked up the few stairs and opened the *aron kodesh* – the Holy Ark. Then, he began to speak.

"My friends, I must tell you a story. Two neighbors once got into an argument over a chicken. Each one claimed the chicken was his. They bickered and brawled for some time before they decided to present their case to the local rabbi.

They went to the *rav* and told him the problem. He, in turn, advised that they place the chicken on the ground with each man standing on different sides and they should wait and observe to see in which direction the chicken walked. To whichever man the chicken went – that would be a sign the chicken was his."

R' Chaim raised his voice and looked heavenward. "Master of the World," he called out in a voice filled with emotion, "Your people are worked to the bone and don't have a moment to rest all day. They barely have strength to make it home. And yet, the minute they are released from their work, in what direction do their feet carry them? Home? To the pubs? No! Directly to You! To Your home! To Your great sanctuary! And do You know why? *Ki anu amecha v'Atah Ro'einu* – Because we are Your sheep and You are our Shepherd!"

The Jews of Moscow cried like they never cried before.

| NETZIV AND R' YITZCHAK ELCHANAN SPEKTOR |
To Glorify G-d's Name

For hundreds of years, the Jewish people suffered under the harsh tyrannical rule of the Russian czars. The anti-Semitic decrees, coupled with an unmitigated hatred for Jews and their laws and customs, made for a life of hardship for every Jew. On many occasions, it was left to the *rabbanim* to travel to the capital city of Petersburg to plead their case on behalf of their unfortunate brethren, not always with favorable results.

One year, an important issue pertaining to the welfare of Russian Jewry came up and none other than the Netziv,

R' Naftali Tzvi Yehuda Berlin *zt"l*, and R' Yitzchak Elchanan Spektor *zt"l*, were called upon to appear before important government officials to represent the Torah community. As is often the case with bureaucracies and their pompous, self-inflated minions, time crawled by with little to show for it. Days turned into weeks and weeks turned into months, and no concrete resolution was attained. Before long, the season of the High Holy Days was upon them and they came to the unpleasant realization that they would be forced to stay in Petersburg for the holiday season.

When deciding where to *daven* for Rosh Hashanah, the two great sages made a surprising choice. On the first day of Yom Tov, they walked to the "Cantonist Shul" - a synagogue comprised of former soldiers in the Russian army who were kidnapped from their families as young children and forced to serve for a minimum sentence of twenty-five years. Due to their circumstances, most of these soldiers were far removed from *Yiddishkeit* and barely knew how to *daven*. They only came to shul on Rosh Hashanah because what else was a Jew supposed to do on the Jewish New Year?

During a break in the *davening*, an older man stood up and asked to be permitted to say a few words. When he had the attention of the congregants, he began in a low, tremulous voice. "I used to be called Moishele. I was taken away from my family as a young child, just like the rest of you, and I spent the best years of my life in the service of the czar." Tears ran down the former soldier's cheeks as he let his emotions spill forth. Oh, how he had longed for this moment, when once again he would see the inside of a *beis haknesses* and join his own brethren in prayer.

"I don't know how to pray," Moishele confessed abashedly. "There was a time when I did know, but due to the so many years now that I have not been permitted to *daven*, I have forgotten how to do so. But in my heart, I want to pray! I want to commune with the L-rd. There is a prayer stored away deep inside my heart, and I want to express it to the Al-mighty."

Not a sound was heard in the cramped synagogue. What would he request from Hashem? Indeed, what spiritual desire did this man store in his heart, a man from whom the czar had robbed both this world and his World to Come?

"Creator of the World! What does every Jew request from You?" Moishele's booming voice filled the room. "Children, life and livelihood! For most people, this is a most basic desire for a satisfying and fulfilling life. But as for me, what should I request? Children? I'm already old, and I do not foresee children in my future. Life? Most of my life has already passed, and even that could not really be called life. Livelihood, perhaps? But the czar provides generously for all the cantonists, enough for their whole lives. What then is left for me to ask for?"

And then, the burly soldier let out an anguished cry. With every ounce of strength, he screamed upwards to the heavens, "What do I want? All I want is to praise the holy Name of the Al-mighty G-d. All I want is to say, '*Yisgadal v'yiskadash Shmei Raba*! May Your great Name be exalted and sanctified!'"

The congregants were dumbfounded. The Netziv and R' Yitzchak Elchanan were astounded and would later recount how moved they were by this man, an unlearned and simple Jew, who by his own admission had nothing left in the world. All he had was one simple request. All he wanted was the glorification of Hashem's Name.

| STEIPLER GAON |

A Small Act – A Great Reward

During the waning days of the rule of Czar Nikolai, revolution and insurrection was in the air all throughout the Russian mainland, and the Russian authorities – chief among them the czar himself – realized the implications if the rebellion was not put down. To that end, anyone deemed a Bolshevik revolutionary was pursued and hunted down with the full force of the Russian army and secret police, and many of the leaders of the revolution were caught and executed without even the benefit of a trial. It was a time rife with fear and terror and Russian citizens trembled and groaned under the weight of the czar's persecution – both Jew and gentile alike.

One of the leaders of the Bolshevik Revolution, a man who would later rise to the highest heights of the newly established Soviet Union, was hunted mercilessly during those dark days and was even tagged with the dubious distinction of being at the top of Russia's "Most Wanted" list.

On one occasion, the czar's men came so close to capturing him that he was forced to flee on the spur of the moment, with nothing more than the clothes on his back. Escaping the city to the outlying villages by horseback was his only option, but even this did not go smoothly and the Russian agents picked up his trail, following him from village to village, until they narrowed their search.

The man was cornered with no place to run, and so he began knocking on doors, begging to be allowed in before he was captured. Time after time, he was turned away, as none of the villagers wanted to be caught aiding and abetting a wanted fugitive; the consequence to their own families was too frightening to imagine.

Finally, he pounded on the door of a small house belonging to a Jewish family. Once again, he pleaded with them to let him in and, this time, the Jewish villager did just that. The Jew understood the gravity of the situation and how the soldiers would be at his doorstep at any moment. He quickly grabbed a *tallis* and wrapped the fugitive in it, pushing him into a corner of the room and handing him a siddur.

"Just make it look like you're a Jew praying with great devotion," he told the man. When the soldiers eventually arrived, they did a room-by-room search but came up with nothing other than a few unsuspicious Jews swaying in their prayer shawls. The man was saved.

His gratitude and words of thanks were effusive, but when he offered to pay the kind Jew for his selfless action, the Jew refused any sort of payment, monetary or otherwise. Just saving a human life was enough, he said, and the revolutionary went on his way, vowing never to forget the kindness this man had done for him.

One day a number of years later, after the fall of the Russian Empire, the firing-squad execution of Czar Nikolai and his family, and the rise to power of the Bolshevik proletariats who eventually formed the Soviet Union, a messenger arrived at the home of the aforementioned Jewish villager with a summons to appear at the palatial home of the Premier of the Politburo. Scared and panicked, the man had no choice but to comply. His fear turned to shock when the man who greeted him was none other than the fugitive revolutionary who had hidden in his home, dressed like a Jew and pretending to pray to fool the bloodthirsty Russian soldiers.

The Soviet leader once again thanked him for his kindness and reminded him of his promise to grant him any wish his heart desired. The Jew, however, again requested nothing and reiterated that he was only too happy to be able to save a fellow man's life. He was sent away with many valuable gifts and a permanent pass to visit the Soviet leader any time his heart desired.

The preceding story was told over by the holy Chafetz Chaim *zt"l*, who would impart to his students the lesson that a small act by one man can go a long way towards reshaping the landscape of the entire world. By unknowingly saving this revolutionary, he enabled a chain of events to go forth, changing the world – for better or for worse – forever!

But that's not the end of the story. In 5681 (1921), a group of eighteen yeshivah students from the Novaradok Yeshivah in Russia were captured while attempting to smuggle across the Russian-Polish border to escape the harsh anti-religious decrees of the Soviets. The boys languished in a cold Soviet prison, undergoing torture and severe conditions, until their trial would take place when they would undoubtedly be sent off to a Siberian gulag for the rest of their lives. The Novaradok *roshei yeshivah* attempted to use all of their influence to have the boys released, but nothing seemed to help.

Eventually, they turned to the *posek hador*, R' Chaim Ozer Grodzenski *zt"l*, for assistance. R' Chaim Ozer remembered the Jew who had saved the Soviet leader and told them, "I believe there is one Jew who can help. He once saved a very important man and never asked for anything in return. Now is the time to have the favor repaid."

The Jewish villager was located and impressed upon to seek the release of the eighteen students. Soon after, the boys were all freed.

"But it wasn't just eighteen yeshivah students who were saved," the famed *maggid*, R' Yaakov Galinsky *shlit"a*, would exclaim. "One of those boys turned out to be none other than the great Steipler Gaon, R' Yaakov Yisroel Kanievsky *zt"l*, whose Torah, *avodah* and righteousness lit up the world from one end to the other!" This act of saving another man's life did not just alter the landscape of Russian life; it changed the world of Torah as well! If not for him, where would we be without the great *tzaddik* and eventual leader of his generation, the holy Steipler Gaon?

| RIBNITZER REBBE |
By Your Blood Shall You Live!

For over eighty years, the Ribnitzer Rebbe, R' Chaim Zanvil Abramowitz *zt"l*, lived as a pious and G-d-fearing Jew – as well as an inspirational leader – in the USSR under the likes of Stalin and the tyrannical Communist regime. He did not forgo any aspect of Torah and *mitzvos* in Russia – even immersing daily in the waters of a *mikvah*, which often involved chopping ice on a frozen river. For years, he continued to spread Torah, to perform circumcisions and *shechitah*, and to encourage Jews to send their children to underground Torah schools. He was interrogated, jailed and even placed in front of a firing squad, but he always seemed to miraculously escape and return to his "counter-revolutionary" activities. From the 1930s until the end of his life, the Ribnitzer Rebbe fasted on all days when it is permitted to do so under Jewish law.

As a *mohel* (circumciser), the Ribnitzer Rebbe performed thousands of circumcisions on Jewish children under the

Communist regime. As one of the only *mohelim* who was not intimidated by the government, he would not hesitate to travel all over the country in order to bring another Jewish child into the covenant of Avraham Avinu.

There was one occasion that stood out, both for the level of danger it entailed and for the miraculous wonder that ensued. The Ribnitzer Rebbe once received a message from the Jewish wife of a Russian general who wished for the rebbe to come clandestinely to her home and circumcise her son. Although she and her husband had nothing to do with organized religion – especially Jewish customs and commandments – nevertheless, the heart of a *Yiddishe neshamah* was beating proudly, if not secretly, inside this woman. She remembered her father and grandfather and their connection to Judaism, and she wished to transmit this connection to her offspring as well. The problem was that her husband, a sworn Communist, was outspokenly opposed to religious practices and the one time she even mentioned circumcising their son to him, he had obstinately refused to hear of it lest his career in the army be jeopardized. She decided to bide her time – and she did not have long to wait. When her husband, the general, was urgently called to the front, she sent a message asking the rebbe to come immediately.

The rebbe undertook the mission, of course, and took along a well-known Chassid, Reb Mendel Futerfas *z"l*, to accompany him. Reb Mendel was a survivor of fourteen years of Siberian exile who maintained an underground network of *Chabad* Torah schools, and he was used to seeing the great *mesirus nefesh* of the Ribnitzer Rebbe.

When they arrived at the Russian woman's home, they were whisked into the cellar, where the child was ready and waiting. Without delay, the rebbe performed the *bris*. Although he was an expert at his craft, the child began bleeding profusely. Neither salve nor medicine was able to stop the bleeding. The child began to turn yellow and shake violently. Upon seeing this, the mother became hysterical and began screaming, "Is this the reward I get for my sacrifice of bringing my son into the covenant of Abraham?" The baby then lost consciousness, whereupon the horrified mother fell down in a dead faint.

Reb Mendel was terrified. He understood the implications and consequences that would follow if something happened to this child, and even worse, the terrible *chillul Hashem* and disgrace it would cause to the Name of G-d. He looked at the face of the rebbe at that moment, and it seemed to be aflame. His head was thrown back and his hands were raised to the heavens in intense prayer. In a loud voice, he called out, "*Va'omer lach b'damayich chayi* – I say to you, by your blood shall you live!" Suddenly, the child, who had previously been completely still and showed no signs of life, awoke, and his bleeding stopped!

Reb Mendel screamed with delight, "It's a miracle, Rebbe," whereupon the Ribnitzer Rebbe responded calmly and humbly, "Eliyahu Hanavi is present at every circumcision. This miracle took place under his jurisdiction!"

| LAYCHI GLUECK AND RICHARD NIXON |
The Ride of a Lifetime

Laychi Glueck was born in the small Hungarian town of Rakmaz. At the age of sixteen, Laychi left home for Budapest where he would spend the next several years learning in the yeshivah of Rabbi Yisroel Weltz, the Tinyer Rav. By the end of 1943, the political situation in Hungary had become sufficiently unstable to prompt Laychi to move his parents and sisters – his brothers had all fled before the outbreak of the war – from their remote hometown to the relative safety of Budapest. When the German army occupied Hungary in March of 1944, Laychi was conscripted into a forced labor brigade from which he soon managed to escape. There followed a lengthy period of day-to-day, moment-to-moment existence during which Laychi lived solely by his wits, often moving from one to another of the various protected houses that had been set up by the Swedish and Swiss governments.

As would be the case until the day of liberation, Laychi's primary concern was the safety of his parents and sisters. For a time, they resided in a holding camp operated by the Swiss consul. On September 13, 1944, however, the Germans removed them from the camp. Laychi's sisters were placed on what would prove to be the last transport to Bergen-Belsen, where one of the three would die of typhus. His parents were taken to the ghetto.

From that time on, the greatest part of Laychi's activities was directed at ensuring that his parents would survive the hunger and terrible living conditions of the ghetto. Disguised in an official-looking uniform topped off by a cap bearing a Red Cross insignia, the tall, imposing-looking young man regularly came and went through the ghetto gates, bringing his parents daily rations of food without which, he believed, they would surely starve.

Shortly after the end of the war Laychi wed Edith Singer and the couple began their married life in a D.P. camp in Germany. Soon after, they moved to Kassal, a large German city. In 1948, they settled in the United States.

Over the next eight years, Laychi began and built up a successful men's clothing business. All the while, he maintained constant contact with his parents, as well as with other members of his extended family, who were still in Hungary, living under the harsh Communist regime. In 1956, by which time he had already become a United States citizen, Laychi traveled to Vienna and put into motion a plan to spirit his parents out of Hungary. While an initial rescue attempt failed, a second try proved successful and the elderly couple was soon reunited with their son.

Yet, when the senior Mr. Glueck stubbornly refused to submit to the medical examination required for admittance to the United States, it looked for a time as if getting them from Vienna to America would be the more difficult part of the mission.

Desperate, Laychi went to the American consulate and loudly demanded to have his case heard. Suddenly, a set of double wooden doors swung open and there stood Vice President Richard Nixon, in Vienna on a fact-finding trip. Ordering his staff to "let the young man speak," Mr. Nixon listened while Laychi explained the circumstances and his dilemma.

"How soon can your parents be ready to leave?" was all the vice president wanted to know.

"In twenty minutes," Laychi replied.

The rest of the story has become something of a legend in the Glueck family. Before Laychi had time to fully understand what was going on, his parents' belongings had been packed and they were being flown - compliments of Richard Nixon and Air Force One - to a new life in the United States.

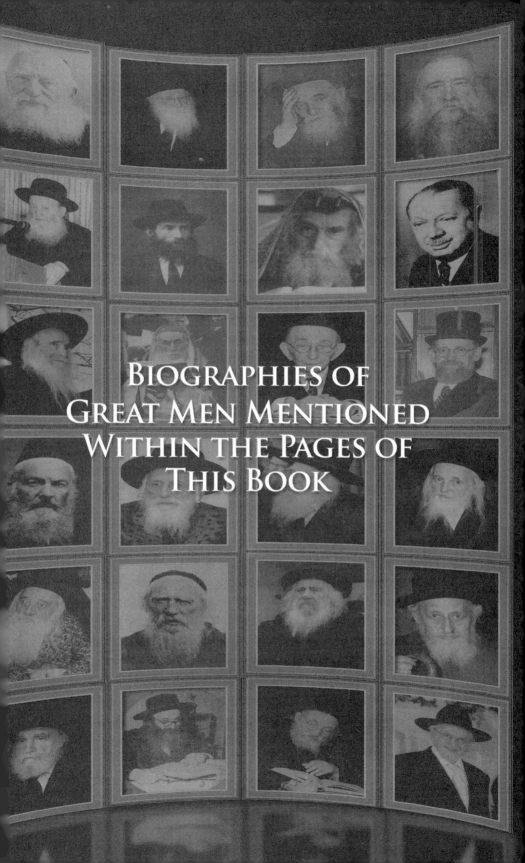

Biographies of Great Men Mentioned Within the Pages of This Book

R' Chaim Stein zt"l
(1912-2011)

R' Chaim Stein zt"l, *rosh yeshivah* of the famed Telzer Yeshivah of Cleveland, was one of the yeshivah world's last remaining links to prewar Europe before he died. He spent his entire life in the universe of the Telzer Yeshivah. At first he was a student; following that he delivered a *shiur* even before he was married; following that he became the *mashgiach ruchani*; and ultimately the *rosh hayeshivah*. Throughout his life little changed in his environment. From the time he entered the yeshivah he saw little outside the pages of the Gemara, and was fluent in all aspects of the Torah. In October 1940, while a member of the Telzer Yeshivah, he led a group of students who escaped from war-torn Lithuania just as it was overrun by the Nazis. R' Chaim and the students he accompanied headed to the Far East via the Trans-Siberian Railroad, having acquired visas from the famous Chiune Sugihara, who risked his life to save Jews who were fleeing the Nazis. Eventually the group landed in Brisbane, Australia, where the local Jewish community welcomed them warmly. A few months later, in 1941, he made his way to the United States and settled in Cleveland, Ohio, where the Telzer Yeshivah had relocated. He taught Torah for over seven decades to many generations of students who cherished his pleasant ways and his brilliant mind. He touched thousands of Jewish souls; not just the thousands of his students, but also those seeking strength and Divine salvation from across the globe.

R' Yoel Teitelbaum zt"l
(1887-1979)

R' Yoel Teitelbaum zt"l, known as "Reb Yoelish," was the saintly Rebbe of Satmar. He was already a highly regarded rebbe in Hungary. When the Nazis invaded Hungary in 1944, he was rescued from death in Nazi-controlled Transylvania as a result of a deal between a Hungarian official, Rudolph Kastner, and a deputy of Adolf Eichmann. Although Kastner intended to rescue only Hungarian Zionists on a special train bound for Switzerland, R' Yoel and a few other religious Jews were also given seats. (It has been said that this was the result of a dream in which Kastner's father-in-law was informed by his late mother that if the Grand Rabbi of Satmar was not included on the train, none of the passengers would survive.) En route, the train was rerouted by the Germans to Bergen-Belsen, where the 1,600 passengers languished for four months while awaiting further negotiations between rescue activists and the Nazi leadership. In the end, the train was released and continued on to Switzerland. R' Yoel lived for a brief period in Jerusalem after World War II, but at the request of some of his Chassidim who had immigrated to the United States, he settled there instead and established a large community in the densely Orthodox neighborhood of Williamsburg, located in northern Brooklyn in New York City.

R' Chaim Dovid Leibowitz zt"l

(1889-1941)

R' Chaim Dovid Leibowitz *zt"l* was a leading disciple of prewar Europe's Slabodka Yeshivah in Lithuania who went on to found the Rabbinical Seminary of America, better known today as "Yeshivas Rabbeinu Yisroel Meir Hakohen" or the "Chafetz Chaim Yeshivah." The yeshivah was named after his great-uncle, R' Yisroel Meir Hakohen Kagan, the great Chafetz Chaim. In his youth, R' Chaim Dovid was known as "Reb Dovid Warshawer." As a teenager, he studied in the Radin Yeshivah, where he held private study sessions with his great-uncle, the founder of the Radin Yeshivah, for twelve hours a day, and helped write the last volume of the *Mishnah Berurah*. He also learned there under R' Naftoli Trop. In 1908, R' Dovid transferred to the Slabodka Yeshivah, where he learned under the Alter of Slabodka, R' Nosson Tzvi Finkel. In 1915, he succeeded his father-in-law as rabbi of Salcininkai. After six years, however, he returned to Slabodka as a founding member of the Slabodka *kollel*. In 1926, he came to the United States to fundraise for the *kollel* and was invited to become the *rosh yeshivah* of Mesivta Torah Voda'ath. Among his students were R' Gedalia Schorr and R' Avraham Yaakov Pam. In 1933, he founded Yeshivas Rabbeinu Yisroel Meir Hakohen, where he successfully transplanted to the United States his unique style of Talmud study as well as the Slabodka school of *mussar*.

R' Yitzchak Lipschutz zt"l

(1870-1943)

R' Yitzchak Lipschutz zt"l, Vyelipolier Rebbe, was born in Wisnicz, Poland in 1870, into a family with great Chassidic lineage. He was the son of R' Nosson Nota zt"l and served as rabbinical judge in Vielipole (Wielipole Skrynskie) between the two world wars. He was a profound Torah scholar who attracted a large following. He was renowned as a great Chassidic rebbe but was forced to leave Vielipole in the 1920s. He moved to Brigel-Brzsezko and from there to Przemyslany. When the war broke out, he ran away to the city of Bochnia and hid in a bunker together with a number of other important *rabbanim* and rebbes. He was eventually captured by the Germans and killed in the Bochnia ghetto at the age of seventy-two. Hy"d.

R' Aharon Rokeach zt"l

(1877-1957)

R' Aharon Rokeach *zt"l* was the fourth Belzer Rebbe in the illustrious line of the Belzer Chassidic dynasty. He was rebbe from 1926 until his passing in 1957. Known for his piety and righteousness, R' Aharon was called the "Wonder Rebbe" by Jews and gentiles alike – even the Nazis – for the miracles he performed. R' Aharon's rule as rebbe saw the devastation of the Belz community during the Holocaust, along with that of many other Chassidic dynasties in Galicia and elsewhere in Poland. During the Holocaust, R' Aharon was high on the list of Gestapo targets as a high-profile rebbe. He and his brother, R' Mordechai of Bilgoray, spent most of the war hiding from the Nazis and moving from place to place, with the support and financial assistance of their Chassidim both inside and outside of Europe. Eventually, they were taken out of Europe via a series of escapes, many miraculous in nature. R' Aharon and R' Mordechai immigrated to the British Mandate of Palestine in 1944. The two lost their entire extended families, including their wives, children, and grandchildren.

R' Elchanan Wasserman Hy"d

(1875-1941)

R' Elchanan Wasserman *Hy"d* was born in Birz, Lithuania and learned in the Telzer Yeshivah under R' Shimon Shkop. In 1907, he joined the Kodshim Kollel of the Chafetz Chaim in Radin. R' Elchanan viewed the Chafetz Chaim as a living Torah and trembled in his presence. The Chafetz Chaim became R' Elchanan's lifetime role model and *rebbi*. In 1910, he became a *rosh yeshivah* in Brisk, and remained at that post until the outbreak of World War I in 1914. In 1921, he became head of Yeshivah Ohel Torah in Baranovitch, where he remained for the rest of his life. Because of his great influence, the yeshivah grew and, despite its abysmal poverty, attracted many hundreds of disciples. He was deeply involved in communal matters, and was active in Agudath Israel. In addition to his *shiurim* and Talmudic writings, he was also a great thinker and interpreter of contemporary events and his ideas were published in *Kovetz Ma'amarim*. He visited America in 1939 to raise money for his impoverished yeshivah, and though he could have remained there and avoided the imminent catastrophe that was to destroy European Jewry, he never considered it a possibility. He felt that he must return to his yeshivah and be with his students. While he was on a visit to Kovno (Kaunas), the Germans declared war on Russia and R' Elchanan was unable to return to his yeshivah. On July 6, 1941, while studying in the house of R' Avraham Grodzenski, in the company of a group of scholars, armed Lithuanians burst in and arrested him together with twelve other rabbis. They were taken to the infamous Ninth Fort and executed two days later.

R' Yekusiel Yehuda Halberstam zt"l

(1905-1994)

R' Yekusiel Yehuda Halberstam *zt"l* was the first Klausenberger Rebbe, founding the Sanz-Klausenberg Chassidic dynasty. He was known for his personal righteousness, kindness toward others, and Torah wisdom that positively influenced whole communities before, during and after the Holocaust. He was a natural leader, mentor, and father figure for thousands of Jews of all ages. The Klausenberger Rebbe became one of the youngest rebbes in Europe, leading thousands of followers in the town of Klausenberg, Romania, before World War II. When the Nazis invaded Romania, he was taken away from his family and incarcerated under terrible conditions in a number of concentration camps. His wife, eleven children, and most of his followers were murdered by the Nazis. He managed to survive through his great faith and encouraged others to believe all throughout the war. After the war, he rebuilt Jewish communal life in the Displaced Persons camps of Western Europe, reestablished the Klausenberg dynasty in the United States and Israel, and rebuilt his own family with a second marriage and the birth of seven more children.

R' Aharon Kotler zt"l
(1891-1962)

R' Aharon Kotler *zt"l* was a prominent *rosh yeshivah* in Lithuania before the war, and later became the leader of the yeshivah movement and *Litvish* Jewry in the United States of America, where he built one of the first and largest *yeshivos* in the U.S. After learning in the famed Slabodka Yeshivah in Lithuania, he joined his father-in-law, R' Isser Zalman Meltzer, to run the yeshivah of Slutsk. When the Soviets took over, the yeshivah moved from Slutsk to Kletzk in Poland. With the outbreak of World War II, R' Aharon and the yeshivah relocated to Vilna, then the major refuge of most *yeshivos* from the occupied areas. Through the intervention of American Jewry, R' Aharon was able to escape Europe for the United States via Siberia, but many of his students did not survive the war. He was brought to America in 1941 by the Va'ad Hatzalah rescue organization and soon assumed its leadership, guiding it during the Holocaust and using any means at his disposal to try to rescue the remnants of European Jewry. In 1943, R' Aharon founded Beis Medrash Govoha in Lakewood, New Jersey and continued to lead American Jewry until his untimely passing in 1962. Today, Beis Medrash Govoha has grown into the largest institution of its kind in America with thousands of students and married *kollel* members, as well as a number of satellite *yeshivos*.

R' Yitzchak Zev Halevi Soloveitchik zt"l

(1886-1959)

R' Yitzchak Zev Halevi Soloveitchik *zt"l*, known throughout the world as the "Brisker Rav" ("rabbi of Brisk"), was the oldest son of the great R' Chaim Soloveitchik *zt"l* of Brisk. He was the rabbi of the Jewish community in Brisk and was the *rosh yeshivah* of its yeshivah. World War II broke out while he was vacationing away from his home and he was unable to return to Brisk. He lived in Warsaw and later moved to Vilna, where he was looked upon for guidance by so many suffering Jews. He was fortunate and was able to flee the Holocaust together with three of his sons. His wife, mother and three small children perished. When the Brisker Rav was in Europe and all was burning, he had a choice of where to escape: America or Palestine. Despite the danger posed by the German army, which at that point had already reached Egypt, he chose to go to Jerusalem, because in Jerusalem, he said, "There is a small group of Jews who truly fight for the honor of *Hashem Yisbarach*." In a place where the Jews never gave up the fight – that would be the guarantee that he would raise good children and future generations. He moved to the Holy Land, where he reestablished the Brisker Yeshivah in Israel. In Jerusalem, he continued educating students as his father did, with what would come to be known as the *Brisker derech* (the "Brisk method" or "Brisk approach") of analyzing Talmud.

R' Chaim Zanvil Abramowitz zt"l
(1890s-1995)

R' Chaim Zanvil Abramowitz *zt"l*, the Ribnitzer Rebbe, was born in the town of Barashan, Romania. He was a main disciple of R' Avraham Matisyahu of Shtefanesht, grandson of the "Holy Rizhiner." The Ribnitzer Rebbe was acknowledged by all Jews across the spectrum as a renowned performer of miracles. He spent much of his life living in Russia under Communist rule. There, under the most difficult circumstances imaginable, he practiced *Yiddishkeit* to its fullest. He served Klal Yisrael as a *mohel, shochet* and *chazzan* for many years. He was jailed, interrogated and even placed in front of a firing squad for his actions. However, somehow he always managed to miraculously escape and continued living as a Torah Jew in the USSR. From the 1930s until the end of his life, the Ribnitzer Rebbe fasted on all days when it is permitted to do so under Jewish law. By 1973, when he was finally allowed to leave Russia, he was the last rebbe of a bygone era. He settled in Israel where he lived in the Sanhedria section of Jerusalem. A number of years later he moved to the United States, where he lived in Miami, Los Angeles, and Brooklyn before eventually settling in Spring Valley, New York.

R' Moshe Feinstein zt"l

(1895-1986)

R' Moshe Feinstein zt"l was a world-renowned *posek* (halachic arbitrator) and was regarded as the supreme rabbinic authority for Orthodox Jewry of North America. R' Moshe grew up Uzda, near Minsk, Belorussia, where his father was rabbi. In 1921, at the age of twenty-six, he became rabbi of Luban, near Minsk, where he served for sixteen years. Under increasing pressure and torment from the Soviet regime, who enacted decrees to limit his authority and control over the community, he moved in 1937 with his family to New York City, where he lived for the rest of his life. Settling on the Lower East Side, he became the *rosh yeshivah* of Mesivta Tifereth Jerusalem. He later established a branch of the yeshivah in Staten Island, New York, now headed by his son, Rabbi Reuven Feinstein. In the Orthodox world, it is universal to refer to him simply as "Rav Moshe" or "Reb Moshe." R' Moshe became the leading halachic authority of his time and his rulings were accepted worldwide. He was a dedicated, selfless and beloved leader for the Jewish people to whom anyone could approach at any time with any problem.

R' Ephraim Oshry zt"l

(1914-2003)

R' Ephraim Oshry zt"l was a young rabbinical scholar in Kovno, the second largest city in Lithuania, when the Nazis invaded on June 23, 1941. After the city's Jews were herded into a ghetto, the Nazis made him custodian of the warehouse where Jewish books were stored for a planned exhibit of "artifacts of the extinct Jewish race." While in the Kovno ghetto, R' Oshry began writing his responsa to the Holocaust, answering very difficult questions and making interpretations of religious law to help people continue to live as Jews in seemingly impossible circumstances. Before the final battle between the Nazis and the Soviets, he buried his responsa in the ground. After the war, he retrieved them and ultimately – in 1959 – he published some of those Hebrew responsa under the title *She'eilos U'teshuvos Mima'amakim*. His first wife and their children died in the camps before the end of the war. In 1949, he married Frieda Greenzweig, a survivor of Auschwitz, and together they left Lithuania and arrived in Rome where he organized a yeshivah for orphaned refugee children. In 1950, he managed to bring all the yeshivah students with him when he moved with his family to Montreal. They came to New York in 1952, where he was invited to be the rabbi of Beth Hamedrash Hagadol, a congregation founded in 1852 in New York City, and led his congregation for over fifty years.

R' Yechezkel Abramsky zt"l

(1886-1976)

R' Yechezkel Abramsky zt"l studied in the *yeshivos* of Telz, Mir, Slabodka and Brisk, under Rabbi Chaim Soloveitchik. At the age of seventeen he became a rabbi, serving, in turn, the communities of Smolyan, Smolevich and Slutsk. Following the Russian Revolution, he was at the forefront of opposition to Communist attempts to repress the Jewish religion and culture. As a result, the Russian government twice refused him permission to immigrate to the Land of Israel and take up the rabbinate of Petach Tikva, in both 1926 and 1928. In 1928, he started a Hebrew magazine, *Yagdil Torah* (lit. "Make [the] Torah Great"), but the Soviet authorities closed it down after two issues appeared. In 1929, he was arrested and sentenced to five years of hard labor in Siberia. However, in 1931 he was rescued by the German government under Chancellor Brüning, who exchanged him for six Communists that they held. He immigrated to London in 1932, where he was appointed rabbi of the Machzikei Hadath community in London's East End. In 1934, he became the senior *dayan* of the London Beth Din, holding the post until he retired to Jerusalem in 1951. While living in Israel, he also served as a *rosh yeshivah* of the Slabodka Yeshivah in Bnei Brak. R' Yechezkel died in Jerusalem on September 19, 1976.

R' Shlomo Halberstam zt"l

(1907-2000)

R' Shlomo Halberstam *zt"l*, the third Bobover Rebbe, reestablished the Bobover dynasty in the United States after World War II. He was the son of Rabbi Benzion Halberstam *Hy"d* (1874-1941) of Bobov, who died in the Holocaust. During World War II, the beautiful *Chassidus* of Bobov was destroyed, the rebbe himself perishing in the Holocaust together with thousands of his followers. His son, R' Shlomo, through *bitachon* and no short supply of cunning, managed to stay one step ahead of the Nazis, miraculously escaping from Poland, where he organized an underground escape route enabling many to get away to Hungary and Czechoslovakia. He, his mother and his young son, Naftali Tzvi (later to succeed his father as Bobover Rebbe), were the only members of his family to survive the Holocaust. After the war, he made his way to Italy, with the intention of immigrating to Palestine, where he was refused entry. Instead, he went to London and urged British Jews to rescue the remnants of European Jewry. Barely three hundred Bobover Chassidim survived, and R' Shlomo took it upon himself to rebuild Bobov. He eventually settled in Boro Park, New York, and married his second cousin, Freidel Rubin, with whom he went on to have five daughters and one son. R' Shlomo was known as a very wise man, a giant in good *middos*, and a true gentleman. He was noted for his steadfastness in not taking sides in disputes. This brought him great popularity and respect.

R' Tzvi Hirsch Meisels zt"l

(1902-1974)

R' Tzvi Hirsch Meisels *zt"l* became the chief *dayan* of the Chassidic community of Weitzun, Hungary, in 1930. Prior to that, he was the *rav* of the Jewish community of Neimark, Galicia. In Neimark, he headed a yeshivah with hundreds of students. In 1944, R' Tzvi Hirsch, along with his entire community, was deported to Auschwitz, where he suffered terribly. He would later recount incredible tales of Jewish heroism in the camp. After his liberation, he was appointed Chief Rabbi of the Bergen-Belsen German/British Section D.P. camp where he established Yeshivah She'aris Yisrael. In 1948, he arrived on American shores, and with the endorsement of his brother-in-law, R' Shlomo Halberstam, the Bobover Rebbe, he settled in Chicago with three of his children, the only members of his family who survived the Holocaust. He established himself on the fast-growing West Side and founded Congregation She'aris Yisrael, a *shtiebel* reminiscent of those in Eastern Europe. He quickly began to build Chicago's Orthodox community after the model of the one he had left in Europe. He also started a kosher *mikvah*, which Chicago was lacking, and was the *mohel* for most of the Jewish families in the area. He married again, to the daughter of a well-known Romanian rabbi, and eventually had eight children.

R' Yosef Shlomo Kahaneman zt"l
(1886-1969)

R' Yosef Shlomo Kahaneman *zt"l* was the founder and *rosh yeshivah* of the Ponevezh Yeshivah. At the age of fourteen, he went to the Telzer Yeshivah, where he learned until he was twenty, under the direct inspiration of Reb Eliezer Gordon, who saw his potential. With the passing of R' Itzele Rabinowitz in 1919, R' Kahaneman was appointed the new rabbi of Ponevezh, one of the largest centers of Jewish life in Lithuania. There, he built three *yeshivos* as well as a school and an orphanage. He was also elected to the Lithuanian parliament. All of his institutions were destroyed and many of his students and family were killed during World War II. R' Kahaneman immigrated to the British Mandate of Palestine in 1940 and built *Kiryat Hayeshivah* ("Town of the Yeshivah") in Bnei Brak and *Batei Avos* orphanages. He traveled widely in the Diaspora to secure financial support for his yeshivah, which he constantly improved and extended. In the face of skepticism and opposition, he succeeded in turning the reestablished Ponevezh Yeshivah into one of the largest in the world. He sought to take care of many orphans and tried to rescue them from the clutches of secular Zionist organizations, especially the *Yaldei Tehran* ("Children of Tehran") – children who escaped from Nazi Europe by walking across Europe to Tehran (including the famous Biala Rebbe – Rabbi Benzion Rabinowitz). R' Kahaneman was a distinguished member of the Council of Torah Sages of Agudath Israel, a man of deep piety and wit.

R' Menashe Klein zt"l

(1924-2011)

R' Menashe Klein zt"l, also known as the Ungvarer Rav, hailed from the town of Ungvar in what was then Czechoslovakia, and what is now the Ukraine. During World War II, he was in Auschwitz-Birkenau, Buna-Auschwitz, and finally in Buchenwald. At Buchenwald, he was sent out to "Stein," a Nazi satellite camp at Eschershausen, but was listed in camp records as returned to Buchenwald, where he was liberated and where he completed a postwar military interview. Subsequently, he was taken with other Buchenwald boys to Ecouis in France and was with the religious complement at Ambloy and Taverny. He came to the United States in 1947, where he served as *rav* in the "Chevrah Liyadi" shul and as principal of Yeshivas She'eiris Hapleitah, under the direction of the Klausenberger Rebbe. In 1964, he founded Yeshivah Beis She'arim in Boro Park, Brooklyn, where he served as *rosh yeshivah*. In 1983, he established Kiryat Ungvar in the Ramot section of Jerusalem. Today, it is a thriving neighborhood with hundreds of inhabitants. R' Menashe would spend many months of the year in Eretz Yisrael in Kiryat Ungvar. In America, his yeshivah and shul was at Sixteenth Avenue and Fifty-Second Street in Boro Park. He was a warm, loving *posek* who inspired tens of thousands with his dedication to Torah and his steadfastness in halachah.

R' Yaakov Yisroel Kanievsky zt"l
(1899-1985)

R' Yaakov Yisroel Kanievsky zt"l was known as the "Steipler Gaon." He was born in the Ukrainian town of Hornisteiple, from which his appellation, "the Steipler," was later derived. At the young age of eleven, he entered the Novaradok Yeshivah, studying under the Alter, R' Yosef Yoizel Horowitz. He progressed rapidly and gained a reputation as a *talmid chacham* and at the age of nineteen was sent to set up a branch of the yeshivah in Rogachov. However, the Bolshevik Revolution was in full swing and he was forcibly conscripted into the Red Army. In spite of the harsh conditions, he continued to strictly observe all the *mitzvos*. After serving under arms for some time, he was discharged and he moved to Bialystok in Poland in order to continue learning Torah unhindered from Communist interference. In 1925, the Steipler published his first *sefer*, *Sha'arei Tevunah*, which was received with great acclaim, and eventually reached the famed Chazon Ish in Vilna. Without even meeting him, the Chazon Ish decided that the author of such a work was worthy of marrying his sister Miriam. The two were soon married and the Steipler was then appointed *rosh yeshivah* of the Novaradok Yeshivah in Pinsk. In 1934, he left Poland and moved to the Holy Land, settling in Bnei Brak, where his brother-in-law, the Chazon Ish, had already been living for a year and a half. Though known as a great Torah scholar, the Steipler shunned publicity and lived in humble surroundings, teaching, writing and devoting himself to Torah and good deeds. Though he held no official position, the Steipler was universally recognized and consulted by individuals from all walks of life on every imaginable problem, with many claiming that he displayed knowledge which was inconceivable by natural means. Over 150,000 mourners attended his funeral in 1985.

Irving M. Bunim z"l
(1901-1980)

Irving M. Bunim z"l was a businessman, philanthropist and a major lay leader of Orthodox Jewry in the United States from the 1930s until his death in 1980. As the trusted assistant to R' Aharon Kotler, he was deeply involved in all aspects of Torah dissemination, philanthropy and Holocaust rescue. Together with other American Orthodox leaders, Bunim established the Va'ad Hatzalah, an organization created to save yeshivah students and teachers from captivity and probable death in Eastern Europe. Later, the Va'ad's scope expanded to include all suffering Jews in Europe and helped them by sending food and other relief supplies, or by giving them refuge in non-European countries of safety. The hardest aspect of his rescue work was negotiating with the Nazis themselves. A series of negotiations called the Musy Negotiations, named after Jean-Marie Musy, the pro-Nazi former president of Switzerland, was initiated. In these negotiations the Va'ad agreed to pay the Nazis a ransom to free Jews from concentration camps. After some dealings the Va'ad agreed to pay $5 million for three hundred thousand Jews or $250,000 each month for twenty months to free fifteen thousand Jews. These negotiations failed, though some one thousand Jews, out of the three hundred thousand Jews promised to be freed, were saved from a certain death. After the war the Va'ad kept working to supply the survivors with food and other relief supplies. Irving Bunim was a philanthropist who gave loans and did the best he could to help people in need. His main goal was spreading the word of the Torah to all Jews who had forgotten it, or never been exposed to it, in America, Israel and the rest of the world. He was devoted to fundraising work. Irving Bunim died in 1980 at his home in New York City.

R' Yaakov Avigdor zt"l
(1896-1967)

R' Yaakov Avigdor *zt"l* was born into a rabbinic family in Tyrawa Woloska, a *shtetl* in the Austrian province of Galicia. As a youth, he studied in a number of *yeshivos*, acquiring a great reputation as an orator and Talmudic scholar. He was named Chief Rabbi of Drohobycz-Boryslaw in southeast Poland (East Galicia) in 1920, where he officiated until the Nazi occupation. After the Nazi occupation in the summer of 1941, he lived in the Drohobycz ghetto until he was deported to the Plaszow camp, and from there to Buchenwald. During the Holocaust, he lost his wife, his two daughters and his brother Dovid, the rabbi of Andrychow, among many family members. After liberation, he was active in the revival of religious life for survivors, and served as a *dayan* on the rabbinical court for Holocaust *agunos*. In 1946, he was asked to take the position of rabbi of the Chovevei Torah synagogue in Brooklyn and to head the Rabbi Shlomo Kluger Yeshivah. Upon immigrating to the U.S. in 1946, he accepted a pulpit in Brooklyn, New York. Six years later, he was offered the rabbinate of Mexico, holding that position until his death in Mexico City in 1967. R' Avigdor was a prolific writer who published dozens of books and articles both before and after the Holocaust and was much consulted on religious and ethical questions by worldwide peers. His writings included religious philosophy, Jewish history and traditions, and a commentary on Biblical text. Most of his prewar works were lost. In Mexico, he became a regular contributor to Yiddish periodicals, and published books in Yiddish, Hebrew and Spanish.

R' Yisroel Spira zt"l

(1889-1989)

R' Yisroel Spira *zt"l*, the Bluzhever Rebbe, was the scion of the illustrious Bluzhever dynasty, of which he remained the sole survivor after the war. He had been the *rav* in the small town of Pruchnik until 1932 and only assumed the title of Bluzhever Rebbe after his arrival in the United States in 1946. His *rebbetzin* and their daughter, with her husband and children, were among the six million who perished. At the outbreak of World War II, R' Yisroel moved from Istrik to Lvov. Lvov was then under Soviet rule due to the Soviet-German Non-Aggression Pact that was signed on August 23, 1939, which effectively divided the soon-to-be conquered country of Poland into two. The eastern half was to fall under the sphere of Soviet influence, while the western sector would be controlled by the invading Germans. Of course, the Germans could not be trusted and in the summer of 1941, the Germans broke the treaty and occupied the Soviet areas. R' Yisroel found himself in the Lvov ghetto, where he lived under horrid conditions until its liquidation in June of 1943, when he and the remaining Jews were deported to Bergen-Belsen and later to the infamous Janowska road camp, from where almost no one survived. R' Yisroel suffered for nearly five years in a succession of labor, concentration, and death camps but was a constant bastion of faith and inspiration in the camps where he helped as many Jews as he was able. After liberation, he immigrated to the U.S., rebuilt the Bluzhever *Chassidus*, and became one of the leading lights of Chassidic Jewry until his death in 1989.

R' Chaim Meir Hager zt"l
(1881-1972)

R' Chaim Meir Hager *zt"l*, the revered Vizhnitzer Rebbe, was a spiritually energizing force in the entire region where he lived. But the war brought all this to an abrupt halt. Miraculously, the rebbe escaped war-torn Romania and survived the war. When the Romanian Jews were deported in 1941 to Transnistria (a death camp in the Ukraine, administered jointly by the Germans and the Romanians from July 1941 to March 1944), R' Chaim Meir threw himself, heart and soul, into the rescue operation, helping to alleviate the suffering in Transnistria and establishing a rescue apparatus that saved thousands of Jewish souls from certain death. Within a short time, the Vizhnitzer Rebbe gathered around him a group of survivors, thirsty for spirituality. He changed their lives, taking broken, despondent refugees on the road to nowhere and turning them into optimistic Chassidim. It did not take long to realize that Europe would no longer yield the harvest of holiness that it had in the past. Consequently, he set his sights on the Holy Land, where he had a huge following, including the thousands of settlers of Shikun Vizhnitz and the hundreds of students of the Vizhnitzer Yeshivah, both in Bnei Brak. He was a member of the Mo'etzes Gedolei HaTorah (Council of Torah Sages) of the Agudath Israel of Eretz Yisrael and he was the scion of a noble Chassidic dynasty; but, perhaps equal to all of these elements, his personal warmth, and the triumph of joy over adversity that he personified, won him vast admiration beyond the confines of any one group.

Lieutenant Meyer Birnbaum z"l

(1919-2013)

Lieutenant Meyer Birnbaum z"l was amongst the American soldiers who took part in the liberation of the Buchenwald and Ohrdruff D.P. camps. He wrote a book titled *Lieutenant Birnbaum*, which describes his life as an American soldier. He grew up in the Brownsville section of Brooklyn during the Depression and joined the U.S. army in 1942. He landed at Normandy on D-Day, and was one of the only Orthodox U.S. army officers commissioned during World War II. After liberating Buchenwald, he remained in Europe to assist at the camps for displaced persons, including Feldafing, Föhrenwald, Landsberg and Dachau, encountering a number of unforgettable Torah giants and survivors, among them the Klausenberger Rebbe. After returning to America and being reunited with his wife and seven children, he worked with the likes of Mike Tress and Irving Bunim, assisting in the Va'ad Hatzalah efforts. He later worked for the Young Israel and went into the poultry business. In 1969, he got remarried to his second wife, Goldie, whose nine children he considered like his own. In 1981, Meyer and his entire family resettled in Israel.

R' Eliezer Zusia Portugal zt"l

(1898-1982)

R' Eliezer Zusia Portugal zt"l, the Skulener Rebbe, succeeded his father as rabbi of Skulen at the age of seventeen upon his father's death in 1915. Before the outbreak of World War II, upon the urging of the Sadigerer Rebbe, the Skulener Rebbe moved to the city of Chernowitz. Chernowitz changed hands several times during World War II, eventually ending up in the Soviet Union. On a number of occasions, the rebbe was persecuted by both the Germans and Russians. More than once his life was in danger. One day he was even taken out to be executed, but he was saved from the Germans by a miracle. The Russians also imprisoned him several times. But despite everything, he never stopped his appointed task. After the war he moved to Bucharest, the capital of Romania, where he opened an orphanage for the orphans left after the Holocaust. When the Communists took over Romania it became dangerous for him to continue to educate the children in the ways of Judaism, yet the rebbe continued. In 1959, the Communists arrested the rebbe and his son, the present rebbe, for teaching religion and for supporting and educating orphans. An international effort to free the Skulener Rebbe and his son was mounted, and eventually, through the intervention of United Nations Secretary-General Dag Hammarskjöld, they were freed and immediately immigrated to the United States. Upon moving to America, the rebbe continued his works helping the underprivileged and began an international charity organization known as *Chessed L'Avraham*. The rebbe authored *Noam Eliezer* and *Kedushas Eliezer*, and composed many popular Chassidic tunes. He died in 1982 and is buried in the Vizhnitzer cemetery in Monsey, New York.

Reb Shmuel Yosef Friedenson z"l
(1922-2013)

Reb Shmuel Yosef Friedenson *z"l* was born in Lodz, Poland. His father, Reb Eliezer Gershon, was a prominent *askan* within Agudath Israel. He helped administer the Bais Yaakov system and edited its monthly *Bais Yaakov Journal*. When World War II broke out, Reb Yossel (as he was fondly called) ended up in the Warsaw ghetto, where he married Gittel Leah Silberman.

He spent over two years in the Starachowice concentration camp, and then was shipped to other camps, including Auschwitz and Buchenwald. On Tishah B'Av of 1944, he and his wife arrived in Auschwitz, where only the intervention of *Hashgachah* ensured their survival. While Mrs. Friedenson remained in Auschwitz until she was liberated by the Russian army in early 1945, Reb Yosef endured death marches, confinement in Ohrdruff and several other concentration camps, and was finally liberated from Buchenwald in April 1945 by the American army. Reb Yosef was reunited with his wife several months later, spent several years in postwar Germany working to help other survivors rebuild their shattered lives, and immigrated to the United States in 1951 where he joined the Agudath Israel led by Mike Tress, establishing himself as one of the world's leading Yiddish writers and Holocaust historians as editor of *Dos Yiddishe Vort*. He was known as "Mr. Friedenson," but in fact was far wiser than many rabbis who assume that title. He was not into titles but into work, on behalf of the Jewish people.

GLOSSARY

Aktion: German for "round-up."

Al Kiddush Hashem: Lit. "To sanctify the Name." Used to describe Jews who died with Hashem's Name on their lips.

Aliyah: Being called up to say a blessing at the Torah reading.

Allies: The nations, including the United States, Britain, France, and the Soviet Union, that joined in the fight in World War II against Germany and the other Axis nations.

Amud: Lectern from which the prayers are led.

Anti-Semitism: Prejudice against Jews.

Appell: German for "roll call."

Arba'ah Minim: Four Species taken on Sukkos, including *lulav, esrog, hadassim* and *aravos.*

Aryan: An ancient people of Central Asia. Used by the Nazis to mean a superior, white gentile.

Auschwitz-Birkenau: Nazi labor and death camp located in Poland.

Avel: Jewish mourner.

Axis: The nations, including Italy and Japan, that fought in World War II alongside Germany against the Allies.

Bachur: Young yeshivah student.

Beis Din: Jewish rabbinical court.

Beis Medrash: Study hall, where Jews go to study Torah.

Baruch Hashem: Lit. "Blessed is the Name."

Bergen-Belsen: Nazi concentration camp located in Germany.

Blitzkrieg: German for "lightning war."

Buchenwald: Nazi concentration camp located near Weimar, Germany.

Cantor/Chazzan: Leader of synagogue prayer.

Chazal: The Sages of blessed memory.

Chol Hamoed Sukkos: Intermediate Days of the holiday of Sukkos when work is permitted.

Churchill, Sir Winston: Prime Minister of Britain during most of World War II (May 1940-July 1945) and again after the war (1951-55).

Concentration Camp: A prison in which "enemies of the German nation" were concentrated. Before the end of World War II, more than one hundred such camps had been set up.

Crematorium: Oven in which death-camp victims' bodies were burned.

Dachau: The first Nazi concentration camp, near Munich, Germany.

Death Camps: Camps built to kill Jews and other "enemies of the German nation." There were six death camps: Auschwitz, Belzec, Chelmno, Majdanek, Sobibor, and Treblinka.

Death Marches: Close to the end of the war, Nazi S.S. forced prisoners in concentration and death camps located in Poland to march to other camps located in Germany.

Deportation: The Jews' forced relocation from their homes to other places, usually ghettos or Nazi camps.

Eibishter: Yiddish term for Hashem.

Eichmann, Adolf: S.S. officer who directed the roundup of Jews and their transport to concentration and death camps. He was captured and executed by the Israelis.

Elul: The Jewish month before the New Year, which signifies repentance and circumspection.

Emunah: Faith and trust in the Al-mighty.

Esrog: Citron, the special fruit used on the holiday of Sukkos to fulfill a mitzvah.

Final Solution: The Nazi term for their plan to murder every Jew in Europe.

Fuhrer: German for "leader." Used in reference to Adolf Hitler.

Gabbai: Hebrew term to define one who assists a rebbe or runs the services in the synagogue.

Gartel: Yiddish term for a belt used by Chassidim for prayer.

Gas Chambers: Sealed rooms in the death camps. Jewish prisoners were crowded into these rooms and poison gas was released, killing the prisoners.

Gemara: Individual part of the Talmud studied by Jews all over the world.

Gestapo: The Nazi secret police.

Ghetto: A closed-off section of a city in which the Jews were forced to live.

Hakadosh Baruch Hu: Lit. "Holy One blessed be He." A glorifying expression of Hashem.

Hakafos: Dancing and singing with the Torah on Simchas Torah, when Jews traditionally circle the *bimah* in shul.

Hitler, Adolf: Nazi party leader, 1919-45. German chancellor, 1933-45. Committed suicide in a Berlin bunker. May his name be blotted out.

Hitler Youth: Nazi youth organization. From 1936 the only legal youth organization in Nazi Germany.

Holocaust: "Destruction by fire." This word came to be used to refer to the Nazi killing of six million Jews, in the years 1933-45.

Hy"d: Acronym for "May G-d avenge his blood."

Juden: German word for "Jews."

Judenrat: "Jewish council." Jews appointed by the Germans to govern the ghettos.

Judenrein: German for "free of Jews."

Kapos: Prisoners within concentration camps who were selected by the Nazis to oversee other prisoners.

Kristallnacht: "Night of Broken Glass." November 9-11, 1938, when there were wholesale arrests of Jews and destruction of Jewish property in Germany and Austria.

Labor Camp: A Nazi concentration camp in which the prisoners were used as slave laborers.

Kol Nidrei: The awesome prayers said at the opening of Yom Kippur.

Lager: German for "camp."

Luftwaffe: German Air Force.

Majdanek: Nazi labor and death camp located in Poland.

Mauthausen: Nazi concentration camp located in Austria.

Mengele, Josef: The medical doctor and S.S. captain who in Auschwitz made "selections" and conducted sadistic medical experiments on prisoners. Escaped to Paraguay after the war, where he was presumed to have died of natural causes.

Mesiras Nefesh: Extraordinary dedication and courage.

Mikvah: A ritual bath, separate for men and women, where Jews go to purify their bodies before prayer and/or performing a mitzvah.

Muller, Heinrich: Gestapo chief, 1939-45. Directly responsible for carrying out the "Final Solution."

Minyan: Quorum of ten men necessary to pray the three daily prayers in shul.

Rabbiner: German for "rabbi."

Rav: Rabbi, teacher.

Rebbetzin: Wife of a rabbi.

Rebbi: One who teaches Torah.

Ribono Shel Olam: Lit. "Master of the Universe." A glorifying expression of Hashem.

Ribbentrop, Joachim von: German foreign minister. Negotiated an agreement between the Soviet Union and Germany in 1939 that neither country would attack the other.

Righteous of the Nations: Righteous gentiles. The term used for gentiles who risked their lives to save Jews from Nazi persecution.

Roosevelt, Franklin Delano: U.S. president from March 1933 until his death in April 1945, almost the entire period of Nazi rule in Germany.

S.A.: Storm troopers, or Brown Shirts. Organized to protect Nazi rallies and to terrorize those not sympathetic to the Nazis.

S'chach: Branches, leaves or bamboo used to cover the sukkah as a makeshift roof.

Sedarim: The special feasts that Jews hold on the first two nights of Pesach, where tales of redemption are recounted and the children are an integral part of the evening.

Sefer: Jewish book.

Sefer Torah: The Torah scroll which is read each Shabbos and Yom Tov.

Selektion: The process of deciding which prisoners in Nazi camps would be sent to their deaths immediately and which would be spared.

Shehecheyanu: Blessing thanking G-d for surviving "until today."

Shivah: The traditional Jewish mourning period.

Shochet: Traditional ritual slaughterer.

Shtiebel: Classic Chassidic synagogue.

Shtreimel: Classic Chassidic headdress.

Simchas Torah: The Festival of the Torah. It follows the holiday of Sukkos and is characterized by dancing, singing and unbridled joy of the Torah. The Torah is read on this day until its completion and then rewound to the beginning where it is started all over again.

Sinas Yisrael: Hatred for Jews.

S.S.: Protection squad, or Black Shirts. Established in 1925 as Nazi protection squads. Included the Gestapo, squads that ran the Nazi concentration and death camps, and squads that fought with the German army.

Stalin, Joseph: Dictator of the Soviet Union, 1929-53.

Tallis: Rectangular cloth with specially prepared fringes (tzitzis). Worn by Jews during prayer.

Tefillin: Phylacteries which Jewish men don each morning during prayers.

Teshuvah: Repentance.

Third Reich: Hitler's name for Germany during his years as dictator, 1933-45.

Treblinka: Nazi death camp located in Poland.

Tzitzis: The fringes or tassels worn on a traditional four-cornered garment by Jewish males.

Vidui: The Jewish confession, usually recited preceding death.

Wehrmacht: The German army.

Yad Vashem: Memorial in Jerusalem to Holocaust victims, and center for Holocaust study.

Yahrtzeit: A day when Jews remember and commemorate the life of a dead loved one. The Kaddish prayer is recited and some eat and drink and bless the memory of their loved one.

Zemiros: Jewish songs which are often sung on Shabbos and holidays during the festive meals.

Zhid: Polish for "Jew."

ZOB: The Warsaw ghetto Jewish fighting organization.

Zt"l: Acronym for "of blessed memory."

WHEN WAS THE LAST TIME YOU READ A GOOD...

- STORY
- DVAR TORAH
- MASHAL
- HALACHAH
- DRUSH
- HASHKAFAH
- MIDDOS/ DERECH ERETZ

?

(over please)

There is something in TORAH TAVLIN

for everyone, every day, every week, every Yom Tov

THE KURZ FAMILY EDITION
THE BAUMAN FAMILY EDITION

TORAH TAVLIN VOL. II

Stories and Sayings, Wit and Wisdom From Our Torah Leaders

Arranged Daily According to the *Parshah* of the Week

Rabbi Dovid Hoffman

By: Rabbi Dovid Hoffman

...Sephardic, Ashkenazic, Litvish, Chassidish, man, woman, young or old – you'll find enjoyment here, among the satisfying pages of Torah Tavlin.

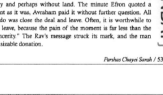
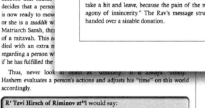

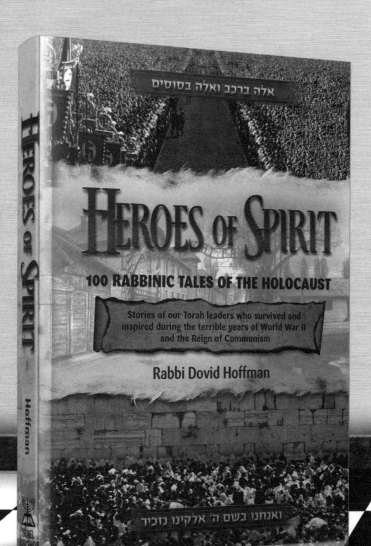

Torah Tavlin
Yamim Noraim

Stories and Sayings, Wit and Wisdom from Our Torah Leaders

Rabbi Dovid Hoffman

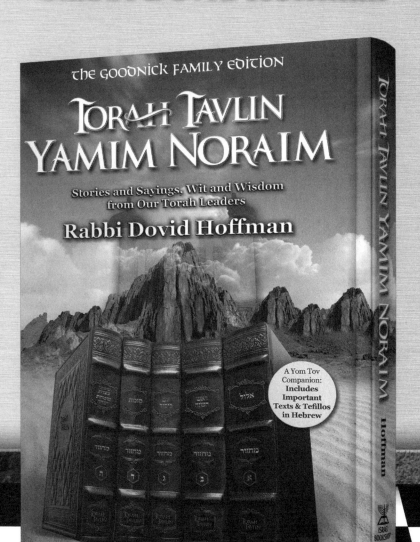

הגדה של פסח
TORAH TAVLIN HAGGADAH

Stories and Sayings, Wit and Wisdom
from our Torah Leaders
on the Haggadah shel Pesach

By:
Rabbi Dovid Hoffman

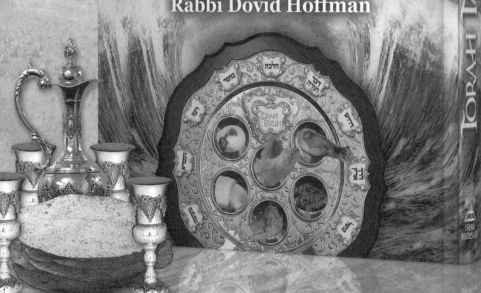

ליקוטי תורה תבלין

רעיונות ופירושים לקחי חיים ודברי תורה ומוסר נסדרו עפ"י פרשיות השבוע ונלקטו
מתורת רבותינו גאונינו אדמורינו וחכמינו לעורר את האדם לעבודת השי"ת